PATHWAYS

Listening, Speaking, and Critical Thinking

2

Becky Tarver Chase
Kristin L. Johannsen

NATIONAL GEOGRAPHIC LEARNING | HEINLE CENGAGE Learning

Australia • Brazil • Japan • Korea • Singapore • Spain • United Kingdom • United States

Pathways 2
Listening, Speaking, and Critical Thinking
Becky Tarver Chase
Kristin L. Johannsen

Publisher: Sherrise Roehr

Executive Editor: Laura Le Dréan

Acquisitions Editor: Tom Jefferies

Senior Development Editors:
Margarita Matte, Mary Whittemore

Director of Global Marketing: Ian Martin

Director of U.S. Marketing: Jim McDonough

Marketing Manager: Caitlin Thomas

Marketing Manager: Katie Kelley

Marketing Coordinator: Jide Iruka

Director of Content and Media Production:
Michael Burggren

Content Project Manager: Daisy Sosa

Manufacturing Manager: Marcia Locke

Manufacturing Buyer: Marybeth Hennebury

Production Intern: Brittney Rizo

Cover Design: Page 2 LLC

Cover Image: Fred Bavendam/Minden Pictures/
National Geographic Image Collection

Interior Design: Page 2 LLC

Composition: Nesbitt Graphics, Inc.

Library of Congress Control Number: 2011911578

International Edition:

ISBN-13: 978-1-111-22299-4

ISBN-10: 1-111-22299-1

U.S. Edition:

ISBN-13: 978-1-111-39863-7

ISBN-10: 1-111-39863-1

National Geographic Learning
20 Channel Center St.
Boston, MA 02210
USA

Cengage Learning is a leading provider of customized learning solutions with office locations around the globe, including Singapore, the United Kingdom, Australia, Mexico, Brazil, and Japan. Locate your local office at:
international.cengage.com/region

Cengage Learning products are represented in Canada by Nelson Education, Ltd.

Visit National Geographic Learning online at **ngl.cengage.com**

Visit our corporate website at **www.cengage.com**

Printed in the United States of America
4 5 6 7 8 15 14 13

ACKNOWLEDGEMENTS

The authors and publisher would like to thank the following reviewers:

UNITED STATES Adrianne Aiko Thompson, Miami Dade College, Miami, Florida; **Gokhan Alkanat**, Auburn University at Montgomery, Alabama; **Nikki Ashcraft**, Shenandoah University, VA; **Karin Avila-John**, University of Dayton, Ohio; **Shirley Baker**, Alliant International University, California; **John Baker**, Oakland Community College, Michigan; **Evina Baquiran Torres**, Zoni Language Centers, New York; **Michelle Bell**, University of South Florida, Florida; **Nancy Boyer**, Golden West College, California; **Carol Brutza**, Gateway Community College, Connecticut; **Sarah Camp**, University of Kentucky, Center for ESL, Kentucky; **Maria Caratini**, Eastfield College, Texas; **Ana Maria Cepero**, Miami Dade College, Florida; **Daniel Chaboya**, Tulsa Community College, Oklahoma; **Patricia Chukwueke**, English Language Institute – UCSD Extension, California; **Julia A. Correia**, Henderson State University, Connecticut; **Suzanne Crisci**, Bunker Hill Community College, Massachusetts; **Katie Crowder**, University of North Texas, Texas; **Lynda Dalgish**, Concordia College, New York; **Jeffrey Diluglio**, Center for English Language and Orientation Programs: Boston University, Massachusetts; **Tim DiMatteo**, Southern New Hampshire University, New Hampshire; **Scott Dirks**, Kaplan International Center at Harvard Square, Massachusetts; **Margo Downey**, Center for English Language and Orientation Programs: Boston University, Massachusetts; **John Drezek**, Richland College, Texas; **Anwar El-Issa**, Antelope Valley College, California; **Anrisa Fannin**, The International Education Center at Diablo Valley College, California; **Jennie Farnell**, University of Connecticut, American Language Program, Connecticut; **Mark Fisher**, Lone Star College, Texas; **Celeste Flowers**, University of Central Arkansas, Arkansas; **John Fox**, English Language Institute, Georgia; **Pradel R. Frank**, Miami Dade College, Florida; **Sally Gearheart**, Santa Rosa Jr. College, California; **Karen Grubbs**, ELS Language Centers, Florida; **Joni Hagigeorges**, Salem State University, Massachusetts; **Valerie Heming**, University of Central Missouri, Missouri; **Mary Hill**, North Shore Community College, Massachusetts; **Harry L. Holden**, North Lake College, Texas; **Ingrid Holm**, University of Massachusetts Amherst, Massachusetts; **Marianne Hsu Santelli**, Middlesex County College, New Jersey; **Katie Hurter**, Lone Star College – North Harris, Texas; **Justin Jernigan**, Georgia Gwinnett College, Georgia; **Barbara A. Jonckheere**, American Language Institute at California State University, Long Beach, California; **Susan Jordan**, Fisher College, Massachusetts; **Maria Kasparova**, Bergen Community College, New Jersey; **Gail Kellersberger**, University of Houston-Downtown, Texas; **Christina Kelso**, Austin Peay State University, Tennessee; **Daryl Kinney**, Los Angeles City College, California; **Leslie Kosel Eckstein**, Hillsborough Community College, Florida; **Beth Kozbial Ernst**, University of Wisconsin-Eau Claire, Wisconsin; **Jennifer Lacroix**, Center for English Language and Orientation Programs: Boston University, Massachusetts; **Stuart Landers**, Missouri State University, Missouri; **Margaret V. Layton**, University of Nevada, Reno Intensive English Language Center, Nevada; **Heidi Lieb**, Bergen Community College, New Jersey; **Kerry Linder**, Language Studies International New York, New York; **Jenifer Lucas-Uygun**, Passaic County Community College, New Jersey; **Alison MacAdams**, Approach International Student Center, Massachusetts; **Craig Machado**, Norwalk Community College, Connecticut; **Andrew J. MacNeill**, Southwestern College, California; **Melanie A. Majeski**, Naugatuck Valley Community College, Connecticut; **Wendy Maloney**, College of DuPage, Illinois; **Chris Mares**, University of Maine – Intensive English Institute, Maine; **Josefina Mark**, Union County College, New Jersey; **Connie Mathews**, Nashville State Community College, Tennessee; **Bette Matthews**, Mid-Pacific Institute, Hawaii; **Marla McDaniels Heath**, Norwalk Community College, Connecticut; **Kimberly McGrath Moreira**, University of Miami, Florida; **Sara McKinnon**, College of Marin, California; **Christine Mekkaoui**, Pittsburg State University, Kansas; **Holly A. Milkowart**, Johnson County Community College, Kansas; **Warren Mosher**, University of Miami, Florida; **Lukas Murphy**, Westchester Community College, New York; **Elena Nehrebecki**, Hudson Community College, New Jersey; **Bjarne Nielsen**, Central Piedmont Community College, North Carolina; **David Nippoldt**, Reedley College, California; **Lucia Parsley**, Virginia Commonwealth University, Virginia; **Wendy Patriquin**, Parkland College, Illinois; **Marion Piccolomini**, Communicate With Ease, LTD, Pennsylvania; **Carolyn Prager**, Spanish-American Institute, New York; **Eileen Prince**, Prince Language Associates Incorporated, Massachusetts; **Sema Pulak**, Texas A & M University, Texas; **James T. Raby**, Clark University, Massachusetts; **Anouchka Rachelson**, Miami-Dade College, Florida; **Lynn Ramage Schaefer**, University of Central Arkansas, Arkansas; **Sherry Rasmussen**, DePaul University, Illinois; **Amy Renehan**, University of Washington, Washington; **Esther Robbins**, Prince George's Community College, Pennsylvania; **Helen Roland**, Miami Dade College, Florida; **Linda Roth**, Vanderbilt University English Language Center, Tennessee; **Janine Rudnick**, El Paso Community College, Texas; **Rita Rutkowski Weber**, University of Wisconsin – Milwaukee, Wisconsin; **Elena Sapp**, INTO Oregon State University, Oregon; **Margaret Shippey**, Miami Dade College, Florida; **Lisa Sieg**, Murray State University, Kentucky; **Alison Stamps**, ESL Center at Mississippi State University, Mississippi; **Peggy Street**, ELS Language Centers, Miami, Florida; **Lydia Streiter**, York College Adult Learning Center, New York; **Nicholas Taggart**, Arkansas State University, Arkansas; **Marcia Takacs**, Coastline Community College, California; **Tamara Teffeteller**, University of California Los Angeles, American Language Center, California; **Rebecca Toner**, English Language Programs, University of Pennsylvania, Pennsylvania; **William G. Trudeau**, Missouri Southern State University, Missouri; **Troy Tucker**, Edison State College, Florida; **Maria Vargas-O'Neel**, Miami Dade College, Florida; **Amerca Vazquez**, Miami Dade College, Florida; **Alison Vinande**, Modesto Junior College, California; **Christie Ward**, Intensive English Language Program, Central Connecticut State University, Connecticut; **Colin S. Ward**, Lone Star College-North Harris, Texas; **Denise L. Warner**, Lansing Community College, Michigan; **Wendy Wish-Bogue**, Valencia Community College, Florida; **Cissy Wong**, Sacramento City College, California; **Kimberly Yoder**, Kent State University, ESL Center, Ohio

ASIA Teoh Swee Ai, Universiti Teknologi Mara, Malaysia; **Nor Azni Abdullah,** Universiti Teknologi Mara, Malaysia; **Thomas E. Bieri**, Nagoya College, Japan; **Paul Bournhonesque**, Seoul National University of Technology, Korea; **Michael C. Cheng**, National Chengchi University, Taiwan; **Fu-Dong Chiou**, National Taiwan University, Taiwan; **Derek Currie**, Korea University, Sejong Institute of Foreign Language Studies, Korea; **Christoph A. Hafner**, City University of Hong Kong, Hong Kong; **Wenhua Hsu**, I-Shou University, Taiwan; **Helen Huntley**, Hanoi University, Vietnam; **Rob Higgens**, Ritsumeikan University, Japan; **Shih Fan Kao**, JinWen University of Science and Technology, Taiwan; **Ikuko Kashiwabara**, Osaka Electro-Communication University, Japan; **Richard S. Lavin**, Prefecturla University of Kumamoto, Japan; **Mike Lay**, American Institute, Cambodia; **Byoung-Kyo Lee**, Yonsei University, Korea; **Lin Li**, Capital Normal University, China; **Hudson Murrell**, Baiko Gakuin University, Japan; **Keiichi Narita**, Hirosaki University, Japan; **Huynh Thi Ai Nguyen**, Vietnam USA Society, Vietnam; **James Pham**, IDP Phnom Penh, Cambodia; **Duncan Rose**, British Council, Singapore; **Simone Samuels**, The Indonesia Australia Language Foundation Jakarta, Indonesia; **Wang Songmei**, Beijing Institute of Education Faculty, China; **Chien-Wen Jenny Tseng**, National Sun Yat-Sen University, Taiwan; **Hajime Uematsu**, Hirosaki University, Japan

AUSTRALIA Susan Austin, University of South Australia; **Joanne Cummins**, Swinburne College; **Pamela Humphreys**, Griffith University

LATIN AMERICA AND THE CARIBBEAN Ramon Aguilar, Universidad Tecnológica de Hermosillo, México; **Livia de Araujo Donnini Rodrigues**, University of São Paolo, Brazil; **Cecilia Avila**, Universidad de Xapala, México; **Beth Bartlett**, Centro Cultural Colombo Americano, Cali, Colombia; **Raúl Billini**, Colegio Loyola, Dominican Republic; **Nohora Edith Bryan**, Universidad de La Sabana, Colombia; **Raquel Hernández Cantú**, Instituto Tecnológico de Monterrey, Mexico; **Millie Commander**, Inter American University of Puerto Rico, Puerto Rico; **Edwin Marín-Arroyo**, Instituto Tecnológico de Costa Rica; **Rosario Mena**, Instituto Cultural Dominico-Americano, Dominican Republic; **Elizabeth Ortiz Lozada**, COPEI-COPOL English Institute, Ecuador; **Gilberto Rios Zamora**, Sinaloa State Language Center, Mexico; **Patricia Veciños**, El Instituto Cultural Argentino Norteamericano, Argentina

MIDDLE EAST AND NORTH AFRICA Tom Farkas, American University of Cairo, Egypt; **Ghada Hozayen**, Arab Academy for Science, Technology and Maritime Transport, Egypt

Dedicated to Kristin L. Johannsen, whose love for the world's cultures and concern for the world's environment were an inspiration to family, friends, students, and colleagues.

Scope and Sequence

Unit	Academic Pathways	Vocabulary	Listening Skills
1 **Staying Healthy in the Modern World** *Page 1* **Academic Track:** Health Science	**Lesson A:** Listening to a Talk about Preventing Heart Disease Giving a Presentation on Health and Exercise Habits **Lesson B:** Listening to an Informal Conversation Keeping a Conversation Going	Understanding meaning from context Using new vocabulary in an everyday context	Listening for main ideas Listening for details **Pronunciation:** Word endings: *–s* and *–es*
2 **Energy and Our Planet** *Page 21* **Academic Track:** Interdisciplinary	**Lesson A:** Listening to a PowerPoint Lecture Discussing Personal Energy Use **Lesson B:** Listening to an Informal Conversation Planning a Group Presentation	Understanding meaning from context Using new vocabulary to complete a text	Listening for specific information Interpreting speakers' tone and attitude Listen for main ideas Listen for speakers' conclusions **Pronunciation:** Stressing key words Using intonation to show feelings
3 **Culture and Tradition** *Page 41* **Academic Track:** Anthropology/ Sociology	**Lesson A:** Listening to a Lecture Giving Information **Lesson B:** Listening to an Assignment and a Student Presentation Planning a Presentation	Understanding meaning from context Using new vocabulary to complete a text	Listening to confirm predictions Listening for details Making inferences Taking notes to remember information **Pronunciation:** Reduced function words
4 **A Thirsty World** *Page 61* **Academic Track:** Interdisciplinary	**Lesson A:** Listening to a Guest Speaker Presenting an Idea **Lesson B:** Listening to a Group Discussion Role-Playing a Meeting	Understanding meaning from context Using a dictionary to understand new words Discussing unit content using new vocabulary	Listen for the main idea Listen for details Taking notes on important facts **Pronunciation:** Syllable stress Suffixes and syllable stress
5 **Inside the Brain** *Page 81* **Academic Track:** Health Science	**Lesson A:** Listening to a Documentary Discussing Problems and Solutions **Lesson B:** Listening to a Conversation between Students Planning a Group Presentation	Understanding meaning from context Using a dictionary to understand new words	Predicting content Listening for main ideas Listening for details **Pronunciation:** Linking sounds

Grammar	Speaking Skills	Viewing	Critical Thinking Skills
Adverbs of frequency Tag questions	Using expressions of frequency Making small talk **Student to Student:** Asking about personal knowledge and experience **Presentation Skills:** Using your notes	**Video:** *Bee Therapy* Using prior knowledge Viewing for general understanding Viewing for specific information	Inferring word meaning from context Discussing healthy habits Identifying the parts of a presentation Predicting content Organizing ideas for a presentation **Critical Thinking Focus:** Supporting a statement
The simple present and the present continuous Modals of advice: *should/shouldn't, ought to, had better*	Giving examples Giving advice and making suggestions **Student to Student:** Taking turns **Presentation Skills:** Organizing ideas for a group presentation	**Video:** *Alternative Energy* Predicting content Viewing for general understanding Viewing for specific information Relating video to personal experiences and opinions	Using a graphic organizer Inferring information not stated in a conversation Drawing conclusions based on a conversation Proposing solutions for efficient energy consumption Analyzing and ranking ideas and providing reasons **Critical Thinking Focus:** Interpreting pie charts
The past continuous tense Adjectives ending in –ed and –ing	Asking for and giving clarification Interrupting politely **Student to Student:** Talking about assignments **Presentation Skills:** Posture	**Video:** *The Gauchos of Argentina* Using prior knowledge Viewing for specific information Discussing the video in the context of previous knowledge	Explaining ideas about culture Creating sentences using new vocabulary Discussing prior knowledge of a topic Inferring information from a listening Classifying new expressions **Critical Thinking Focus:** Inferring meaning from context
The passive voice Superlative adjectives	Talking about priorities Expressing opinions **Student to Student:** Showing surprise **Presentation Skills:** Speaking at the right volume	**Video:** *More Water for India* Predicting content Viewing for general understanding Viewing for specific information	Creating questions using the passive voice Understanding visuals Explaining how a PlayPump works Choosing a presentation topic with a group Discussing advantages and disadvantages **Critical Thinking Focus:** Predicting content
Infinitives after verbs	Making suggestions Making suggestions during group work **Student to Student:** Presenting your ideas in a small group **Presentation Skills:** Pausing to check for understanding	**Video:** *Memory Man* Viewing for specific information Giving an informed opinion based on the video	Relating personal experience to unit content Using verbs that relate to mental activities Analyzing problems and proposing solutions Interpreting a flow chart Recalling key information from a listening passage **Critical Thinking Focus:** Using context clues

Scope and Sequence

Unit	Academic Pathways	Vocabulary	Listening Skills
6 **What We Eat** *Page 101* **Academic Track:** Health and Nutrition	**Lesson A:** Listening to a Seminar Participating in a Mini-Debate **Lesson B:** Listening to a Group Discussion Using Visuals to Support a Presentation	Understanding meaning from context Using new vocabulary to complete a diet quiz and label graphics	Listening for the main idea Listening for details Listening for intonation **Pronunciation:** Intonation of finished and unfinished sentences
7 **Our Active Earth** *Page 121* **Academic Track:** Earth Science	**Lesson A:** Listening to an Earth Science Lecture Giving a News Report **Lesson B:** Listening to a Group Discussion Giving a Group Presentation	Understanding meaning from context Using new vocabulary to interpret a diagram, form questions, and summarize an article	Listening for main ideas Note-taking Listening for details **Pronunciation:** Syllable stress review and syllable number
8 **Ancient Peoples and Places** *Page 141* **Academic Track:** Anthropology and Sociology/ Archaeology	**Lesson A:** Listening to a Guided Tour Presenting an Ancient Artifact **Lesson B:** Listening to a Conversation between Students Giving a Summary	Understanding meaning from context Using new vocabulary to discuss unit content	Listening for main ideas Listening for details Making inferences **Pronunciation:** Question intonation
9 **Species Survival** *Page 161* **Academic Track:** Life Science	**Lesson A:** Listening to a Biologist's Talk about Birds Discussing Endangered Species **Lesson B:** Listening to a Conversation about a Science Experiment Planning and Presenting a Research Proposal	Understanding meaning from context Using new vocabulary to paraphrase statements	Taking brief notes Using graphic organizers for note-taking Listening for specific expressions **Pronunciation:** Full and reduced vowel sounds and secondary stress
10 **Entrepreneurs and New Businesses** *Page 181* **Academic Track:** Business and Economics **Independent Student Handbook** *Page 201*	**Lesson A:** Listening to a PowerPoint® Lecture Discussing New Business Ideas **Lesson B:** Listening to a Case Study and a Conversation Creating a Commercial	Understanding meaning from context Using new vocabulary to discuss unit content	Listening for main ideas Listening for details Note-taking **Pronunciation:** Thought groups

Grammar	Speaking Skills	Viewing	Critical Thinking Skills
The real conditional with the present The real conditional with the future	Interrupting and returning to topic Managing a discussion **Student to Student:** Expressing thanks and appreciation **Presentation Skills:** Talking about visuals	**Video:** *The Food and Culture of Oaxaca* Viewing to confirm predictions Viewing for specific information Note-taking while viewing	Identifying visuals Interpreting nutritional guidelines Discussing results using grammar from the unit Categorizing new expressions using a T-chart Developing an argument for a mini-debate **Critical Thinking Focus:** Supporting reasons with examples
Imperatives Gerunds as subjects and objects	Using transitions Refusing politely **Student to Student:** Polite refusals **Presentation Skills:** Speaking slowly	**Video:** *Volcano Trek* Viewing for specific information Making inferences Relating a video to personal opinion	Interpreting a map Understanding diagrams Identifying imperatives Developing instructions for an emergency or important event Using a chart to organize notes for a presentation **Critical Thinking Focus:** Predicting exam questions
The passive voice with the past Phrasal verbs	Using the passive voice to talk about famous sites Discussing problems **Student to Student:** Voicing a small problem **Presentation Skills:** Oral summaries	**Video:** *The Lost City of Machu Picchu* Viewing for specific information Viewing for general understanding Making inferences	Interpreting information from a map Discussing prior knowledge of a topic Analyzing and discussing information Categorizing new vocabulary Inferring points of view and rationalizing them **Critical Thinking Focus:** Making Inferences
The simple present with facts Phrasal verbs: review	Explaining causes and effects Congratulating **Student to Student:** Congratulating **Presentation Skills:** Choosing information to support your topic	**Video:** *A Disappearing World* Using prior knowledge Viewing for specific information Evaluating content from the video	Comparing notes with a partner Explaining a process Using a graphic organizer to list pros and cons Relating prior knowledge and personal experience to a listening passage Developing a research proposal **Critical Thinking Focus:** Using a graphic organizer to take notes
The infinitive of purpose The present perfect tense	Speculating about the future Using the present perfect to start conversations **Student to Student:** Giving compliments **Presentation Skill:** Showing enthusiasm for your topic	**Video:** *Making a Deal in Fes* Relating the video to personal experience Viewing for specific information Viewing for general understanding	Discussing statistics Evaluating business ideas Identifying reasons Applying new grammar and vocabulary to discussions and informal conversations Synthesizing content from the unit **Critical Thinking Focus:** Using questions to evaluate information

Each unit consists of two lessons which include the following sections:

Building Vocabulary
Using Vocabulary
Developing Listening Skills
Exploring Spoken English
Speaking (called "Engage" in Lesson B)

An **academic pathway** is clearly labeled for learners, starting with formal listening (e.g., lectures) and moving to a more informal context (e.g., a conversation between students in a study group).

The **"Exploring the Theme"** section provides a visual introduction to the unit and encourages learners to think critically and share ideas about the unit topic.

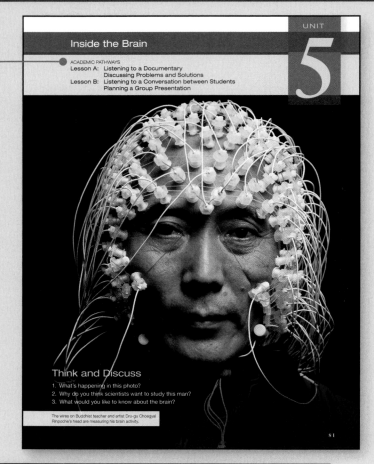

UNIT 5

Inside the Brain

ACADEMIC PATHWAYS
Lesson A: Listening to a Documentary
Discussing Problems and Solutions
Lesson B: Listening to a Conversation between Students
Planning a Group Presentation

Think and Discuss
1. What's happening in this photo?
2. Why do you think scientists want to study this man?
3. What would you like to know about the brain?

The wires on Buddhist teacher and artist Dru-gu Choegyal Rinpoche's head are measuring his brain activity.

81

Exploring the Theme:
Inside the Brain

Look at the photos and read the captions. Then discuss the questions.
1. What are some things your brain helps you do?
2. What happens to your brain when you learn something new?
3. What is your *hippocampus*?

How Does Learning Affect Our Brains?

How Do We Remember Information?

Studies show that when we learn something new, it changes the structure of our brains.

Glen McNeill spends six or seven hours a day riding his motor bike through the streets of London, England so he can become a taxi driver. When he finishes his training, his *hippocampus*, the area of the brain used for memory, will be larger than most adults'.

A laurel maze at Glendurgal in Cornwall, England

Key academic and high-frequency vocabulary is introduced, practiced, and expanded throughout each unit. Lessons A and B each present and practice 10 terms.

A **"Developing Listening Skills"** section follows a before, during, and after listening approach to give learners the tools necessary to master listening skills for a variety of contexts.

Listening activities encourage learners to listen for and consolidate key information, reinforcing the language and allowing learners to think critically about the information they hear.

USING VOCABULARY

A | Complete each sentence with the correct form of a word in blue from exercise **A** on page 84. Use each word only once.

1. The heart has a very important _____. It moves blood through the body.
2. The new art museum is a very interesting _____. It's made of glass and shaped like a pyramid.
3. Airplanes move at very high _____. Most planes fly at about 500 miles (805 kilometers) per hour.
4. It's amazing that water, wind, and our brains can all _____ electricity!
5. Brain cells are very _____. You can't see them without a microscope.
6. When you are driving and you see a red traffic light, it's a _____ to stop.
7. Allen seems like he's in a bad _____ today. I think it's because his team lost last night.
8. Our landlord _____ the heat in our apartment. We can't change it ourselves.
9. My hotel room doesn't have an Internet _____, so I can't send email.
10. Russian is a very _____ language. It has a different alphabet and the grammar and pronunciation are very difficult.

B | **Discussion.** With a partner, discuss the questions below.

1. Look at the facts on page 84. Which facts do you think are most interesting? Explain.
2. Your *amygdala* helps you "read" other people's faces and understand their moods. How can doing this be useful?
3. What things put you in a good mood? What things put you in a bad mood?
4. What are some signals you can give someone to show you're happy? To show you understand? To show you agree?

Your amygdala helps you "read" other people's faces and understand their moods.

Before Listening

Predicting Content. Discuss the question with a partner.

You are going to listen to a documentary about the human brain. Which of these topics do you expect to hear about in the documentary? Circle your ideas.

exercise	learning	food
neurons	memory	intelligence

An image of the human brain

Listening: A Documentary

A | Listen to the documentary and check your predictions.

B | **Listening for Main Ideas.** Listen again and put a check (✔) next to the main ideas.

☐ Your brain is a very important and complex organ.
☐ Your brain tells your muscles what to do.
☐ Your brain is very powerful.
☐ You brain can send messages very quickly.
☐ Your brain helps you protect your pets.
☐ Learning changes your brain.
☐ Exercise helps you learn.

C | **Listening for Details.** Read the statements below. Then listen again and circle **T** for *true* or **F** for *false*.

1. Your brain weighs five pounds. **T F**
2. Computers can process information more quickly than our brains can. **T F**
3. Your brain contains about 100 million neurons. **T F**
4. Motor neurons can send information at 200 miles per hour. **T F**
5. Exercise can improve your mood. **T F**
6. Exercise produces chemicals that make it easier to learn. **T F**

After Listening

Discussion. With a partner, discuss the questions below.

1. What are some activities or skills that were difficult for you at first, but are easy for you now (e.g., riding a bicycle)?
2. Do you agree that exercise improves your mood? Explain.
3. Do you think that exercise helps you study or solve problems more easily? Explain.

Pronunciation

Linking Sounds

When people speak quickly, they do not stop or pause after each word. In fact, you often hear words that are joined or linked together. Three common types of linking are:

Consonant sound → Vowel sound

It's a fascinating job.

Vowel sound → Vowel sound

I knew it was the right answer.
The book will certainly be interesting.

Consonant sound → Same consonant sound

What was your reason for being late?

Collaboration. Work with a partner. Listen to the sentences. Then take turns saying the sentences. Identify the types of linking used in each sentence. Write **C-V** for consonant-vowel, **V-V** for vowel-vowel, and **C-SC** for consonant-same consonant.

1. Your brain controls everything you do. *C-V*
2. Your brain generates enough energy to power a light bulb. _____
3. The activity in your brain never stops. _____
4. Your brain sends a message to your foot to shake the bee off quickly. _____
5. Any exercise that makes your heart beat faster can help your mood. _____
6. Your body produces a chemical that makes it easier to learn. _____

EXPLORING SPOKEN ENGLISH

Grammar

Infinitives after Verbs

We can use infinitives after certain transitive verbs.
I'll *try* **to study** more tonight.
Last night I *needed* **to sleep**.
I *forgot* **to bring** my notebook to class.

Note: Verbs cannot have other verbs as objects.
✗ Volkan and Begum **plan take** a vacation in August.
✔ Volkan and Begum **plan to take** a vacation in August.

A | Take turns asking and answering the questions with a partner. Notice the underlined words in each sentence.

1. What do you <u>want to do</u> next weekend?
2. What do you <u>need to do</u> tonight?
3. What do you always <u>remember to do</u> in the morning?

B | Complete each sentence with an appropriate infinitive.

1. I promise not ____to spend____ too much money on my vacation.
2. Pablo tried _____ his friend John with his homework.
3. My daughter sometimes forgets _____ her teeth in the morning.
4. If you want _____ a new vocabulary word, you should write it down.
5. The Norton family decided _____ a new car.
6. Lee is pretending _____ sick so he can stay in bed all day.
7. Do you want _____ our presentation this afternoon?
8. I really hope _____ Amy next time she comes to New York.

C | **Discussion.** Practice asking and answering the questions with a partner.

1. What do you try to do every day?
2. What do you need to do tomorrow?
3. What do you want to do this weekend?
4. What do you hope to do this summer?

What do you try to do every day?

I try to go to the gym every day.

D | Look at the photos and read the captions. Notice the verbs in **bold**.

They are **planning** to take a vacation.

She **learned** to play the violin.

They are **deciding** what to order.

You must **remember** to be on time for a job interview.

E | **Self-Reflection.** Finish the sentences about yourself. Then read your sentences to a partner.

1. I plan to _____
2. In this class, I'm learning to _____
3. I really want to _____
4. Yesterday, I remembered to _____
5. I've decided to _____
6. In the future, I hope to _____

F | Say any verb from the box below to your partner. Your partner must quickly say a correct sentence using that verb. Then switch roles. Repeat the process as many times as possible in two minutes.

remember	learn	plan	want	decide	need
choose	hope	prepare	promise	try	forget

forget

I forgot to bring my notebook to class today.

The **"Exploring Spoken English"** section allows students to examine and practice specific grammar points and language functions from the unit while enabling them to sharpen their listening and speaking skills.

Lesson A closes with a **full page of "Speaking" activities** including pair and group work activities, increasing learner confidence when communicating in English.

A variety of activity types simulates the academic classroom where multiple skills must be applied simultaneously for success.

SPEAKING

Discussing Problems and Solutions

A | Read the information about the different problems people have.

Josh
"My wife and I are from different countries. We can't decide where to live after our children are born."

Maya
"I already speak English. Now I want to learn Japanese, but I don't have time to take classes because of my busy work schedule."

Toby
"I spend too much money on video games, music, and electronics. Every time I see a new game, I want to buy it. I'm spending too much money!"

Ken
"Every time I want to leave my apartment, I have to look for my keys. I never remember to put my keys in the same place so I can find them."

Renata
"I don't want to live alone in this house anymore. My husband died five years ago, and my son and daughter are married now and have their own houses and families. This house feels too big for me now."

B | **Brainstorming.** What should these people do? Brainstorm possible solutions to each person's problem in your notebook.

C | Form a group with four other students. Choose one of the people from exercise **A** to role-play. Take turns talking about your problems and making helpful suggestions. Use your own words and the expressions from page 90.

My wife wants to be closer to her family when our children are born.

You could spend a few years in one country and then move.

Or try to convince your wife to live in your country.

● The **"Viewing" section** works as a content-bridge between Lesson A and Lesson B and includes two pages of activities based on a fascinating video from National Geographic.

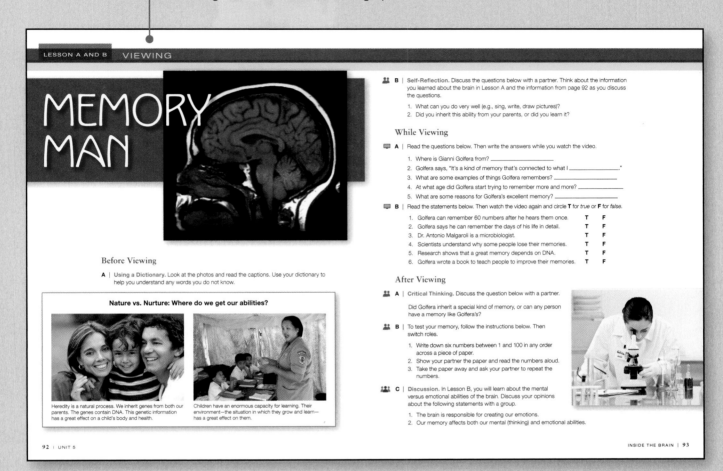

LESSON A AND B   VIEWING

MEMORY MAN

Before Viewing

A | **Using a Dictionary.** Look at the photos and read the captions. Use your dictionary to help you understand any words you do not know.

Nature vs. Nurture: Where do we get our abilities?

Heredity is a natural process. We inherit genes from both our parents. The genes contain DNA. This genetic information has a great effect on a child's body and health.

Children have an enormous capacity for learning. Their environment—the situation in which they grow and learn—has a great effect on them.

B | **Self-Reflection.** Discuss the questions below with a partner. Think about the information you learned about the brain in Lesson A and the information from page 92 as you discuss the questions.

1. What can you do very well (e.g., sing, write, draw pictures)?
2. Did you inherit this ability from your parents, or did you learn it?

While Viewing

A | Read the questions below. Then write the answers while you watch the video.

1. Where is Gianni Golfera from? _____
2. Golfera says, "It's a kind of memory that's connected to what I _____."
3. What are some examples of things Golfera remembers? _____
4. At what age did Golfera start trying to remember more and more? _____
5. What are some reasons for Golfera's excellent memory? _____

B | Read the statements below. Then watch the video again and circle **T** for *true* or **F** for *false*.

1. Golfera can remember 60 numbers after he hears them once.   **T   F**
2. Golfera says he can remember the days of his life in detail.   **T   F**
3. Dr. Antonio Malgaroli is a microbiologist.   **T   F**
4. Scientists understand why some people lose their memories.   **T   F**
5. Research shows that a great memory depends on DNA.   **T   F**
6. Golfera wrote a book to teach people to improve their memories.   **T   F**

After Viewing

A | **Critical Thinking.** Discuss the question below with a partner.

Did Golfera inherit a special kind of memory, or can any person have a memory like Golfera's?

B | To test your memory, follow the instructions below. Then switch roles.

1. Write down six numbers between 1 and 100 in any order across a piece of paper.
2. Show your partner the paper and read the numbers aloud.
3. Take the paper away and ask your partner to repeat the numbers.

C | **Discussion.** In Lesson B, you will learn about the mental versus emotional abilities of the brain. Discuss your opinions about the following statements with a group.

1. The brain is responsible for creating our emotions.
2. Our memory affects both our mental (thinking) and emotional abilities.

92 | UNIT 5   INSIDE THE BRAIN | 93

● **A DVD for each level** contains 10 authentic videos from National Geographic specially adapted for English language learners.

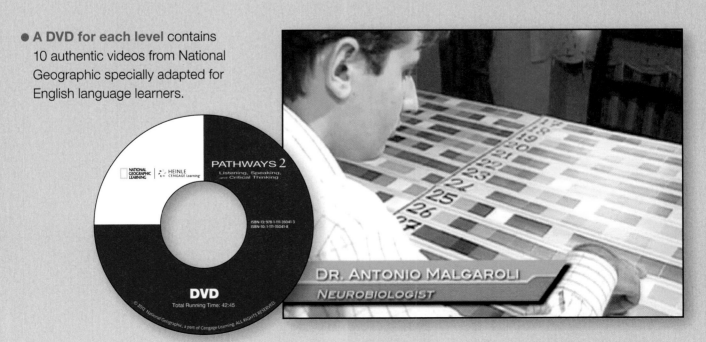

NATIONAL GEOGRAPHIC LEARNING   HEINLE CENGAGE Learning

PATHWAYS 2
Listening, Speaking, and Critical Thinking

ISBN-13: 978-1-111-35041-3
ISBN-10: 1-111-35041-8

DVD
Total Running Time: 42:45

© 2012 National Geographic, a part of Cengage Learning. ALL RIGHTS RESERVED.

DR. ANTONIO MALGAROLI
NEUROBIOLOGIST

Critical thinking activities are integrated in every unit encouraging continuous engagement in developing academic skills.

An **"Engage" section** at the end of the unit challenges learners with an end-of-unit presentation project. Speaking tips are offered for formal and informal group communication, instructing students to interact appropriately in different academic situations.

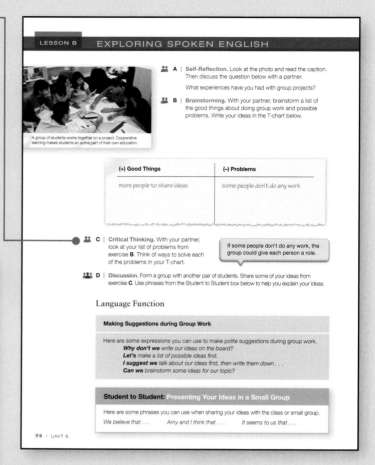

LESSON B   EXPLORING SPOKEN ENGLISH

A | **Self-Reflection.** Look at the photo and read the caption. Then discuss the question below with a partner.

What experiences have you had with group projects?

B | **Brainstorming.** With your partner, brainstorm a list of the good things about doing group work and possible problems. Write your ideas in the T-chart below.

A group of students works together on a project. Cooperative learning makes students an active part of their own education.

(+) Good Things	(−) Problems
more people to share ideas	some people don't do any work

C | **Critical Thinking.** With your partner, look at your list of problems from exercise **B**. Think of ways to solve each of the problems in your T-chart.

> If some people don't do any work, the group could give each person a role.

D | **Discussion.** Form a group with another pair of students. Share some of your ideas from exercise **C**. Use phrases from the Student to Student box below to help you explain your ideas.

Language Function

Making Suggestions during Group Work

Here are some expressions you can use to make polite suggestions during group work.
Why don't we write our ideas on the board?
Let's make a list of possible ideas first.
I suggest we talk about our ideas first, then write them down . . .
Can we brainstorm some ideas for our topic?

Student to Student: Presenting Your Ideas in a Small Group

Here are some phrases you can use when sharing your ideas with the class or small group.
We believe that . . .   Amy and I think that . . .   It seems to us that . . .

98 | UNIT 5

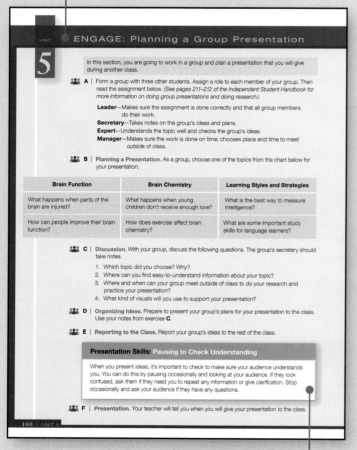

UNIT 5   ENGAGE: Planning a Group Presentation

In this section, you are going to work in a group and plan a presentation that you will give during another class.

A | Form a group with three other students. Assign a role to each member of your group. Then read the assignment below. *(See pages 211–212 of the Independent Student Handbook for more information on doing group presentations and doing research.)*

Leader—Makes sure the assignment is done correctly and that all group members do their work.
Secretary—Takes notes on the group's ideas and plans.
Expert—Understands the topic well and checks the group's ideas.
Manager—Makes sure the work is done on time; chooses place and time to meet outside of class.

B | **Planning a Presentation.** As a group, choose one of the topics from the chart below for your presentation.

Brain Function	Brain Chemistry	Learning Styles and Strategies
What happens when parts of the brain are injured?	What happens when young children don't receive enough love?	What is the best way to measure intelligence?
How can people improve their brain function?	How does exercise affect brain chemistry?	What are some important study skills for language learners?

C | **Discussion.** With your group, discuss the following questions. The group's secretary should take notes.

1. Which topic did you choose? Why?
2. Where can you find easy-to-understand information about your topic?
3. Where and when can your group meet outside of class to do your research and practice your presentation?
4. What kind of visuals will you use to support your presentation?

D | **Organizing Ideas.** Prepare to present your group's plans for your presentation to the class. Use your notes from exercise **C**.

E | **Reporting to the Class.** Report your group's ideas to the rest of the class.

Presentation Skills: Pausing to Check Understanding

When you present ideas, it's important to check to make sure your audience understands you. You can do this by pausing occasionally and looking at your audience. If they look confused, ask them if they need you to repeat any information or give clarification. Stop occasionally and ask your audience if they have any questions.

F | **Presentation.** Your teacher will tell you when you will give your presentation to the class.

100 | UNIT 5

"Presentation Skills" boxes offer helpful tips and suggestions for successful academic presentations.

A 19-page **"Independent Student Handbook"** is conveniently located in the back of the book and provides helpful self-study strategies for students to become better independent learners.

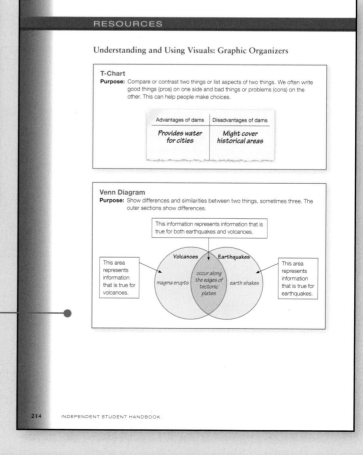

RESOURCES

Understanding and Using Visuals: Graphic Organizers

T-Chart
Purpose: Compare or contrast two things or list aspects of two things. We often write good things (pros) on one side and bad things or problems (cons) on the other. This can help people make choices.

Advantages of dams	Disadvantages of dams
Provides water for cities	Might cover historical areas

Venn Diagram
Purpose: Show differences and similarities between two things, sometimes three. The outer sections show differences.

This information represents information that is true for both earthquakes and volcanoes.

This area represents information that is true for volcanoes.

Volcanoes — magma erupts

occur along the edges of tectonic plates

Earthquakes — earth shakes

This area represents information that is true for earthquakes.

214   INDEPENDENT STUDENT HANDBOOK

For the Teacher:

Perfect for integrating language practice with exciting visuals, **video clips from National Geographic** bring the sights and sounds of our world into the classroom.

A **Teacher's Guide** is available in an easy-to-use format and includes teacher's notes, expansion activities, and answer keys for activities in the student book.

The Assessment CD-ROM with Exam*View*® is a test generating software program with a data bank of ready-made questions designed to allow teachers to assess students quickly and effectively.

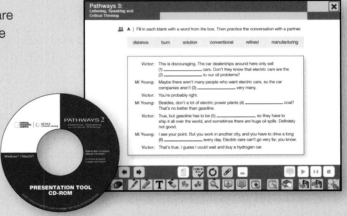

Bringing a new dimension to the language learning classroom, the **Classroom Presentation Tool CD-ROM** makes instruction clearer and learning easier through interactive activities, audio and video clips, and Presentation Worksheets.

For the Student:

The **Student Book** helps students achieve academic success in and outside of the classroom.

Audio CDs contain the audio recordings for the exercises in the student books.

ELT. Powered by MyELT, the **Online Workbook** has both teacher-led and self-study options. It contains 10 National Geographic video clips, supported by interactive, automatically graded activities that practice the skills learned in the student books.

Visit elt.heinle.com/pathways for additional teacher and student resources.

CREDITS

LISTENING AND TEXT

4: Adapted from "New Wrinkles on Aging": National Geographic Magazine, November 2005, **14:** Adapted from "Misery for all Seasons," by Jennifer Kahn: National Geographic Magazine, February 2007, **25:** Adapted from "Saving Energy Starts at Home," by Peter Miller: National Geographic Magazine, March 2009, **26-27:** Adapted from "Global Footprints", **25-35:** Adapted from "Saving Energy Starts at Home" by Peter Miller: National Geographic Magazine, March 2009, **34:** Adapted from "Saving Energy Starts at Home" by Peter Miller: National Geographic Magazine, March 2009, **35:** Adapted from "Saving Energy Starts at Home" by Peter Miller: National Geographic Magazine, March 2009, **46-47:** Adapted from "21st Century Cowboys: Why the Spirit Endures," by Robert Draper: National Geographic Magazine, December 2007, **66:** Adapted from "China's Three Gorges Dam," National Geographic News, June 2006 by Brian Handwerk, **74:** Adapted from "Australia's Dry Run," by Robert Draper: National Geographic Magazine, April 2009, **76-77:** Adapted from "Australia's Dry Run: Parched Lands," by Martin Gramache: National Geographic Magazine, April 2009, **76:** Adapted from "Changing Rains: Outlook: Extreme, by Elizabeth Kolbert": National Geographic Magazine, April 2009, **86:** Adapted from "Your Amazing Brain": National Geographic Kids Web site, November 2005, **94:** Adapted from "Love," National Geographic Magazine, February 2006, by Lauren Slater, **124:** Adapted from "Active Earth," National Geographic Magazine, February 2010 by Beth Geiger, **124-125:** Adapted from "Safe Houses," National Geographic, June 2010, by Chris Carroll, **134:** Adapted from "Volcano Culture," National Geographic Magazine, by Andrew Marshall, **144-145:** Adapted from "The Dawn of the Maya Gods and Kings," National Geographic Magazine, January 2006, by William Saturno, **156-157:** Adapted from "Geographica: Vietnam Unearths its Royal Past," National Geographic Magazine, June 2005, **164:** Adapted from "Darwin's First Clues," National Geographic Magazine, February 2009, by Matt Ridley, **165:** Adapted from "Massive Genetic Study Supports "Out of Africa Theory," National Geographic New, February 2008, **171:** Adapted from "Lifeline for the Iberian Lynx," National Geographic Magazine, May 2010, by Jennifer Holland, **174-175:** Adapted from "Scanning Life," National Geographic Magazine, May 2010 Big Idea, by Robert Kunzig, **178:** Adapted from "Discovery in the Foja Mountains," National Geographic Magazine, June 2010, by Mel White, **186-187:** Adapted from "Flower Trade," National Geographic Magazine, April 2001, by Vivienne Walt

PHOTOS

1: David Mclain, **2-3:** Randy Olson/National Geographic Image Collection, **3:** John Burcham/National Geographic Image Collection, **3:** Justin Guariglia/National Geographic Image Collection, **3:** Greg Dale/National Geographic Image Collection, **4:** David Mclain/National Geographic Image Collection, **4:** David Mclain/National Geographic Image Collection, **5:** David Mclain/National Geographic, **6:** Dean Mitchell/Shutterstock.com, **7:** Susan Seubert/National Geographic Image Collection, **8:** Bill Hatcher/National Geographic Image Collection, **9:** rj lerich/Shutterstock.com, **10:** Bill Hatcher/National Geographic Image Collection, **11:** Mika Heittola/Shutterstock.com, **12:** Lynn Johnson/National Geographic Image Collection, **12:** Siberian Lena/Shutterstock.com, **13:** Joe Petersburger/National Geographic Image Collection, **13:** O. Louis Mazzatenta/National Geographic Image Collection, **14:** Steve Peters/National Geographic Images, **14:** Jason Stitt, 2009/Shutterstock.com, **15:** Robert Madden/National Geographic Images, **16:** David Mclain, **17:** Pete Mcbride/National Geographic Images, **19:** Daniel Laflor/iStockphoto.com, **20:** Yuri Arcurs/Shutterstock.com, **21:** Tyrone Turner/National Geographic Society/Corbis, **22-23:** Jason Hawkes/National Geographic Image Collection, **23:** Joel Sartore/National Geographic Image Collection, **23:** Sarah Leen/National Geographic Image Collection, **24:** Greg Dale/National Geographic Image Collection, **24:** imagebroker/Alamy, **26:** Heiner Heine/imagebroker/Alamy, **26:** Andy Z, 2010/Shutterstock.com, **26:** Lori Epstein/National Geographic Image Collection, **27:** Jodi Cobb/National Geographic Image Collection, **27:** Jodi Cobb/National Geographic Image Collection, **27:** Jodi Cobb/National Geographic Image Collection, **27:** Jodi Cobb/National Geographic Image Collection, **27:** Jodi Cobb/National Geographic Image Collection, **27:** Jodi Cobb/National Geographic Image Collection, **28:** Adeel Halim/Bloomberg/Getty Images, **29:** Karine Aigner/National Geographic Image Collection, **32:** Daniel Karmann/dpa/Landov, **32:** Gene Chutka/iStockphoto.com, **33:** Fuse/Jupiter Images, **33:** Eugene Suslo, 2010/Shutterstock.com, **34:** Pichugin Dmitry/Shutterstock.com, **35:** Joel Sartore/National Geographic Image Collection, **37:** Kohlerphoto/iStockphoto.com, **37:** Ilya Andriyanov, 2010/Shutterstock.com, **37:** Baloncici, 2010/Shutterstock.com, **37:** Joseph McCullar, 2010/Shutterstock.com, **37:** Hywit Dimyadi, 2010/Shutterstock.com, **37:** Windzepher/iStockphoto.com, **38:** Katerina Evseyeva/National Geographic Image Collection, **39:** YinYang/iStockphoto.com, **41:** Konrad Wothe/Minden Pictures, **42:** Justin Guariglia/National Geographic Image Collection, **42:** Gordon Wiltsie/National Geographic Image Collection, **42:** Michael Moxter/vario images/Alamy, **43:** Frans Lanting/National Geographic Image Collection, **43:** Chuck Place/Alamy, **43:** Kobby Dagan, 2010/Shutterstock.com, **45:** Grey Villet/Time Life Pictures/Getty Images, **46:** David Scott Smith/PhotoLibrary, **47:** Robb Kendrick/National Geographic Image Collection, **47:** Robb Kendrick/National Geographic Image Collection, **48:** Steve Von Bokern/iStockphoto.com, **50:** Simone van den Berg, 2010/Shutterstock.com, **50:** Monkey Business Images, 2009/Shutterstock.com, **51:** David South/Alamy, **51:** David L. Moore-Hawaii/Alamy, **51:** Kobby Dagan, 2010/Shutterstock.com, **52:** James P. Blair/National Geographic Image Collection, **52:** Beth Wald/National Geographic Image Collection, **53:** O. Louis Mazzatenta/National Geographic Image Collection, **53:** James P. Blair/National Geographic Image Collection, **54:** Stephen Sharnoff/National Geographic Stock, **55:** Chris Hill/National Geographic Image Collection, **56:** Christophe Bluntzer/Photolibrary, **58:** moodboard RF/PhotoLibrary, **58:** Kimberly Cubero/iStockphoto.com, **58:** James Estrin/The New York Times/Redux Pictures, **60:** Pictorial Press Ltd/Alamy, **60:** Toby Jacobs/Lebrecht Music and Arts Photo Library/Alamy, **60:** Mario Kos/iStockphoto.com, **60:** Lebrecht Music and Arts Photo Library/Alamy, **61:** Lynn Johnson/National Geographic Image Collection, **62:** George F. Mobley/National Geographic Image Collection, **62:** Gideon Mendel/Corbis News/Corbis, **62-63:** Jonas Bendiksen/National Geographic Image Collection, **64:** Jennifer Sharp/iStockphoto.com, **64:** Amit Dave/Reuters/Landov, **65:** Bates Littlehales/National Geographic Image Collection, **67:** Thomas Barrat, 2010/Shutterstock.com, **67:** David Evans/National Geographic Images, **70:** Gideon Mendel/Corbis, **71:** Q DRUM, **71:** Watercone.com, **71:** Kickstart International, **71:** Vestergaard Frandsen, **72:** AP Photo/Rajesh Kumar Singh, **72:** Mickael David/Author's Image Ltd/Alamy, **73:** Helene Rogers/Art Directors & TRIP/Alamy, **73:** Paul Springett 06/Alamy, **74:** Ian Waldie/Getty Images, **75:** Amy Toensing/National Geographic Image Collection, **75:** Karen Kasmauski/National Geographic Image Collection, **76:** Amy Toensing/National Geographic Image Collection, **76:** Amy Toensing/National Geographic Image Collection, **76:** Amy Toensing/National Geographic Image Collection, **76:** Amy Toensing/National Geographic Image Collection, **78:** Dusan Zidar/iStockphoto.com, **78:** Feng Yu, 2010/Shutterstock.com, **78:** Soubrette/iStockphoto.com, **78:** Kostiantyn Lievoshko/iStockphoto.com, **81:** Cary Wolinsky/National Geographic Image Collection, **82:** Greg Dale/National Geographic Image Collection, **82:** Cary Wolinsky/National Geographic Image Collection, **82-83:** Bob Krist/Corbis, **84:** O. Louis Mazzatenta/National Geographic Image Collection, **85:** Frans Lanting/National Geographic Image Collection, **85:** mamahoohooba/iStockphoto.com, **85:** Joel Sartore/National Geographic Image Collection,

continued on p. 226

Staying Healthy in the Modern World

Think and Discuss

1. What is the man in the photo doing?
2. Why do you think he is doing this?
Give at least two reasons.
3. Do you think you can do this? Why,
or why not?

An elderly man in Okinawa, Japan

Exploring the Theme:
Staying Healthy in the Modern World

Look at the photos and read the captions. Then discuss the questions.

1. What are some activities you see that can help you stay healthy?
2. What are some things you see that can cause health problems?
3. What do you do every day to stay healthy?

This street in Kolkata, India is filled with traffic and people going to and from their homes and jobs.

Reduce Stress

Tai chi is a form of exercise that uses slow, gentle movements. It can help reduce stress and other health problems.

Exercise Regularly

Exercising three times per week for 30 minutes can help keep you strong and healthy.

Eat a Healthy Diet

Eating a healthy diet that includes a lot of fresh fruits and vegetables is one way to prevent health problems such as heart disease.

track 1-2
A | **Meaning from Context.** Read and listen to the information about the people in Sardinia and Okinawa. Notice the words in blue. These are words you will hear and use in Lesson A.

The Secret to a Long Life

A 75-year-old shepherd in Sardinia stays healthy by keeping active.

What's the secret to a long, healthy life? It begins with genes[1] but also depends on good habits. Experts studied groups of people living in places where many people live to be 100 years old—including Sardinia, Italy, and Okinawa, Japan. People in these places suffer from fewer diseases and are more likely to live to be 100 than people in other parts of the world.

Sardinia

In Sardinia, many people, especially men, live longer than in other parts of the world. In general, women live longer than men. In fact, in the United States, there are four times as many 100-year-old women as men. However, in Sardinia, an equal number of men and women live to be 100. One of the reasons may be that men have a stress-free life there. The men typically work in the hills, which provides daily exercise and helps keep them strong. The women look after the house and money. "I do the work," says Tonino, a native Sardinian. "My wife does the worrying."

Okinawa

In Okinawa, people have very low rates of cancer and heart disease compared to Americans. One of the reasons for this is *Ikigai*, a Japanese word that translates to "reason for living." *Ikigai* may help prevent stress, which can cause high blood pressure. Okinawans also eat a healthy, low-calorie diet that consists of a lot of fresh vegetables. "A full plate of Okinawan vegetables, tofu, and a little fish or meat has fewer calories than a small hamburger," says Makoto Suzuki of the Okinawa Centenarian[2] Study. "And it will have many more healthy nutrients."

An elderly woman from Okinawa gets her exercise by growing vegetables.

[1]Genes are the parts of cells in living things that control physical characteristics.
[2]A centenarian is someone who is 100 years old or older.

B | Write each word in blue from exercise **A** next to its definition.

1. _____ (n.) a difficulty in life that makes you worried
2. _____ (adj.) in good health, with good muscles
3. _____ (adj.) probably true or going to happen
4. _____ (n.) things that you do often or regularly
5. _____ (n.) illnesses which affect people, animals, or plants
6. _____ (v.) to make something happen
7. _____ (n.) force
8. _____ (adj.) well and not sick
9. _____ (n.) the type of food you eat regularly
10. _____ (v.) to move your body energetically to stay healthy

A | Complete each sentence with the correct form of a word from exercise **B** on page 4.

1. Do you think chicken and fish are _____ foods?
2. Is running or walking a better kind of _____?
3. My grandmother is 90 and very healthy. I think she's _____ to live to 100.
4. Ed has a lot of _____ in his life right now. I think he needs to relax more.
5. George is very _____. He can lift 150 pounds! (68 kilograms)
6. The typical Sardinian _____ includes a lot of fish and fresh vegetables.
7. Eating too many hamburgers can _____ health problems.
8. Smoking is a very bad _____. You should quit.
9. Today a lot of people in the United States suffer from heart _____.
10. Larry's blood _____ is too *low*. That's unusual!

A 102-year-old woman lifts weights to keep fit.

B | **Discussion.** Form a group with two or three other students and discuss the questions below.

1. What other cultures do you know of that have a very **healthy diet**?
2. What are some ways that people can prevent health problems like heart **disease** and cancer?
3. What kinds of health problems can **stress cause**?
4. Why do you think women are more **likely** to live to 100 than men?
5. What **habits** do you think can help you live a long, **healthy** life?

> Do you exercise for 30 minutes or more a day?

> Yes, I do. I exercise for an hour every morning.

C | Find out how likely you are to live to be 100. Take turns asking and answering the questions below with a partner. Take notes on your partner's answers.

Questionnaire: How likely are you to live to be 100?

Question	Yes	No	Explain
1. Do you have a stress-free life?	☐	☐	_____
2. Do you have a few close friends that are very important to you?	☐	☐	_____
3. Do you exercise for 30 minutes or more a day?	☐	☐	_____
4. Has anyone in your family lived to be 90 or 100?	☐	☐	_____
5. Does your diet include a lot of fruits and vegetables?	☐	☐	_____
6. In general, do you think you have good, healthy habits?	☐	☐	_____

Answer: *The more questions you answered with "yes," the more likely you are to live to be 100!*

Pronunciation

 A | Read and listen to the sentences below. Notice the –s and –es word endings.

1. Frank exercises every day. He plays sports and lifts weights.
2. There are 16 doctors and 37 nurses at the hospital.

Word Endings –s and –es

For most words, an –s or –es ending does not add an extra syllable to the word. Examples:

leg (1 syllable)	legs (1 syllable)
like (1 syllable)	likes (1 syllable)
refer (2 syllables)	refers (2 syllables)

But if a word ends in an /s/, /sh/, /ch/, or /x/ sound, an –s or –es ending is pronounced /iz/ and adds an extra syllable to the word.

bus (1 syllable)	buses (2 syllables)
surprise (2 syllables)	surprises (3 syllables)
exercise (3 syllables)	exercises (4 syllables)

 B | Read and listen to an excerpt from a talk by a public health nurse. <u>Underline</u> the words with –s and –es endings.

Tara: Hello, everyone, and thanks for coming. I'd like to introduce myself. I'm Tara Sorenson, and I'm a public health nurse. Public health nurses are like other nurses, but we take care of more than one person. Our job is to keep everyone in the community healthy. I know—it's a *big* job! Mostly, I do this through education. Tonight, I have 45 minutes to teach you about heart disease.

 C | With a partner, take turns saying the sentences with the words you underlined from exercise **B**.

Before Listening

A | **Prior Knowledge.** Check (✔) the words and phrases you already know. Use your dictionary to help you with the words and phrases you don't know. Write the definitions in your notebook or vocabulary journal. *(See page 208 of the Independent Student Handbook for more information on keeping a vocabulary journal.)*

❏ blood vessel   ❏ narrow   ❏ overweight   ❏ coronary   ❏ medication   ❏ prevent

B | Predicting Content. Discuss the question below with a partner.

Which of these topics do you expect to hear about in a talk about preventing heart disease? Circle your ideas.

blood pressure	diet	education
exercise	music	stress

Listening: A Talk about Preventing Heart Disease

A | Listen to the talk and check your predictions from exercise **B** above.

track 1-6

Eating a diet that includes fresh fruits and vegetables can help prevent heart disease.

B | Listening for Main Ideas. Read the questions below. Then listen again and check (✔) the main ideas you hear.

track 1-6

1. What advice does the nurse give for preventing heart disease?

❏ Get your blood pressure checked.   ❏ Eat less salt and sugar.   ❏ Get enough exercise.
❏ Visit your doctor.   ❏ Drink a lot of water.   ❏ Read more about heart disease.

2. What does the nurse say are some common causes of heart disease?

❏ high blood pressure   ❏ smoking   ❏ living alone   ❏ high blood sugar

C | Listening for Details. Listen again and choose the correct word or phrase to complete each sentence.

track 1-6

1. According to the nurse, if you have high blood pressure, you need to _____.
   a. do something about it   b. take medication
2. According to _____, healthy eating habits can keep your weight and your blood pressure down.
   a. medical journals   b. government reports
3. To deal with stress, the nurse suggests going for a walk or _____.
   a. talking to a friend   b. taking a yoga class

After Listening

Critical Thinking. Discuss the questions with a partner.

1. What new information did you learn from the talk?
2. Do you plan to take any of the nurse's advice? Explain.

Grammar

 A | **Prior Knowledge.** Read and listen to some habits people have for exercising safely. Then answer the questions that follow.

track 1-7

A woman rides her bike down a hill on South Island, New Zealand.

Manuel:	I <u>always</u> drink plenty of water before I exercise.
Jenny:	I <u>never</u> ride my bike without wearing a helmet.
Samir:	I <u>usually</u> warm up for five to ten minutes before I exercise.
Monica:	My friends and I <u>often</u> bring healthy snacks such as fruit and peanuts when we go hiking.
Erik:	I <u>always</u> make sure to wear comfortable clothing. I don't want to be too hot or too cold.

1. Which of the underlined words have similar meanings?
2. Where do these words appear in the sentence?

Adverbs of Frequency	
100 percent	always
	usually
	often
	sometimes
	not often/seldom
0 percent	never

- One-word adverbs go before the main verb.
  *Mike **never** exercises.*
- One-word adverbs go after the verb *be*.
  *She is **often** tired.*

B | Unscramble the words to form sentences.

1. go I never gym the to ___I never go to the gym___.
2. always Kim golf on plays Saturdays _____.
3. Luigi doesn't football often play _____.
4. basketball sometimes I play _____.
5. the weekend goes usually swimming Amy on _____
   _____.
6. often We yoga do _____.

C | **Self-Reflection.** Complete the following sentences about yourself and your own exercise routine or habits. Then say your sentences to a partner.

1. I always _____.
2. I am usually _____.
3. I never _____.
4. I sometimes _____.
5. I often _____.

Language Function

Using Expressions of Frequency

We use these expressions to talk about frequency.

once a(n)
twice a(n)   hour / day / week / month / year
three times a(n)

I exercise **three times a week**.
She takes vitamins **once a day**.
Anita visits her grandparents in Chile **twice a year**.

We also use **every** to talk about frequency. *Every* has a similar meaning to *each*.

every   hour / day / week / month / year
           Monday / Tuesday / Wednesday
           six months / five years

Laura plays tennis **every Saturday**.
I go to the dentist **every six months**.
Angela goes to the gym **every day**.

A | **Critical Thinking.** Work with a partner. Look at the photo and read the caption. Then answer the question below.

How do you think Matthew helps people stay healthy?

Matthew Douglas works at a university Sports Medicine program. He teaches people about athletic training.

B | Collaboration. Work with a partner. What advice might Matthew give people? Write a list of things you think he might tell people.

1. _Everyone should exercise at least three times a week._
2. _____
3. _____
4. _____

C | Note-Taking. Form a group with two or three other students. Take turns interviewing the students in your group. Find out about their exercise routines and habits. What kind of exercise do they do? How often do they do it? Use the chart below to take notes. *(See pages 206-207 of the Independent Student Handbook for more information on note-taking.)*

A kayaker paddles in the Hope Arm of mountain ringed Lake Manapouri, New Zealand.

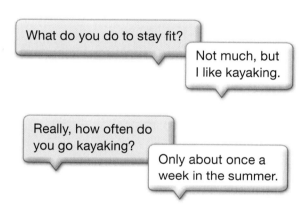

What do you do to stay fit?

Not much, but I like kayaking.

Really, how often do you go kayaking?

Only about once a week in the summer.

Name	Type of Exercise	Frequency
Alberto	kayaking	once a week/summer

D | Presentation. As a group, report your findings to the class.

Alberto doesn't exercise much, but he likes kayaking. He goes about once a week in the summer.

Giving a Presentation on Health and Exercise Habits

A | Self-Reflection. Answer the questions with information about your own habits.

1. What do you do every day to stay healthy? _____
2. Which kinds of exercise do you do? _____
3. How often do you do them? _____
4. How do you plan to stay healthy in the future? _____

B | Planning a Presentation. Use your notes from exercise **A** to plan a short presentation about your health and exercise habits. Your presentation should include the following four parts:

1. An introduction
2. Information about your personal health and exercise habits
3. Your plans for the future
4. A *thank you* to your audience for listening

track 1-8

C | Read and listen to the example of a student presentation below. Identify the four parts of the presentation. Write the correct number from exercise **B** next to each part of the presentation. You will need to use some numbers more than once.

Example:

Hello, my name is Megan Schwarz. (____)

To stay healthy, I exercise—but not every day. I usually exercise four or five days a week. I also take vitamins every day. (____)

For exercise, I usually go jogging two or three times a week. And I also walk, of course—I walk to class every day, actually. Sometimes I go biking, but I don't have my own bike, so I can only ride on weekends in the park. They rent bikes in the park on Saturdays and Sundays. (____)

In the future, I want to have a healthier diet. Now, I live in a very small apartment with no kitchen. I eat a lot of fast food because I can't cook for myself. After I graduate, I plan to move to a bigger apartment with a kitchen. I also want to buy my own bike so I can bike every day. (____)

Thank you very much. (____)

D | Practice your presentation with a partner. Make sure your presentation includes the four parts from exercise **B**.

E | Presentation. Give your presentation to the whole class. Use your notes from exercise **A** to help you.

Presentation Skills: Using Your Notes

When you give a presentation, do not read directly from your notes. Just use your notes to help you remember the information you want to talk about and when you want to talk about it. Not reading directly from your notes will help make your presentation more interesting. *(See pages 211–213 of the Independent Student Handbook for more information on giving presentations in class.)*

A beekeeper with honeycombs of honey and bees.

BEE THERAPY

Before Viewing

A | **Discussion.** Lesson A of this unit talked about different ways to stay healthy—from good eating habits to preventing heart disease. You are going to watch a video that talks about using bees to help people with certain kinds of illnesses. Discuss the questions with a partner.

1. When you are sick, do you turn to modern medicine for help? Explain.
2. Have you ever tried traditional medicine such as acupuncture? Explain.
3. Which kind of medicine works better, modern or traditional? Explain.

B | **Using a Dictionary.** You will hear these words in the video. Work with a partner and match each word with its definition. Use your dictionary to help you.

1. nerve (n.)	___	a.	hurt from an injury or illness
2. sting (v.)	___	b.	to put a liquid into a person's blood or under the skin
3. therapy (n.)	___	c.	the part of the body that carries messages between the brain and other parts of the body.
4. inject (v.)	___	d.	to cut into the skin, usually with venom (poison)
5. pain (n.)	___	e.	treatment of an illness over time

C | **Prior Knowledge.** Read about two illnesses. What do you know about them? Do you know anyone who has these illnesses?

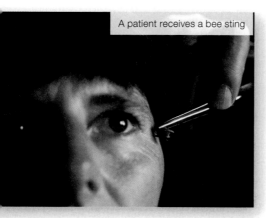

A patient receives a bee sting

Illness: Multiple sclerosis (MS)

Symptoms: It affects the nervous system (brain and spinal cord), so people with MS may not be able to walk, or may be in a lot of pain.

Illness: Arthritis

Symptoms: It affects the joints in the hands, knees, and other parts of the body. It causes pain, and is common in older adults.

While Viewing

A | Match each person's name to the information below.

1. Mr. Chen 　　　 2. Hso-rong Chen 　　　 3. Mr. Chen's wife

a. _____	b. _____	c. _____
had arthritic pain	has multiple sclerosis	bee-sting therapy master
could not cook	couldn't move for six months	used to be afraid of bees

A woman receives acupuncture treatment around her ears.

B | Watch the video again and complete the sentences below with the numbers you hear.

1. Every week, Mr. Chen and his assistants treat _____ patients and sacrifice _____ honeybees.
2. After _____ bees, you will look _____ years younger than your contemporaries.
3. Many think it is based on the _____-year-old practice of acupuncture.
4. After _____ months, her red blood cell count increased. Her headache disappeared.
5. After _____ months of bee-sting therapy, Hso-rong Chen has seen a dramatic change.

After Viewing

A | **Discussion.** Work with a partner and match each special expression below with its meaning. Then discuss how each expression was used in the video.

1. taboo ___
2. labor of love ___
3. a new lease on life ___

a. work that is not done for the money
b. a good attitude about the future
c. something most people avoid

B | **Critical Thinking.** Form a group with two or three other students and discuss the questions.

1. What other kinds of traditional or natural medicine do you know about? What kinds of illnesses do they cure?
2. Do you think modern or traditional medicine is more effective in curing serious illnesses like heart disease and cancer? Explain.
3. In Lesson B, you will learn about a growing health problem— allergies. Why do you think so many people suffer from allergies?

A | **Meaning from Context.** Read and listen to the information and look at the diagram. Notice the words in blue. These are words you will hear and use in Lesson B.

Allergies

What are allergies? If you have a particular *allergy* to something, you become sick, or have an *allergic reaction*, when you eat, smell, or touch it. Many people have allergies to pollen.[1] The diagram below shows what happens when there is an allergic reaction to pollen.

Yellow pollen covers the underside of a bee.

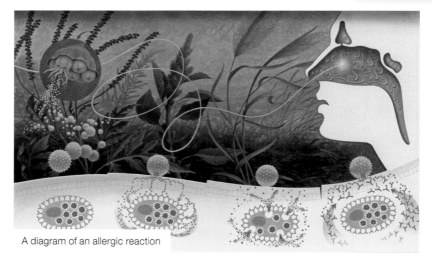
A diagram of an allergic reaction

1. First, pollen enters the body through the nose.
2. Second, the body's immune system responds to the pollen with IgE antibodies.[2] These antibodies attach to a mast cell. A mast cell is a cell that usually defends your body against health problems.
3. The next time the same pollen enters the body, the IgE antibodies "tell" the mast cell. The mast cell "thinks" there is a problem and tries to defend the body.
4. When this occurs, the mast cell produces substances in the body that cause allergic reactions, such as sneezing, itching, and breathing problems.

B | Write each word in blue from exercise **A** next to its definition. Use your dictionary to help you.

1. _____ (n.) the smallest part of an animal or plant
2. _____ (v.) goes into
3. _____ (v.) makes or creates
4. _____ (v.) reacts by doing something
5. _____ (v.) protects
6. _____ (v.) happens

Mast cells produce substances in the body that cause allergic reactions such as sneezing.

[1]**Pollen** is a powder produced by flowers to fertilize other flowers.

[2]**Antibodies** are substances your body produces to fight disease.

track 1-10

C | **Meaning from Context.** Read and listen to the information below. Notice the words in **blue**. These are words you will hear and use in Lesson B.

Allergies and the Hygiene Hypothesis

A dairy farmer stands near his cows, USA

Many people work very hard to keep their houses clean. But can too much cleanliness cause health problems?

One **theory** is that dirt is good for us. Dirt on farms, for example, **contains** substances that exercise our immune systems when we're very young. **Research** shows that allergies are not **common** among people who live with farm animals.

Of course, there are many causes of allergies. For example, if your parents have allergies, you're more likely to have them, too. The pressure and stress of modern life could be another cause. But if the hygiene hypothesis is correct, it might be a good idea to have a cow at your house—or at least not to worry so much about cleanliness.

D | Write each word in **blue** from exercise **C** next to its definition. Use your dictionary to help you.

1. _____ (v.) has something inside
2. _____ (adj.) usual
3. _____ (n.) work that involves studying something
4. _____ (n.) an idea used to explain something

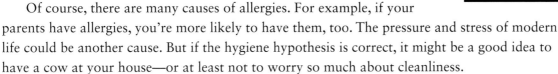

E | Work with a partner. Complete each sentence with a word from the box. You may need to change the form.

cell	contain	enter	produce	respond
common	defend	occur	research	theory

1. Pollen always _____ the body through the nose.
2. The human body is made of millions of tiny _____.
3. Being too clean is just one _____ to explain why people suffer from allergies.
4. An allergic reaction _____ when the body "thinks" there's a problem.
5. Colombia _____ delicious coffee.
6. Milk _____ a lot of important vitamins and nutrients.
7. The immune system usually _____ the body against diseases.
8. Scientists are now doing _____ to learn more about allergies.
9. A cold is a very _____ illness.
10. John usually _____ to my phone messages by email.

Before Listening

 | **Discussion.** Read part of a conversation. Then discuss the questions below with a partner.

Raymond:	I had no idea that allergies were so serious. And so common!
Elena:	Yeah, they are. I'm allergic to strawberries, peanuts, and chocolate—and I *love* chocolate.

1. What is Raymond surprised about?
2. Do you think Elena's food allergies make her life difficult? Explain.
3. Why might food allergies be a serious problem?

Listening: An Informal Conversation

track 1-11

A | **Listening for Main Ideas.** Listen to the conversation. What are the speakers most concerned about? Check (✔) your answers.

❏ air pollution   ❏ asthma   ❏ cats   ❏ food allergies   ❏ peanuts

track 1-11

B | **Listening for Details.** Listen again. Answer each question with a word or phrase from the conversation.

1. What is something that causes Elena's asthma to "act up"? _____
2. What percent of children have food allergies nowadays? _____
3. What is the "new" allergy problem? _____
4. Which food are many people allergic to? _____
5. When did the number of people with food allergies grow quickly? _____

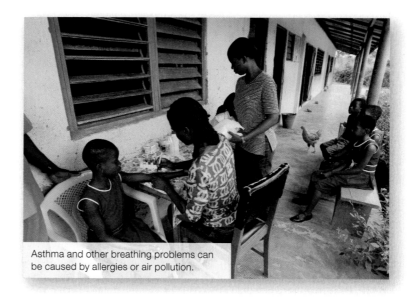

Asthma and other breathing problems can be caused by allergies or air pollution.

After Listening

When you make a statement in an academic setting, such as a lecture or a paper, you need to support the statement with evidence. Some types of evidence include:

Numbers and statistics:
*The number of malaria cases has dropped **39 percent** in the past two years.*
*About **4000** people in this country die from asthma each year.*

Experts:
***Research shows** that allergies are uncommon among people who live on farms.*
***Clinic director Paula Sanders recommends** getting several injections before the allergy season begins.*

Images:
***This picture shows** IgE antibodies on a mast cell.*
***In the video, you will see** children playing near the river.*

A | **Critical Thinking.** Which kind of evidence from the chart above do you think is the strongest? Why?

B | For each statement below, write a follow-up sentence with supporting evidence.

1. Food allergies are a growing problem these days. (numbers and statistics)

_____

2. There are new theories about the causes of asthma. (experts)

_____

3. Over time, the artery becomes narrow. (images)

_____

C | **Critical Thinking.** Compare your sentences with a partner's. Which evidence gives stronger support for each statement?

D | **Discussion.** With your partner, discuss what evidence you see in your daily life that supports the statement below.

Allergies are a growing problem.

Medical treatments such as injections can help people who suffer from allergies enjoy daily activities. This woman is enjoying a walk outdoors with her dog in Aspen, Colorado.

Grammar

Tag Questions

Forming Tag Questions

Affirmative statements have negative tag questions.

You're going to the gym, **aren't you?**

Negative statements have affirmative tag questions.

She doesn't have any health problems, **does she?**

Answering Tag Questions

We answer tag questions in the same way as other questions.

You did your homework, **didn't you?**

Yes, I did (if you did it), or **No, I didn't** (if you didn't do it).

Pronunciation

We use rising intonation when we're really not sure of the answer.

Peter's coming to class, **isn't he?**
(The speaker expects an answer.)

We use falling intonation when we think we already know the answer, or think the listener will agree.

They were late again, **weren't they?**
(The speaker is emphasizing a statement and expects you to say yes.)

track 1-12 **A** | Complete each sentence with a tag question. Then listen to check your answers.

1. John took the bus, _____?
2. They're tired, _____?
3. You called her last night, _____?
4. Tina likes pizza, _____?
5. That man is your friend, _____?
6. He's late again, _____?

track 1-12 **B** | Listen again. Decide whether the speaker is not sure **(NS)** of the answer or already knows **(AK)** the answer. Write **(NS)** or **(AK)** next to each question in exercise **A**.

C | Write sentences with tag questions for a partner to answer. Write tag questions about three things you already know about your partner and three things you do not know. Then ask your partner the questions.

1. _____
2. _____
3. _____
4. _____
5. _____
6. _____

You're from Mexico, aren't you?

Yes, I am.

Language Focus

Making Small Talk

"Small talk" is friendly conversation, often between classmates, neighbors, coworkers, or strangers. Good topics for small talk include:

The weather: *Wow! It's really hot today.*

Sports: *Did you watch the game last night?*

The present situation: *A lot of people are waiting to see the doctor today.*

Small talk is usually not about important topics such as political beliefs, and it should not be too personal.

Tag questions can be useful for making small talk.
It's a beautiful day, isn't it?
You're a new student, aren't you?

A | Read the conversations. Then practice them with a partner.

1. **A:** It's a nice day, isn't it?
   B: Beautiful!
   A: I'm happy to see the sun.
   B: Me, too.

2. **A:** Did Cameroon win yesterday?
   B: I'm not sure. They played Denmark, didn't they?
   A: Yes, but I don't know who won.

3. **A:** There are a lot of vocabulary words to learn.
   B: Yes, but they look useful.
   A: I agree.
   B: It's good to learn new words, isn't it?
   A: Yes, it is.

B | With your partner, take turns making small talk of your own.

Engage: Keeping a Conversation Going

In this activity, you are going to have a conversation about health and practice keeping the conversation going.

A | Read the information below about keeping a conversation going.

Keeping a conversation going is often considered polite in social and business situations. Here are some ways to help keep a conversation going.

Showing the speaker that you are listening.
Oh, really? That's interesting!

Asking a follow-up question about something the speaker said.
What was on the test?
The bus driver didn't really say that, did he?

Avoid *yes/no* questions. Use *wh–* questions instead. *Wh-* questions require speakers to give more information in their answers.
What do you think about that?
How often do you take a vacation?

 B | **Discussion.** Work with a partner. Choose one of the topics below. Keep your conversation going as long as you can.

Heart Health	Traditional Medicine	Allergies
What are some things people can do in their daily lives that can help prevent heart disease?	Why do people turn to bee therapy and other types of traditional medicine?	What are your experiences with allergies? (e.g., Do you or someone you know have them?)

 C | Form a group with four to six other students. Have a conversation contest. Follow the instructions below.

1. Choose one person to be the timekeeper and watch the clock.
2. In pairs, keep a conversation going for as long as possible about one of the topics in exercise **B**.
3. The timekeeper decides when the conversation has stopped and tells you how long the conversation lasted.
4. The pair that had the longest conversation wins!

Student to Student: Asking about Personal Knowledge and Experience

Asking about personal experiences can also help to keep a conversation going. You can use expressions like these to ask classmates about their personal knowledge and experiences.
Do you know anything about . . . ?
Does anyone in your family (have) . . . ?
What about you?

Energy and Our Planet

ACADEMIC PATHWAYS

Think and Discuss

1. What do you think the colors in this photo mean?
2. Look at the information on this page. What do you think you will learn about in this unit?

Thermal image of a house in New Haven, Connecticut, USA

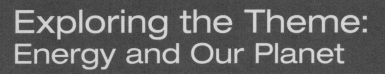

Exploring the Theme:
Energy and Our Planet

A | Look at the photos and read the captions. Then discuss the questions.

1. What kinds of energy or fuel do you see on these pages?
2. How is our energy use affecting the environment?
3. What are some examples of renewable energy?

B | Look at the pie charts. Then discuss the questions.

1. How much of the world's production of non-renewable energy comes from oil?
2. How much of the world's production of renewable energy comes from wind power?

London, England, at night

Fossil Fuels and The Environment

A grizzly bear and her cubs walk along an oil pipeline in Prudhoe Bay, Alaska. Our use of fossil fuels is impacting the environment in a variety of ways.

Renewable Forms of Energy

Wind turbines at Middelgrunden Wind Park in Copenhagen, Denmark, provide a renewable form of energy. Many countries are using renewable forms of energy such as wind, hydroelectric, and solar power.

Our Increasing Demand for Energy

World Energy Production

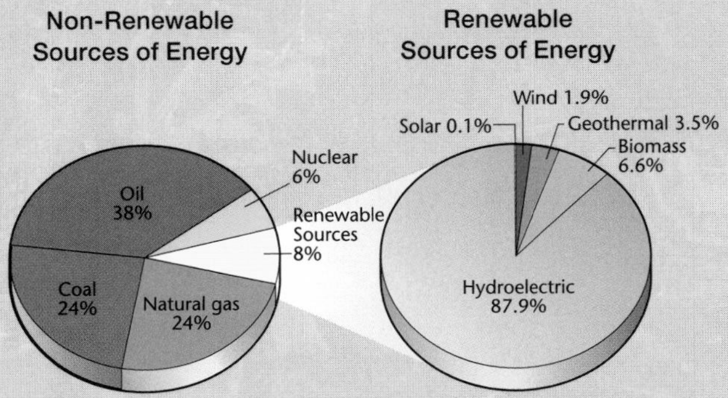

Non-Renewable Sources of Energy

Oil 38%
Coal 24%
Natural gas 24%
Nuclear 6%
Renewable Sources 8%

Renewable Sources of Energy

Solar 0.1%
Wind 1.9%
Geothermal 3.5%
Biomass 6.6%
Hydroelectric 87.9%

These pie charts show the world's production of renewable and non-renewable sources of energy. Each section represents a different source of energy. The numbers show what percent each source of energy makes up of all energy production.

The world is hungry for energy. Our use of coal and gas has increased by 100 percent since the 1970s, and our use of electricity has gone up by 200 percent. And still it isn't enough—more than 1.5 million people in the world today live without electricity. If our demand for energy doesn't change, the world's energy use could increase by another 50 percent by 2030. What can we do? To save our climate and environment, we need to produce more renewable energy such as **wind**, **solar**, and **hydroelectric** power.

track 1-13 **A** | **Meaning from Context.** Read and listen to the information about the process of global warming. Notice the words in blue. These are words you will hear and use in Lesson A.

The Process of Global Warming

Natural gas is a fossil fuel used for many daily activities such as cooking.

This coal-fueled power plant is sending carbon into the atmosphere.

1. Our **demand** for fossil fuels such as oil and natural gas is growing.
2. This growing need for **energy** causes us to burn more and more fossil fuels.
3. Burning fossil fuels such as coal puts **carbon** into the air.
4. Carbon dioxide, or CO_2, and other gases **reduce** the amount of heat that goes out into space.
5. When less heat goes out into space, it means that more heat stays in the earth's **atmosphere**.
6. When more heat stays in the earth's atmosphere, the average temperature **increases**, making it warmer.
7. A **significantly** higher average temperature leads to climate change and changes to the weather.
8. Climate change can have a negative **impact** on people's lives. For example, climate change can make it difficult to grow food in some places.
9. People are starting to **conserve** energy by making changes that cause them to use less fuel. For example, people are buying smaller cars.
10. Smaller cars are more **efficient** because they use less gas and oil.

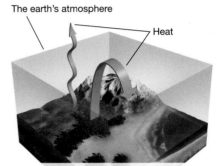
The earth's atmosphere

Heat

This diagram shows how CO_2 impacts the amount of heat that goes into the atmosphere. The blue box represents the earth's atmosphere. The yellow arrows represent amounts of heat.

B | Write each word in blue from exercise **A** next to its definition.

1. _____ (v.) to make smaller or less
2. _____ (n.) the power from oil, gas, and electricity
3. _____ (n.) the need for something
4. _____ (n.) the chemical element that coal is made from
5. _____ (n.) a strong effect on something
6. _____ (v.) makes larger or more
7. _____ (adv.) importantly
8. _____ (n.) the air around the earth
9. _____ (adj.) able to do something without using too much time or energy
10. _____ (v.) to use something carefully so that it lasts a long time

A | Read the article and fill in each blank with the correct form of a word in blue from exercise **A** page 24. Use each word only once.

The Impact of Our Energy Use on the Earth's Climate

Map Key

Least impact   Most impact

This map shows the amount of (1) _____ and other greenhouse gases that people in each country put into the (2) _____ by burning fossil fuels. These gases have (3) _____ changed the weather in many parts of the world.

Every year, the world is using more (4) _____, especially from fossil fuels like gas and oil. Some countries like China and India don't use much energy now, but their (5) _____ for energy is growing. In fact, it (6) _____ each year as they become more modern.

There are two important ways that countries can (7) _____ the amount of energy they use. One way countries can (8) _____ energy is by developing new sources of energy, such as wind or solar energy. The other way countries can use less energy is by manufacturing more (9) _____ cars that use less fuel. If countries work harder to decrease the amount of carbon they produce, it will have a positive (10) _____ on the earth's climate and weather.

B | **Understanding Visuals.** Look at the map in exercise **A**. Then discuss the questions below with a partner.

1. Find your country on the map. Do people in your country produce a little or a lot of carbon?
2. Which areas of the world produce the most carbon? Which areas produce the least?
3. What surprises you the most about this map?

Pronunciation

Stressing Key Words

track 1-14

English speakers put extra emphasis on the key words in a sentence by saying them more loudly and more clearly than other words. Key words are content words (*nouns, verbs, adjectives,* and *adverbs*) that give the listener important information.

Speakers usually stress the last content word in a sentence.
> Where is Karen **going**?

Speakers also use stress to disagree or contradict.
> *Is the meeting in Simpson Hall?*
> *No, the meeting is at the* **Student Union** *this week.*

track 1-15

Listen to the conversation. <u>Underline</u> the words in the conversation that the speakers stress. Then practice the conversation with a partner.

Katelyn:	Are you going to the Environmental Club meeting?
Dan:	Maybe. What is it about?
Katelyn:	It's a presentation about energy around the world. A photographer is going to talk about different families and how they live.
Dan:	Sounds interesting! What time is the meeting?
Katelyn:	It starts at seven.
Dan:	Is it in the science building?
Katelyn:	No, it's at the Student Union this time.

Before Listening

 Prior Knowledge. Work with a partner. Match the names of places with the photos below. In which of these places do you think people use the most energy? Explain.

Maun, Botswana (Africa)	Las Vegas, Nevada (USA)	Jaipur, Rajasthan (India)

a. _____   b. _____   c. _____

Listening: A PowerPoint Lecture

 A | **Listening for Main Ideas.** Listen to the talk and number the families in the order that you hear about them. Then write the country where each family lives.

_____ The Panchal family

country _____

_____ The Chuma family

country _____

_____ The Nelson family

country _____

B | **Listening for Details.** Listen again and complete the notes about each family.

The Chuma Family	The Nelson Family	The Panchal Family
wash _____ by hand, hang them in the sun to dry	wash and dry their clothes in _____	have a _____ for their clothes
children _____ to school or use a _____	parents _____ the children to school	want to build another _____ in their house
use _____ for lights and radio	use _____ of gasoline every day	Lalita goes to work by _____
they have _____ impact on the environment	to save energy, they bought _____ appliances	hopes the family will _____
sometimes they don't have _____ because of the dry climate	put _____ carbon into the atmosphere	more than 300 _____ middle-class people in India

After Listening

Critical Thinking. In your notebook, list the families in order of their energy use (from the most to the least). Then write three ways each family can conserve energy.

Language Function

Giving Examples

An example is something that represents a group of things.

Petroleum *is an example of a* **fossil fuel.**

Examples give specific information that can help support statements and make ideas clearer and easier to understand.

Many countries are trying to conserve energy. For example, **people in Japan are buying smaller cars.**

Here are some expressions speakers use when giving examples.
For instance, . . . , For example, . . . , such as . . .

A | Underline the expression used for giving an example in each sentence. Then circle the example.

1. The Chumas use fossil fuels for a few important things such as electric lights and a radio.
2. But global warming is having a big effect on people in Botswana, and the Chuma family is an example of this.
3. The Nelsons want to conserve energy, and they have done several things to save energy. For example, they bought more efficient appliances.
4. Changes in their way of life will make a big impact on the world's greenhouse gases. For instance, by 2050, India will have more than 600 million cars.

B | Look at the words you underlined in exercise **A** and answer the questions with a partner.

1. Which expressions come at the beginning of a sentence?
2. Which expressions come at the end of a sentence?
3. Which expressions come in the middle of the sentence?
4. Which expressions have a comma after them?

Traffic in India is increasing every day. Using fossil fuels such as oil puts carbon into the atmosphere.

C | Read each sentence and then write a specific example for the underlined word or words.

Many wild animals can now be found in American cities.

Specific example: *For example, the other day I saw an opossum in my backyard.*

1. I enjoy watching many kinds of sports.

   Specific example: _____

2. My daughter is learning about African animals in her science class.

   Specific example: _____

3. Using public transportation can help conserve energy.

   Specific example: _____

4. Burning fossil fuels causes greenhouse gases.

   Specific example: _____

A young opossum climbing a tree.

D | **Discussion.** With a partner, discuss the topics below. Try to teach your partner something new about yourself or your country. Give specific examples to explain your ideas.

| music | food | energy | interesting places | exercise | your idea _____ |

> I love Brazilian music. For example, I enjoy listening to Bossa Nova when I study.

> Really? I didn't know that. I like it, too.

Grammar

The Simple Present and the Present Continuous

We use the simple present to talk about facts or situations that are generally true.
> *The Nelsons **live** in Las Vegas.*
> *Burning fossil fuels such as coal **puts** carbon into the atmosphere.*

We also use the simple present to talk about habits and routines.
> *They **drive** to work every day.*

We use the present continuous to talk about actions in progress but that may not be happening right now.
> *Jennifer **is saving** money to buy a car.*

We also use the present continuous to talk about actions that are happening right now at the time of speaking.
> *Jim **is working**.*

A | Circle the correct form of the verb in parentheses.

1. Jeff (rides/is riding) his bike right now.
2. Turn off the TV. Nobody (watches/is watching) it.
3. The earth (receives/is receiving) less sunlight because of air pollution.
4. I (drink/am drinking) coffee every morning.
5. It (takes/is taking) a lot of energy to heat our apartment because it is so big.

B | Write sentences using the correct form of the verb and the words in parentheses.

1. I/exercise/(every morning) _I exercise for an hour every morning._
2. Paul/study/(right now) _____
3. Isabel/take/(four classes) _____
4. I/turn off/(my computer at night) _____
5. Carmen and Luis/speak/(three languages) _____
6. We/take/(English classes) _____

C | Work with a partner. Complete the conversations. Then practice saying them.

1. **A:** What are you doing here? You usually (drive/are driving) to work.
   B: Yes. But this week we _are taking the train_____.

2. **A:** We always (walk/are walking) to school when the weather is nice.
   B: But today it _____.

3. **A:** What (do you do/are you doing)?
   B: I _____.

4. **A:** (Does Marissa go/Is Marissa going) to school with you?
   B: Yes. But this week she _____.

5. **A:** Hello?
   B: Hi, Kim. (Do I call/Am I calling) at a bad time? (Do you eat dinner/Are you eating dinner)?
   A: No, I'm not. I _____.

Discussing Personal Energy Use

Critical Thinking Focus: Interpreting Pie Charts

Pie charts show us the different parts of something in a clear and visual way. Each section of a pie chart shows a different piece of information. For example, the pie chart in exercise **A** below shows the different ways that energy is used in an Australian household. *(See page 216 of the Independent Student Handbook for more information on understanding pie charts.)*

A | Understanding Visuals. With a partner, look at the pie chart and discuss the questions below.

1. The pie chart shows what people in Australia use energy for at home. What do the numbers in the chart show?
2. Which activities use the most energy? Which activities use the least energy?
3. Does any information in this chart surprise you? Explain.

B | Self-Reflection. Write your answers to the questions below in your notebook.

1. What appliances do you use?
2. How often do you use them?
3. What activities do you do that use a lot of energy?

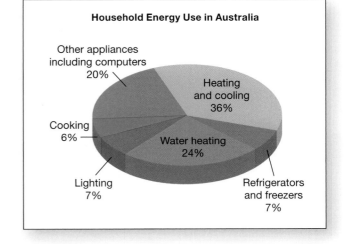

Household Energy Use in Australia

Other appliances including computers 20%
Heating and cooling 36%
Cooking 6%
Water heating 24%
Lighting 7%
Refrigerators and freezers 7%

C | Critical Thinking. Create a *Household Energy Use* pie chart in your notebook that shows what you use energy for. Use the chart from exercise **A** as an example and your answers from exercise **B** to help you. Follow these steps:

1. Draw a circle. Then draw sections in the circle to represent what you use energy for at home. Label each section.
2. Write a percentage in each section that represents how much energy you think you use for each activity. You don't have to be exact. Just make your best guess.
3. Check and make sure that the numbers in your chart equal 100 percent.

D | Discussion. Compare your pie chart with a partner's. Then discuss the questions below.

1. What do you use the most energy for? Explain your reasons and give examples.
2. Which of these uses of energy is most important in your life? Explain.
3. If you wanted to use less energy, which part would be the easiest to change? Which would be the most difficult?

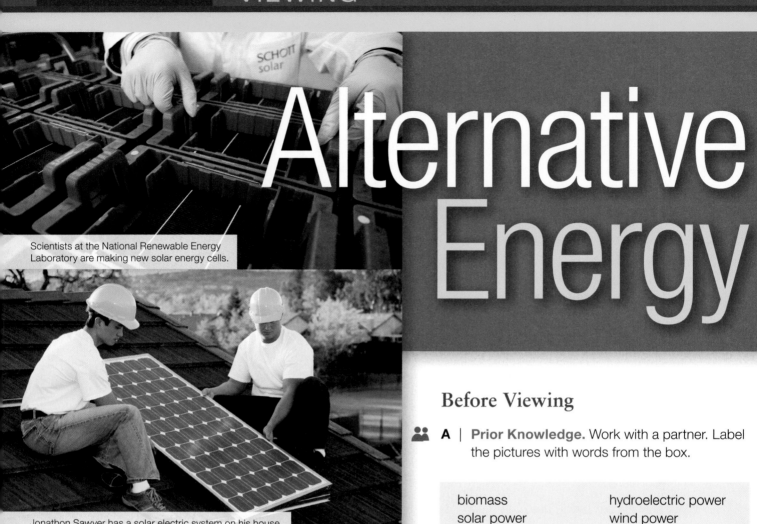

Scientists at the National Renewable Energy Laboratory are making new solar energy cells.

Alternative Energy

Jonathon Sawyer has a solar electric system on his house.

Before Viewing

A | **Prior Knowledge.** Work with a partner. Label the pictures with words from the box.

biomass	hydroelectric power
solar power	wind power

Kinds of Renewable Energy

_____   _____   _____   _____

B | **Predicting Content.** Look at the photos and captions and think about the information from Lesson A. With your partner, list words you think you will hear in the video.

_____

While Viewing

A | Watch the video. Circle any words you hear from your list from exercise **B** in the Before Viewing section.

B | Read the statements. Then watch the video again and circle **T** for *true* and **F** for *false*.

1. Some scientists think that wind power will be much more important in the future. **T** **F**
2. The National Renewable Energy Laboratory is new. **T** **F**
3. About 50 percent of people think we should use more solar energy. **T** **F**
4. Solar power has been around for a long time. **T** **F**
5. Experts think we need more small renewable energy projects. **T** **F**
6. Many countries in Europe use wind turbines to generate power. **T** **F**

In Europe, several countries use wind turbines to produce electricity for many homes, schools, and businesses.

C | Watch the video again and complete the sentences.

1. Scientists are looking to the wind, sun, and _____ products to power the future.
2. Many people say they would like to use more solar power, but they think it's something for the _____, not now.
3. It's so efficient that he actually _____ electricity back to his local power company.
4. Researchers claim that for _____ energy to truly make a difference, it must be used on a large scale.
5. The cost of fuel in many_____ has increased significantly over the past few years.

After Viewing

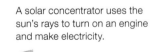

A solar concentrator uses the sun's rays to turn on an engine and make electricity.

Critical Thinking. Discuss the questions with a partner.

1. What is the main idea of this video?
2. Do people use renewable energy in your country now? What do they use it for?
3. Do you think you will use more renewable energy 10 years from now? Explain.
4. The video and Lesson A discussed some ways that countries can help conserve energy. Lesson B will discuss what individual people can do to conserve energy. What are some ways that countries and individual people can conserve energy?

track 1-17 **A** | **Meaning from Context.** Read and listen to the advertisement. Notice the words and phrases in **blue**. These are words and phrases you will hear and use in Lesson B.

Tips for Saving Energy and Protecting Our Environment

Scientists believe that the earth's temperature is increasing. They believe this increase in temperature is having a negative impact on our environment. You might think that protecting the planet is too big a job for you, but it isn't. There are many small and practical ways you can conserve energy and help protect the environment. Here are some helpful tips.

Yoho National Park, British Columbia, Canada

- Cut back on driving by taking public transportation or walking more often. You will save a lot of gas if you drive to work two or three days a week instead of five!

- Shop at local stores close to your home. You will drive less, so you can spend less money on gas and more money on food.

- Turn off lights and electronics when you aren't using them, so you don't waste electricity.

- Replace your old appliances like refrigerators and dishwashers with new, efficient models. Old appliances consume more energy than new ones.

- Keep track of the electricity and gas you use and how you use it. Write down the different activities you do that use gas or electricity and how often you do them in an "energy journal."

- Use your energy journal to help you set a lower target for your energy use each month. For example, if your energy bill is $100 one month, try lowering your bill to $80, or by 20 percent the next month.

- Try to reduce the amount of energy you use by making gradual changes to your lifestyle. You will see that making small changes each month can have a big impact on the amount of energy you use—and help protect our beautiful planet!

B | Match each word or phrase in **blue** from exercise **A** with its definition.

1. practical (adj.) _____
2. cut back on (v.) _____
3. local (adj.) _____
4. waste (v.) _____
5. replace (v.) _____
6. keep track of (v.) _____
7. consume (v.) _____
8. target (n.) _____
9. gradual (adj.) _____
10. percent (n.) _____

a. to put something new in the place of an old one
b. parts out of a hundred (%)
c. from or related to the place where you live
d. to use
e. happening slowly
f. to reduce, make less
g. to pay attention to what is happening to something
h. a goal; something you want to do
i. to use too much of something without a good reason
j. useful in a real situation

A | Read the ideas below and fill in each blank with the correct form of a word in **blue** from exercise **A** on page 34. Then rate how difficult or easy each idea would be for you to do. Write **E** for *easy*, **M** for *medium*, and **D** for *difficult*.

More Energy-Saving Ideas

1. Don't _____ energy drying your dishes in the dishwasher. Dry them by hand instead of using energy by drying them in the dishwasher. (_____)

A woman drying her dishes by hand.

2. _____ your use of hot water. Take a five-minute shower, or use only four inches (10 centimeters) of water in your bath. (_____)

3. Buy more food that comes from _____ farms. Food that is produced near your home uses less energy for transportation. (_____)

4. _____ your electric bills. Make a chart of how much energy you use, and watch the numbers go down every month. (_____)

5. Recycle all of your cans, bottles, and paper. Recycled materials _____ much less energy than new materials. (_____)

6. _____ all of the light bulbs in your house with modern, energy-efficient light bulbs. (_____)

7. Unplug computers, printers, TVs, and cell-phone chargers when you aren't using them. They use electricity even when they are turned off—up to eight _____ of your electric bill! (_____)

8. Make _____ changes to your diet that will help save energy. Try eating less meat and more locally grown fruits and vegetables each month. Producing meat uses more energy than producing other kinds of food. (_____)

9. For most people, it isn't _____ to replace all your electronic appliances. But when you need to buy a new refrigerator, computer, or air conditioner, look for brands that use less energy. (_____)

10. Set a _____ for using public transportation more often. Try to take the train or bus instead of driving at least two days a week instead of five. (_____)

B | **Discussion.** Compare your answers from exercise **A** with a partner's. For ideas that you rated as *difficult*, explain your reasons.

C | **Critical Thinking.** Form a group with another pair of students and choose the three ideas that you think could save the most energy.

D | **Reporting to the Class.** Explain your ideas and reasons from exercise **C** to the class.

Pronunciation

Using Intonation to Show Feelings

track 1-18

In English, speakers often use intonation (make their voices go up or down) to show how they feel. Listening to a speaker's intonation can help you understand if they feel happy, afraid, upset, nervous, angry, or surprised about what they are saying. Examples:

Our energy bill is 200 dollars this month. (showing surprise)

Our energy bill is 200 dollars this month. (showing anger)

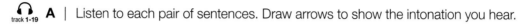

A | Listen to each pair of sentences. Draw arrows to show the intonation you hear.
track 1-19

1. **Speaker A:** The earth's temperature might increase by five degrees.

   Speaker B: The earth's temperature might increase by five degrees.

2. **Speaker A:** Americans produce twice as much carbon as Europeans.

   Speaker B: Americans produce twice as much carbon as Europeans.

3. **Speaker A:** Oh, you bought a new TV.

   Speaker B: Oh, you bought a new TV.

B | Listen to the sentences again and circle how each speaker feels.
track 1-19

1. **Speaker A:** The earth's temperature might increase by five degrees. (angry/surprised)

   Speaker B: The earth's temperature might increase by five degrees. (upset/afraid)

2. **Speaker A:** Americans produce twice as much carbon as Europeans. (surprised/nervous)

   Speaker B: Americans produce twice as much carbon as Europeans. (angry/surprised)

3. **Speaker A:** Oh, you bought a new TV. (happy/angry)

   Speaker B: Oh, you bought a new TV. (surprised/nervous)

C | Complete the conversation below with a partner. Decide how each speaker feels. Then practice the conversation using the correct intonation.

A: What are you doing?

B: I'm looking at our electric bill.

A: Oh, is it lower than last month's bill?

B: No, it's actually higher.

A: _____

B: _____

A: _____

D | **Presentation.** Form a group with another pair of students. Take turns presenting your conversations. Listen for the intonation and try to guess how each speaker feels.

Before Listening

Prior Knowledge. Label the household appliances below. Which do you think uses the most electricity and produces the most carbon in a year? Work with a partner and rank them from 1 (the most) to 6 (the least).

| air conditioner | clothes dryer | computer | hair dryer | refrigerator | TV |

a. _____

c. _____

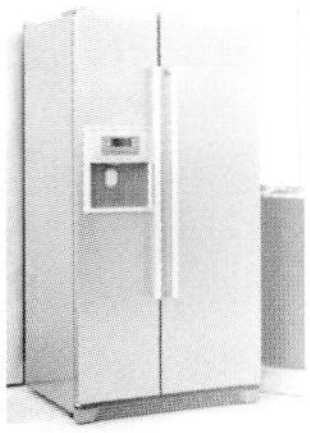

e. _____

b. _____

d. _____

f. _____

Listening: An Informal Conversation

A | Listening for Main Ideas. Listen to the first part of the conversation and answer the questions.

track 1-20

1. Who is talking? _____
2. How does the man feel? _____
3. Why does he feel this way? _____

B | Listening for Details. Listen to the rest of the conversation. Which ideas do the speakers talk about? Check (✔) the ideas you hear.

track 1-21

❑ replacing the light bulbs   ❑ eating cold food more often   ❑ taking shorter showers
❑ using solar energy   ❑ not using the clothes dryer   ❑ turning the computers off at night
❑ buying a new refrigerator   ❑ keeping track of their energy use   ❑ not using the hair dryer

C | Listen again. Circle the ideas in exercise **B** that the speakers decide to try.

track 1-21

After Listening

Critical Thinking. Discuss the questions with a partner.

1. Which ideas that the speakers decided to try from exercise **C** do you think will be easy, medium, or difficult for them? Explain.
2. What other ideas do you have for this family?

Grammar

Modals of Advice: *Should/Shouldn't, Ought to, Had Better*

We use *should* and *shouldn't* to ask for and give advice.
> **Should** I replace my light bulbs?
> You **should** keep an energy journal.
> You **shouldn't** leave your computer on all night.

We also use *should* to talk about what is generally accepted as the right thing to do.
> Everyone **should** try to save on energy.

We also use *ought to* and *ought not to* for giving advice. *Ought to* is stronger than *should*. We rarely use *ought to* in questions or negative statements.
> You **ought to** get a new refrigerator.

We use *had better* to give strong advice or give a warning. We use *had better* when a negative consequence may result.
> **I'd better** pay my energy bill today, or they will cut off the power.

Note: We do not use *had better* for questions. The negative of *had better* is *had better not*.

A | Complete the sentences with the correct form of the modal in parentheses. Circle your answers.

1. You (should/shouldn't) turn off your computer every night. You could save a lot of electricity.
2. Tom (had better/had better not) forget to turn off the lights. Last time he went away he left them on for a week.
3. We (ought/ought not) to call the energy company. I think there's a mistake on our bill.
4. You really (should/shouldn't) drive your car to the store. It's only two blocks away.
5. We (had better/had better not) stop burning fossil fuels. It's bad for the environment.

B | Work with a partner. Take turns giving advice for the situations below.

1. Your partner has an important test tomorrow.
2. Your partner has a very bad cold.
3. Your partner's car is making a strange noise.
4. Your partner keeps missing class.

> I have a very bad cold.

> I'm sorry to hear that. You should drink hot tea.

Language Function

Giving Advice and Making Suggestions

Here are some other expressions we use to give advice and make suggestions.

You look sick. ***Why don't you*** *go to the doctor?*
If I were you, *I would ask the teacher.*
Let's *try to cut back on the amount of energy we use.*
Why don't we *take the bus to school instead of driving?*

A | **Self-Reflection.** Write down three or four problems you have or situations you want to change.

1. My apartment is very expensive.
2. _____
3. _____
4. _____

B | Work with a partner. Take turns asking for and giving advice and suggestions for the situations you wrote down in exercise **A**.

> *My apartment is very expensive. Do you have any advice?*

> *Why don't you get a roommate?*

> *I lost my cell phone yesterday.*

> *If I were you, I would call campus security.*

C | **Role-Playing.** Read the information below. Then role-play the situation with your partner.

Situation: You are roommates sharing an apartment. Your energy bill is very high and is getting higher every month. You need to find ways to lower your bill. Each of you has a computer and a TV set. You like to keep your apartment very warm in the winter. You have a washing machine and clothes dryer in your apartment. You each do your laundry about twice a week. You are having a conversation about ways you can reduce the amount of energy you use and lower your energy bill.

In this section, you will work with a group to plan a presentation on ways to conserve energy.

A | Form a group with two or three other students. Read the information below and complete the exercises that follow.

> **Situation:** You are members of your school's "Green[1] Committee." The director of your school wants you to present the four most important ways that your school can save energy and reduce its carbon footprint.[2] You are going to meet to discuss your ideas and then present them to your director.

B | **Brainstorming.** With your group, brainstorm a list of ideas in your notebook of how your school can save energy and reduce its carbon footprint.

> We should turn off all lights at night.
>
> The school ought to use fewer school buses.

Presentation Skills: Organizing Ideas for a Group Presentation

When planning a group presentation, it is important to decide in which order each person will speak. Make sure everyone in your group understands who is presenting first, second, third, and so on. Organizing your ideas will help make your presentation go smoothly and will make the presentation easier for your audience to follow.

C | Look at your list of ideas from exercise **B**. Discuss which ideas you think are the best. Put a check (✔) next to your four best ideas. Take notes on why you think each idea is important.

D | **Planning a Presentation.** Decide which member of your group will present each idea. Each member of your group should talk about one idea.

E | **Presentation.** Present your ideas to the class.

[1] In this case **green** means environmental or concerned with the environment.
[2] A **carbon footprint** is the total amount of greenhouse gas emission caused by a person, organization, or product.

Student to Student: Taking Turns

When you are having a conversation or group discussion, taking turns can help you keep the discussion going and make sure that everyone has an opportunity to talk about his or her ideas. Here are some expressions you can use for taking turns.

What do you think?
What's your idea?
Did you want to say something?
OK, your turn.
Marta?

Culture and Tradition

ACADEMIC PATHWAYS
Lesson A: Listening to a Lecture
             Giving Information
Lesson B: Listening to an Assignment and a Student Presentation
             Planning a Presentation

Think and Discuss

1. Look at the photo. What do you know about cowboys?

2. In which countries do cowboys live and work?

A cowboy and cowgirl herding horses in Oregon, USA

Exploring the Theme:
Culture and Tradition

Look at the photos and read the captions. Match each photo with a place on the map. Then discuss the questions.

1. Where do these people live?
2. How are these people similar?
3. What are some cultures that interest you? Why?
4. What are some things that make your own culture special?

f
A Sherpani

The *Sherpa* people live in the Himalaya region of Nepal. The word *Sherpa* means "eastern people." The word *Sherpani* is used for female *Sherpas*. Many *Sherpas* work as guides and help people climb mountains, particularly Mount Everest.

a
A Geisha

In Japan, *geisha* are female entertainers. The word *geisha* means "art person." *Geisha* spend a lot of time studying how to perform traditional Japanese music and dances.

Lambert Azimuthal Equal-Area Projection

0 mi   1000
0 km   1000

b
A Roma (Gypsy)

The Roma people lived in India before they moved to Europe. Today, there are many Roma people living in Romania, Hungary, and other European countries. When Roma children go to a school where people speak a different language, they often stop speaking their Roma language. Scientists estimate that 3000 languages might disappear in the next 100 years as people stop speaking their native languages.

NORTH AMERICA

PACIFIC OCEAN

OCEAN

SOUTH AMERICA

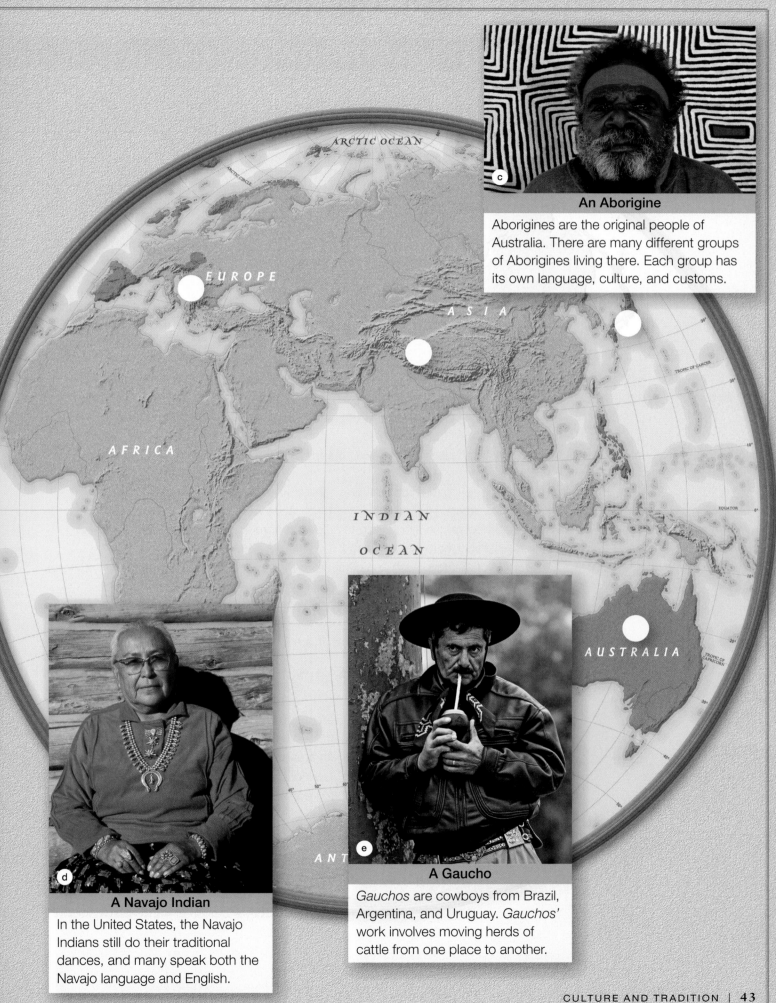

An Aborigine

Aborigines are the original people of Australia. There are many different groups of Aborigines living there. Each group has its own language, culture, and customs.

A Navajo Indian

In the United States, the Navajo Indians still do their traditional dances, and many speak both the Navajo language and English.

A Gaucho

Gauchos are cowboys from Brazil, Argentina, and Uruguay. *Gauchos'* work involves moving herds of cattle from one place to another.

Critical Thinking Focus: Inferring Meaning from Context

When you see a word you do not know, you can often infer, or guess its meaning from the context, or words around it.

---

track 1-22

A | **Meaning from Context.** Read and listen to the sentences. Notice the words in blue. Circle the correct word or phrase in parentheses. Then listen and check your answers. These are words you will hear and use in Lesson A.

1. Women in Japan **still** wear a kimono for their wedding. They (have/haven't) stopped wearing these beautiful clothes.
2. In Korea, people eat **traditional** food such as rice cakes on New Year's Day. They have done this for a (short/long) time.
3. We are **developing** a program to teach foreigners about our culture. Now we are (making plans for/selling tickets for) this program.
4. In my country, we have a **custom** of giving money to children on their birthdays. We (usually/never) give them money.
5. In the future, many languages might **disappear**. (Many people/No one) will speak these languages.
6. A group of people called the Inuit live in the cold **regions** of the world. They live in cold (cities/areas).
7. The Navajo people use storytelling to help **preserve** their language and traditions. They use storytelling to (keep/change) their language and traditions.
8. Some kinds of animals, such as tigers, are **endangered** today. They might (all die/kill people).
9. Scientists **estimate** that there are over 7000 languages in the world. They (know/don't know) the exact number.
10. Television is a **factor** in cultural change. It is a (cause of/result of) these changes.

B | Match each word in blue from exercise **A** with its definition. Use your dictionary to help you.

1. still (adv.)   ___   a. an action or practice that is common to a person or group
2. traditional (adj.) ___   b. an area of a country or the world
3. develop (v.)   ___   c. has continued and exists now
4. custom (n.)   ___   d. to keep or protect
5. disappear (v.)   ___   e. something that lets another thing happen
6. region (n.)   ___   f. likely to soon disappear
7. preserve (v.)   ___   g. to guess
8. endangered (adj.) ___   h. to make grow
9. estimate (v.)   ___   i. to no longer exist or be visible
10. factor (n.)   ___   j. something that is customary and has existed for a long time

A | Read the article. Complete each sentence with the correct form of a word in blue from exercise **A** on page 44. Use each word only once.

Cowboy Life and Culture

In the 1800s, cowboys worked with cattle all across the Western (1) _____ of the United States. An important (2) _____ in the cowboys' work was the railroad. Most cattle were in Texas, but the railroad was more than 1000 miles (1609 kilometers) away. Cowboys moved the cattle there in big cattle drives.[1] Experts (3) _____ that in a cattle drive, only 10 cowboys could take more than 3000 cattle to a railroad town. Cowboys typically worked for about four months and received all their pay at the end. Then they spent it very quickly in the town. The average cowboy was only 24 years old.

Working alone with their cattle, cowboys (4) _____ some very interesting (5) _____. For example, at night, some cowboys would sing to the cattle to keep them quiet. Some (6) _____ American songs came from these singing cowboys.

Cowboys have not (7) _____ completely, but there are not nearly as many as there were in the past. One reason for this is very few young people want to work so hard for so little money, so the cowboys' way of life is (8) _____. Although the number of actual cowboys has decreased, there are many people who help (9) _____ aspects of the cowboy culture. For example, cowboy hats and boots are very popular, especially in the western part of the United States, and many places (10) _____ have rodeos.[2]

A cowboy working on a cattle drive

[1] A **cattle drive** is the process of moving cattle from one place to another.
[2] A **rodeo** is a public event where cowboys show their skills.

B | **Self-Reflection.** Complete the sentences with your own ideas. Then discuss your ideas with a partner. Ask questions to get more information.

1. In my country today, _____ is/are endangered.
2. A traditional food that I like is _____.
3. Some people in my country still _____.
4. A holiday custom that I enjoy is _____.
5. In my country, _____ has/have disappeared.
6. I think it's really important to preserve _____.

> Some people in my city still live in traditional houses.

> Really? What do they look like?

Pronunciation

Reduced Function Words

Some unstressed words in a sentence are *reduced*—they are said quickly, and the vowel sound is shortened. Articles (*a, an, the*), prepositions (e.g., *to, for, of*), conjunctions (e.g., *and, or, but*), auxiliary verbs (e.g., *is, have, can*), pronouns, and *be* as a main verb are often reduced. Examples:

track 1-23

I hear <u>the</u> phone ringing.
There's <u>a</u> message <u>for</u> Molly.
What <u>are you</u> reading?

A | Read the first part of a lecture about cowboys. Try to guess the function words that are reduced. Circle the words.

> One of the oldest traditions in North and South America is the cowboy. As you know, cattle eat grass—a *lot* of grass—so a herd must be moved often to new places with more grass. The people who move them are called cowboys.

track 1-24
B | Listen and check your answers from exercise **A.**

C | Read the paragraph in exercise **A** to a partner. Use the reduced pronunciations for the function words.

Before Listening

A | **Using a Dictionary.** Work with a partner. Match these words with their definitions. Use your dictionary to help you.

1. cattle (n.) ___
2. ranch (n.) ___
3. grass (n.) ___
4. shack (n.) ___
5. herd (n.) ___
6. generation (n.) ___

a. all the people in a family who are about the same age
b. a very small, simple house
c. a very large farm
d. a large group of animals of one kind
e. a plant that cows and horses eat
f. cows

Cowboys still work on ranches in the western United States.

B | **Prior Knowledge.** Discuss the questions with your partner.

1. Besides North America, do you know of any other regions that have cowboys? What are they called in those places?
2. What else would you like to learn about cowboys?

Listening: A Lecture

track 1-25 **A** | **Listening for Main Ideas.** Listen to the lecture. Listen for the answers to the questions below.

    1. Where is Tyrel from? _____

    2. Where is Manuel from? _____

track 1-25 **B** | **Listening for Details.** Listen again. Complete the notes about the two cowboys.

Tyrel Tucker

- got his first horse when he was _____
- one winter, he worked alone with his _____ on a ranch
- they took care of _____ cattle
- lived in a shack with no _____
- he _____ the work

Manuel Rodriguez

- started working with his father when he was _____
- _____ generations of his family have worked on the same ranch
- got _____ and moved to the city
- wants to _____ back to the countryside and work as a *vaquero* again

track 1-25 **C** | **Making Inferences.** Read the statements below. Listen again and circle **T** for *true* or **F** for *false*. The professor does not say the answers directly. You will need to think about what you hear.

    1. Tyrel liked school.   **T**   **F**

    2. Tyrel and his brother ate a healthy diet.   **T**   **F**

    3. Both of these cowboys would be very unhappy living in a big city.   **T**   **F**

    4. The two men want to get better jobs.   **T**   **F**

After Listening

Critical Thinking. Discuss the questions with a partner.

    1. Why do you think Robb Kendrick used an old kind of camera for his pictures?

    2. What kinds of people want to be cowboys now?

    3. Why do you think they like the cowboy's way of life?

    4. Would you like this way of life? Explain.

Language Function

Asking for and Giving Clarification

When you are listening to a lecture or participating in a conversation, you will sometimes need to get clarification on information you did not hear or understand. The conversation below shows examples of some of the language we use for asking for and giving clarification.

 A | The students are talking to the teacher after the lecture about cowboys. Read and listen to the conversation. Then form a group with two other students and practice the conversation.

At a *charreada* in Mexico, cowboys called *charros* compete in teams.

Emily: You said that Mexico had the first real cowboys. <u>Are there still cowboys today?</u>

Prof. Daley: Yes, there are. They're workers who live with the cattle and take care of them. Some ranches are very large, and cattle need to be moved from place to place, so yes, there are still cowboys.

Li: You also talked about two kinds of cowboys in Mexico. <u>Could you explain that?</u>

Prof. Daley: Sure. The most famous cowboys in Mexico are the *charros*. They ride their horses in contests called *charreadas.* The other kind of cowboys are the *vaqueros*—the ones who work with cattle every day.

Li: <u>I still don't understand.</u>

Prof. Daley: <u>Let me explain:</u> Some Mexican cowboys do it as a hobby, and others do it as a job. For the *charros*, it's mostly a sport, or a hobby. For the *vaqueros*, it's their work.

Li: <u>So, what you mean is that</u> Manuel Rodriguez is a *vaquero* and not a *charro*.

Prof. Daley: Exactly!

Emily: <u>Do you mean that</u> *charros* aren't really cowboys?

Prof. Daley: No, *charros* are a part of the tradition, but many of them don't do it as actual work. <u>What I mean is</u>, they are cowboys—but it isn't a job.

B | Write the <u>underlined</u> expressions from the above conversation in the correct part of the T-chart. *(See pages 210–211 of the Independent Student Handbook for more useful expressions.)*

Asking for Clarification	Giving Clarification
Do you mean that . . . ?	*Let me explain. . .*

C | Read the sentences and complete them with your own ideas. Take turns reading them to a partner. Then take turns asking for and giving clarification. Use clarification from your T-chart in exercise **B** on page 48.

1. An important tradition in my country is _____.
2. A tradition that is now disappearing is _____.
3. A traditional kind of clothing from my country is _____.
4. I think one of the main reasons why traditions disappear is _____.
5. My favorite food from my country is _____.

> My favorite food from my country is *shish kebab.*

> What is *shish kebab*?

Grammar

The Past Continuous Tense

We use the past continuous to talk about actions in progress at a certain time in the past.

> Sumi **was living** in New York in 2003.
> In 2007, Ana **was working** for a computer company.

We use the past continuous with the simple past to show that one action happened when another action was in progress.

> I **was taking** a shower when you **called.**
> We **saw** a beautiful bird while we **were walking** home.

We also use the past continuous to talk about two actions that were in progress at the same time.

> Jason **was studying** while his friends **were watching** videos.
> I **was listening** to music while I **was cooking** dinner.

A | Look at these sentences from the exercises in the Listening section on pages 46–47. Circle the past continuous verbs. Then with a partner, discuss why each sentence uses the past continuous.

1. Tyrel was working on a ranch at that time.
2. He was working outside while all his classmates were playing computer games.
3. He was riding horses before he could walk.

B | Complete each sentence with the past continuous form of a verb (or verbs) from the box below.

clean	drink	eat	exercise	live	rain
ride	sleep	study	talk	wait	watch

1. Rick wasn't at home last night because he _____was studying_____ in the library.
2. In 1995, Marta _____ with her parents in Mexico City.
3. I _____ the house while my son _____ TV.
4. It (not) _____ when the soccer game started.
5. When I saw Brandon, he _____ for the bus.
6. You _____ when Sue called, but you didn't wake up.
7. Carl _____ a sandwich while he _____ on the phone. That's very impolite!
8. I saw Lisa walking down Main Street when I _____ my bike to work.
9. Matt _____ at the gym all afternoon. Now he's very tired.
10. Why _____ you _____ coffee at ten o'clock last night?

C | With a partner, take turns asking and answering questions about what you were doing at the times below. Use the past continuous tense.

1. this morning—at eight o'clock
2. last night—at six o'clock
3. last night—at twelve o'clock
4. yesterday—at two o'clock
5. in 2006
6. (your own idea)

What were you doing yesterday at six o'clock?

I was making dinner.

What were you doing yesterday at two o'clock?

I was having lunch with my family.

Giving Information

A | Form a group with two other students. Have each member of your group read about one kind of cowboy.

B | **Note-Taking**. Take turns telling each other about the information you read. Close your book and take notes as you listen. Ask for and give clarification if you need to.

A stockman from Australia

Student 1

In Australia, people who work with animals on ranches are called stockmen. Stockmen work with both cattle and sheep. Stockmen live on huge stations. *Station* is the Australian word for ranch. There is one cattle station in Australia that's bigger than the country of Belgium. Australian stockmen ride horses, and they use dogs to help them. Now some stockmen use trucks instead of horses because the areas where they work are so large. In some places, it takes a whole day to drive to the nearest house.

A *paniolo* from Hawaii

Student 2

Hawaii has traditional cowboys called *paniolos. Paniolo* means Spanish in the Hawaiian language. In 1838, the king of Hawaii invited some *vaqueros* from Mexico to come to Hawaii. *Vaquero* means cowboy in Spanish. The king invited the *vaqueros* because some of them gave him cattle as a gift, but he did not know how to take care of them. Now there are only a few big ranches in Hawaii, and the last *paniolos* are very old, but people still enjoy listening to their music and wearing their costumes.

A *gaucho* from Uruguay

Student 3

Gauchos are the cowboys of Brazil, Argentina, and Uruguay. In the past, gauchos were very poor. The people who owned the ranches didn't want beef. There were no refrigerators to keep the meat, so they couldn't sell it. As a result, the *gauchos* ate meat three times a day. Today *gauchos* still work in South America, but their lives are much better than they were in the past.

C | **Critical Thinking.** Discuss the questions with your group.

1. What parts of the cowboys' lives are probably the same as they were 100 years ago? What parts are probably different?
2. Why do you think some people want to work as cowboys today?

The Gauchos of Argentina

Argentine *gauchos*, or cowboys, herd black Aberdeen Angus cattle through a field.

A *gaucho* on horseback rides past a shed on a sheep ranch.

Before Viewing

A | **Using a Dictionary.** You will hear these words in the video. Work with a partner and match each word with its correct definition. Use your dictionary to help you.

1. self-reliant (adj.) ____   a. severe
2. terrain (n.) ____   b. leather coverings worn over a cowboy's trousers
3. remote (adj.) ____   c. able to take care of oneself without outside help
4. harsh (adj.) ____   d. far away or distant
5. chaps (n.) ____   e. land, landscape

B | **Prior Knowledge.** The video you are going to see is about *gauchos*. In Lesson A, you learned some information about *gauchos,* and maybe you already knew some information about them. Circle the correct words to complete each sentence.

1. *Gauchos* are cowboys from (South America/the United States).
2. *Gauchos* live in (big cities/remote places).
3. Their lives are very (similar to/different from) the lives of other people.
4. *Gauchos* are part of (an old and proud tradition/a new, modern culture).
5. (Airplanes and trucks/Animals) are part of every *gaucho's* life.

While Viewing

A | Watch the video and check your answers from exercise **B** in the Before Viewing section.

B | Read the statements below. Then watch the video again and circle **T** for *true* and **F** for *false*.

1. *Gauchos* live the same way all over Argentina.   **T**   **F**
2. Don José Ansola believes he treats his horses well.   **T**   **F**
3. A *rhea* is a kind of horse.   **T**   **F**
4. *Gauchos* share a strict code of ethics.   **T**   **F**
5. Some *gauchos* herd sheep.   **T**   **F**
6. Many *gauchos* speak English.   **T**   **F**

Argentine *gauchos* ride across a lake near Beron de Astrada.

C | Watch the video again and complete each sentence with the number you hear.

1. *Gauchos* have lived in the same way for _____ centuries.
2. Don José Ansola is _____ years old.
3. His ranch is _____ square miles.
4. There are about _____ *gauchos* in Argentina.
5. Jimmy and Eduardo's ancestors came to Patagonia in the _____ century.
6. Salta is about _____ miles north of Patagonia.

After Viewing

Critical Thinking. Form a group with two or three other students and discuss the questions. Ask for and give clarification as needed.

1. According to the video, most people in Argentina think of the *gaucho* as a hero or a legend. What do you think the reason is for this?
2. Are there any people in your country who live a different and traditional way of life? What do you know about their way of life?
3. In your opinion, why do some people want to preserve old traditions?
4. In Lesson B, you will discuss music from around the world. How do you think music can help preserve cultures and traditions?

Gauchos at a cattle auction in La Cruz, Argentina

A | **Meaning from Context.** Read and listen to the class assignment. Notice the words in **blue**. These are words you will hear and use in Lesson B.

track 1-27

Anthropology 106:   Culture and Music

Assignment: Oral Presentation

For this assignment, you will **select** a kind of music from another country and teach your classmates about it. You should plan to do the following in your presentation:

- **Describe** how the music sounds. Does it have a nice melody[1] that's easy to listen to? Is the **rhythm** fast or slow? What kinds of **instruments** do the musicians play? Does the music typically have **lyrics**? Are the lyrics usually happy or sad? Play an example of the music for your audience so they can hear it.
- **Explain** where and when people typically listen to this kind music. Do they listen to it at weddings or on special holidays?
- **Compare** this kind of music to another kind of music you know about. How are they similar? Then **contrast** the two kinds of music. How are they different?
- **Define** any words you think your classmates may not know.
- In your conclusion, **summarize** the most important ideas of your presentation. Answer any questions, and remember to thank your audience.
- Your presentation should be at least two minutes.

[1]A **melody** is a series of musical notes, or the tune of a song.

B | Match each word in **blue** from exercise **A** with its definition.

1. select (v.)   ___   a. to tell the meaning of a word
2. describe (v.)   ___   b. to use facts or examples to prove your idea
3. rhythm (n.)   ___   c. to discover the similarities or differences between two things
4. instruments (n.) ___   d. the words of a song
5. lyrics (n.)   ___   e. to choose
6. explain (v.)   ___   f. to show the difference between two things
7. compare (v.)   ___   g. a series of sounds
8. contrast (v.)   ___   h. to tell the most important points in a short way
9. define (v.)   ___   i. objects used to produce music
10. summarize (v.)   ___   j. to tell what something is like

A musician plays his guitar on a street in Barcelona, Spain.

A | Complete each sentence with the correct form of a word in blue from exercise **A** on page 54. Use each word only once.

1. I have to _____ which classes I'm going to take next semester. It's a very difficult decision!

2. Can you _____ your favorite music for me? What does it sound like?

3. Taru didn't understand the assignment, so she asked her professor to _____ it again.

4. In the first part my presentation, I'm going to _____ two kinds of music, *reggae* and *calypso*. I'm going to talk about how they are similar.

5. In the second part of my presentation, I'm going to _____ these two kinds of music and talk about how they are different.

6. If you don't understand a new word, you can use your dictionary to help you or ask your teacher to _____ it for you.

7. When you _____ a book or a movie, you retell the most important information in a few sentences. You shouldn't include details or opinions.

8. I don't play a musical _____, but my brother plays the piano very well.

9. *Samba* music has a fast, happy _____ that is fun to dance to.

10. The _____ to Portuguese *fado* songs are typically sad, but beautiful. Many *fado* songs are about the sea or the lives of poor people.

B | **Discussion.** Take turns talking about the topics below with a partner. Try to talk about each topic for at least 30 seconds. Your partner will time you.

1. **Describe** a kind of music you like to listen to.
2. **Explain** how you learn new vocabulary words.
3. **Summarize** a book or movie you enjoyed.
4. **Compare** and **contrast** two people you know.

A traditional Irish musician playing the fiddle.

Before Listening

 You are going to listen to an assignment and then to a student's presentation about the music of the Roma people. Read the information and answer the questions that follow with a partner.

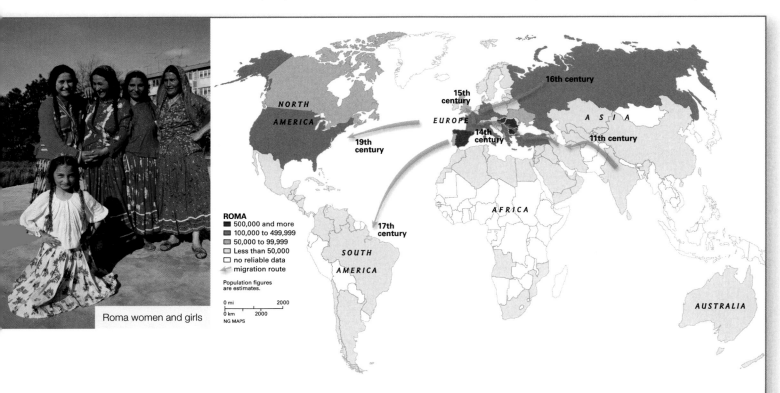

Roma women and girls

ROMA
- 500,000 and more
- 100,000 to 499,999
- 50,000 to 99,999
- Less than 50,000
- no reliable data
- migration route

Population figures are estimates.

The Roma people are sometimes called *gypsies.* They were living in India before they moved into Europe about 1000 years ago. Now they live in many different countries, but they have kept their own culture and language. There are many Roma people in Bulgaria, Hungary, and Romania, but they also live in other European countries. The Roma are famous as musicians and dancers, and they have been very important to jazz, classical, and flamenco music.

1. What do you know about the Roma people?
2. Are you familiar with gypsy music?
3. What would you like to know about the Roma people?
4. Look at the map. Which areas of the world did the Roma people move from? Which areas did they move to?
5. Which places have large populations of Roma people?
6. According to the map, what's the population of Roma people in your country?
7. Does anything surprise you about the information from the paragraph or the map?

Listening: An Assignment and a Student Presentation

track 1-28
A | **Note-Taking.** Listen to the professor as he explains the assignment. Complete the notes about what the students have to do.

Assignment: A Presentation

1. _____ a kind of _____ to present

2. talk about the _____ the music comes from

3. _____ the music and _____ which aspects are _____ and which aspects are new, or _____

4. compare and _____ it with another kind of _____ we have studied

5. _____ a sample of the music for the class

6. summarize the _____ ideas and answer any _____ from your classmates

track 1-29
B | **Listening for Main Ideas.** Now listen to one student's presentation. Circle the numbers in exercise **A** for the parts of the assignment that the student included. Which part(s) of the assignment did he not include in his presentation?

track 1-29
C | **Listening for Details.** Listen to the student's presentation again and circle the correct answers below.

1. Shukar Collective is a group of musicians and DJs from eastern (Europe/Asia).
2. One thing the Roma people are very famous for is (singing/music).
3. Traditional Roma music usually has a very (fast/slow) rhythm.
4. The lyrics show very (strong/happy) feelings.
5. Shukar Collective is made up of three traditional singers and four (modern/electronic) musicians.
6. They call their music electro-gypsy-dance, and it's very (famous/popular) in dance clubs all over Europe.

After Listening

Critical Thinking. Discuss the questions with a partner.

1. Do you know about any other kinds of traditional music that people are playing in new ways?
2. What kind of music is traditional in your country? Is it still popular? Do people still play it the same way, or is it changing?
3. Do you think it's OK to change traditional music, or should we try to keep it the same?

Language Function

Interrupting Politely

When you are listening to a lecture or a presentation, or are participating in a class discussion, you sometimes need to interrupt the speaker to ask a question or get clarification. Here are some polite expressions you can use to interrupt, or get the speaker's attention.

Excuse me, I have a question.   *Sorry to interrupt, but I have a question.*
Could I ask a question?   *I have another question.*
There's one thing I'm not sure about.

Note: Sometimes in a lecture or presentation, the speaker will ask the audience to "hold all questions" (wait to ask questions) until the end of the lecture. When a speaker does this, you should not ask questions during the lecture or presentation.

A | Read the information about two traditional musical instruments. Take turns reading your information aloud slowly to a partner. Your partner will stop you to ask for clarification as needed, using polite expressions. Try to answer your partner's questions, and then continue reading.

Student A   bagpipes

Bagpipes are a very old musical instrument. They have a bag that holds air, and one or more small pipes that make the notes of the music. The player blows air into the bag, and then the air comes out slowly through the pipes to make the sound. There are holes in the pipes that the player covers with his or her fingers to play different notes.

Bagpipes have a long history. Musicians in ancient Rome played a similar instrument with an airbag and pipes. Today, the most famous bagpipes are in Scotland and Ireland, but there are many different instruments like this in different regions of Europe, North Africa, and the Middle East.

Student B   steel drum

Steel drums are an instrument from the island of Trinidad, in the Caribbean. They are made from old steel oil barrels. The steel drum is not a very old instrument—the first steel drums were made in about 1947. But musicians in Trinidad loved the sound and quickly started using them in their traditional music.

The sound of a steel drum is very light and happy. The drum has different sections, and each one makes a different note. The player holds two or three sticks in his or her hands and uses them to hit different notes. Usually, steel drums are played by groups of musicians called a *steel band*. They play all kinds of music on their drums at the *Carnival* festival in Trinidad every spring.

B | Discussion. With your partner, discuss the questions below.

1. What instruments do you like to listen to? Explain.
2. Do you play any musical instruments? Explain.
3. Are you interested in learning how to play an instrument? Explain.

Grammar

Adjectives Ending in *–ed* and *–ing*

We usually use adjectives that end in *–ed* to describe how a person feels.

> I was very **excited** to hear so much Roma music at tonight's concert.
> I'm **interested** in learning more about the Roma people.

We usually use adjectives that end in *–ing* to describe the thing that causes the feeling.

> I think gypsy traditions and customs are very **exciting.**
> I think they are very **interesting.**

A | Circle the correct adjective form to complete each sentence.

1. I was a little (bored/boring) in class today.
2. I was (surprised/surprising) to learn that steel drums are made from oil barrels.
3. I am very (worried/worrying) about tomorrow's assignment on traditional music.
4. Doing the research for our oral presentation tomorrow was (tired/tiring).
5. I gave my presentation yesterday. Now I feel (relaxed/relaxing).
6. Are you really (interested/interesting) in traditional music?

B | Role-Playing. With a partner, role-play the situations below. Then change partners and practice them again.

1. You have a speaking test in a few days. You're explaining to a friend how you feel.
2. Your friend took his/her final exams yesterday. You want to ask him/her how it went.

Student to Student: Talking about Assignments

You can use informal expressions like these when you want to talk with other students about your assignments.

Are you interested in practicing our presentation after class?
Aren't you worried at all about tomorrow's presentation?
I thought your presentation was really interesting. Great job!
What did you think of the presentation yesterday?

Note: You can use the topic of assignments as a topic for *small talk* or to start a conversation with students you don't know very well.

You are going to prepare and give a group presentation on a type of music.

A | **Brainstorming.** Form a group with two or three other students. Brainstorm a list of as many kinds of music as you can think of. Use the ideas below to help you get started.

Afropop   Celtic   hip-hop   rai   reggae   salsa

B | Select a kind of music from your list as the topic for your presentation.

C | **Collaboration.** Read and discuss the instructions below for your presentation. As a group, write notes about what you will say for each part of your presentation.

Assignment: _____

Title: _____

1. Introduce the members of your group and tell the class the topic of your presentation. Tell the class what kind of music your group selected and explain why.

2. Describe the music you selected. Explain where it is from, what instruments it uses, and what it sounds like. Play a sample of the music (if possible).

3. Compare and contrast it with another kind of music you know.

4. Summarize the most important information from your presentation.

5. Answer any questions and thank your audience.

Presentation Skills: Posture

Posture means how you hold your body. When you speak in front of the class, you should stand up straight on both feet. If you aren't holding notes, use your hands for simple gestures as you speak. This shows that you are confident and well-prepared.

D | **Presentation.** Give your presentation to the class. Give clarification and answer questions if you need to.

A Thirsty World

People and a donkey get water from a trough in a village in Kenya.

Think and Discuss

1. Look at the photo. What are these people doing? Why?
2. Which do you think is a bigger problem—too much water, or not enough water?

Exploring the Theme:
A Thirsty World

Look at the photos and read the captions. Then discuss the questions.

1. How do dams help people?
2. How do PlayPumps help people?
3. What are some things you need water for in your daily life?

Controlling Water and Providing Power

Some countries are building dams to manage the water they have. Dams can help prevent dangerous floods and provide hydroelectric power. The Hoover Dam borders the U.S. states of Nevada and Arizona and generates about 4 billion KWh of energy every year.

Providing Clean Water and Fun

PlayPumps make collecting clean water easy and fun. They use the energy of children playing to pump clean water. Adults can collect fresh, clean water while their children play.

The reservoir at the Karahnjukar Dam in Iceland

track 1-30

A | **Meaning from Context.** Read and listen to the statements in the quiz below. Notice the words in **blue**. These are words you will hear and use in Lesson A.

People gather to get water from a huge well in the village of Natwargadh, India.

WATER: What do you know?

1. Brazil has more fresh water **available** for its people than any other country.   **T**   **F**

2. Farmers **require** 911 gallons (3450 liters) of water to produce 2.2 pounds (1 kilogram) of rice.   **T**   **F**

3. **Clean** water is very important for staying healthy. About 1 million people die each year from drinking dirty water.   **T**   **F**

4. Melting snow and ice is a fast and easy way to **provide** drinking water for people in cold places.   **T**   **F**

5. China has built more than 22,000 dams to **manage** water for different uses such as electricity.   **T**   **F**

6. Scientists say that 13 gallons (50 liters) of water per day is **enough** for one person.   **T**   **F**

7. You can **collect** water in a desert with just a sheet of plastic and an empty can.   **T**   **F**

8. Water is a renewable **resource**, so we can use the same water again and again.   **T**   **F**

9. The Nile River in Africa (the longest river in the world) **flows** through four different countries.   **T**   **F**

10. People in Australia use the smallest **amount** of water of any country in the world.   **T**   **F**

B | Match each of the words in **blue** from exercise **A** with its definition. Use your dictionary to help you.

1. collect (v.) ___	a. materials people can use
2. manage (v.) ___	b. how much there is of something
3. clean (adj.) ___	c. free from dirt
4. require (v.) ___	d. sufficient
5. enough (det.) ___	e. moves slowly without stopping
6. amount (n.) ___	f. to bring together
7. available (adj.) ___	g. able to be used or found
8. flow (v.) ___	h. to need
9. resource (n.) ___	i. to give something that people need
10. provide (v.) ___	j. to use carefully

C | Take the quiz from exercise **A**. Circle **T** for *true* and **F** for *false*. Then check your answers on page 65. Which of these facts surprised you? Explain.

A | Complete the sentences with the correct form of a word in **blue** from exercise **A** on page 64.

1. The Amazon River _____ into the Atlantic Ocean.

2. Some plants _____ a lot of water. You have to water them twice a day!

3. Water is a valuable _____. We should be careful how we use it.

4. We put a box in the cafeteria to _____ plastic water bottles for recycling.

5. The water in my city is not very _____, so we have to drink bottled water.

6. Many rivers _____ electricity and clean drinking water for the people who live near them.

7. The _____ of clean water on Earth is decreasing, so we need to find ways to conserve it.

8. I don't think the city should _____ how much water we use. I think we should decide.

9. If we use too much of the earth's water supply now, we won't have _____ in the future.

10. Clean water isn't _____ to many people in their homes, so they have to go to other places to get it.

The Amazon River

B | **Discussion.** With a partner, discuss the questions below.

1. Do you usually drink bottled water? Why, or why not?
2. How often do you think about the **amount** of water you use and try to conserve?
3. Does your country have problems with **providing enough clean** water to people?

Before Listening

 Using a Dictionary. You will hear these words in the talk. Work with a partner and check (✔) the words you already know. Use your dictionary to help you with the words you don't know.

❏ benefit (n.) ❏ dam (n.) ❏ engineer (n.) ❏ flood (n.) ❏ reservoir (n.) ❏ risk (n.)

Listening: A Guest Speaker

🎧 track 1-31 **A** | **Listening for Main Ideas.** Listen to the guest speaker's talk and check the main idea.

❏ The Three Gorges Dam is the biggest dam in the world.
❏ Building the Three Gorges Dam caused many problems.
❏ There are both benefits and risks to the Three Gorges Dam.
❏ The Three Gorges Dam will help China's economy.

🎧 track 1-31 **B** | **Listening for Details.** Listen to the talk again and complete the notes.

Three Gorges Dam (Yangtze River, China)—Dr. Paul Benjamin

Size: _____ miles long and _____ feet tall

Reservoir _____ miles long

Workers: more than _____

Benefits/Reasons for Building the Dam:

- provides a _____ of energy
- control floods on Yangtze: in the 20th century _____ people were killed
- river deeper, so _____ can travel farther up the river

Risks:

- will put a lot of _____ underwater
- many _____ and villages will probably disappear
- over _____ people have already lost their homes
- many very _____ historical and cultural sites will be underwater
- significant impact on the _____

Conclusion:

- one of the world's _____ dams
- built in order to provide important _____
- there are also some significant _____

After Listening

 Critical Thinking. Work with a partner. Decide who would agree with each sentence. Check (✔) the columns. Then give reasons for the sentences you agree with.

	The Guest Speaker	A Farmer Who Lost His Land	The Owner of a Shipping Company	You
1. More countries should build very large dams to manage their water.				
2. Saving historical sites is very important.				
3. It's OK to destroy a lot of homes if it helps more people.				
4. The benefits of the dam are greater than the risks.				

Pronunciation

The Three Gorges Dam in China is one of the largest dams in the world.

> **Syllable Stress**
>
> In words with more than one syllable, one syllable is stressed more than others. The stress makes the syllable sound louder or stronger.
>
> **track 1-32**
>
> en**ough**   **re**source   **in**terested
>
> Stressing the right syllable is part of correct pronunciation, and listening for syllable stress can help you understand what you hear.

track 1-33 **A** | Listen to the words and circle the stressed syllable. Then practice saying the words with a partner.

1. a vai la ble   2. sig ni fi cant   3. in for ma tion   4. un der stand   5. vo ca bu la ry
6. pro nun ci a tion   7. dif fi cult   8. im por tant   9. ne ces sa ry   10. con ser va tion

track 1-34 **B** | Listen to the sentences from the talk. Circle the stressed syllable in each **bold** word.

1. The water from this river is a **val u able re source**.
2. But if it is not **ma naged** well, it can be very **dan ger ous**.
3. Another reason the dam was built was to help China's **e con o my**.
4. Many towns and villages will **pro ba bly dis ap pear**.

A tree in a Yangtze river flood

Language Function

Talking about Priorities

A priority is the most important thing you have to do or achieve in a situation. Here are some expressions we use to talk about priorities.

The most important thing is to provide clean water for everyone.
My highest priority is studying for my exam.
The main thing is to try to conserve water.
The most important issue to think about is our health.
A priority for our city is building a larger reservoir.

A | Read the sentences below. Then underline the expressions used to talk about priorities.

1. Protecting people's lives is a priority.
2. The main thing is to understand that there are both benefits and risks to this kind of enormous engineering project.
3. The most important consideration is providing water for more people to use.

B | Look at the lists of priorities. Put a check (✔) next to the most important one for you in each list. Add some of your own ideas.

Priorities for Good Health:	Priorities for a Healthy City:	Priorities for Improving My English:
❑ enough sleep	❑ enough water	❑ learning more vocabulary
❑ exercise every day	❑ clean air	❑ improving my grammar
❑ a good diet	❑ enough healthy food	❑ speaking more fluently
❑ seeing the doctor often	❑ good weather	❑ improving my pronunciation
❑ _____	❑ _____	❑ _____

C | **Discussion.** Compare and discuss your ideas with a partner. Use expressions from the chart and exercise **A**.

D | **Self-Reflection.** Think about your city. In your opinion, what do you think the highest priority should be for each topic?

1. Education: _____
2. The environment: _____
3. Business and the economy: _____
4. Transportation: _____
5. Entertainment: _____

E | Form a group with two or three other students. Compare and discuss your ideas from exercise **D**.

Grammar

The Passive Voice

We use the active voice when we want to focus on the person or thing doing the action.
> The dam **provides** electricity for many people.

We use the passive voice when we want to focus on the person or thing receiving the action, or the result.
> Electricity **is provided** by the dam.

We often use the passive voice to talk about processes.
> Water **is collected** in buckets and used for washing clothes.
> The best apples **are selected** and then sent to local markets.

We use *by* with the passive when we want to specify *who* or *what* did the action.
> These books were given to us **by the school.**

A | Rewrite the sentences in the passive voice.

1. Children in many countries play soccer.
   Soccer is played by children in many countries.

2. My sister made this.
   _____

3. Over 1 billion people speak Chinese.
   _____

4. The teacher asked Isabel to give a presentation.
   _____

5. Oscar baked this delicious cake.
   _____

6. A friendly man owns that restaurant.
   _____

B | **Discussion.** Take turns asking and answering the questions with a partner. Then ask some of your own questions. Use the passive voice.

1. Who wrote your favorite book?
2. Which countries produce coffee?
3. Who invented the telephone?
4. Who made your clothing?
5. Which country won the last World Cup?

> My favorite book was written by Arundhati Roy.

Student to Student: Showing Surprise

Here are some expressions you can use to express surprise about something.

Some people take water from their showers and use it in their gardens.

You're kidding! Wow! Really? Seriously? That's unbelievable/incredible!

C | **Understanding Visuals.** Read the information about PlayPumps and look at the diagram and the photo.

PlayPumps

Many small villages in Africa don't have access to clean water. People must walk five miles (eight kilometers) to get water and carry very heavy containers that weigh about 40 pounds (18 kilograms). A new invention called the PlayPump is changing life in many villages. It uses a children's toy called a merry-go-round to provide clean water.

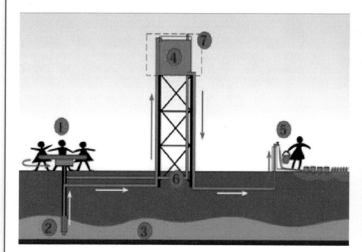 

Source: http://kids.nationalgeographic.com/kids/stories/peopleplaces/playpumps/

D | Work with a partner. Take turns explaining how a PlayPump works. Use the cues below and the diagram to help you. Use the passive voice.

1. the merry-go-round/turn/by the children
2. the energy/use/to pump water
3. 369 gallons (1400 liters) of clean water/pump/in one hour
4. the water/store/in a big tank
5. the water/carry/to people's houses
6. water/pump/up to the tank
7. ads/paint/on the sides of the tank

> The merry-go-round is turned by the children.

Presenting an Idea

 A | Form a group with two or three other students. Read the situation and the information about four water devices. Then choose which device you will present.

> **Situation:** You work for an organization called Safe Water Now. Your organization wants to spend $1 million for a new device that will help provide clean water for people. You have to give a presentation to the directors of your organization that explains which device is best and why.

Device 1 Q Drum

- carries 13 gallons (50 liters) of water easily
- drum/use to bring clean water to houses
- rope/put through hole
- drum/pull/not carry
- drums/make in South Africa
- drums/sell for $60

Device 2 Water Cone

- makes dirty or salty water drinkable
- salty water/put in the blue pan
- clear plastic top/put over the pan
- water/made into gas/by heat from the sun
- clean water/collect in the bottom of the cone
- 0.4 gallons (1.5 liters) clean water/produce in 24 hours

Device 3 KickStart Pump

- helps farmers provide more water for their crops
- pump/sell to farmers in Africa
- pump/operate with your feet
- more crops/grow with the water
- money from crops/use for family's health and education
- pumps/make in Kenya

Device 4 LifeStraw

- provides clean water for one person
- LifeStraw/use any kind of dirty water
- one end/put in a person's mouth
- the LifeStraw/makes water clean
- enough water/provide for one person for a year
- LifeStraw/sell for $2

 B | **Planning a Presentation.** Follow the instructions below with your group. Write notes and decide which information each group member will present.

1. Explain which device you chose and how it works. Use the passive voice.
2. Explain how the device will help people and why it is the best choice for your organization.

 C | **Presentation.** Present your device to the class.

The Yamuna River in New Delhi, India

Alwar is in a very dry region of India.

Before Viewing

A | **Using a Dictionary.** You will hear these words in the video. Match each word with the correct definition. Use your dictionary to help you.

1. earthen (adj.) ___
2. monsoon (n.) ___
3. organization (n.) ___
4. village (n.) ___
5. well (n.) ___

a. a group of houses and other buildings in the country
b. a season in Southern Asia where there is a lot of rain
c. made of dirt or clay
d. a hole in the ground that provides water
e. an official group of people or business

Critical Thinking Focus: Predicting Content

Before listening to or viewing information, you can use the information available to you to help you predict the content you will hear and see. Some ways you can do this is by reading titles and photo captions, or by looking at photos, charts, or images related to the content.

B | **Predicting Content.** Look at the title of the video and the photos. List five words you expect to hear in the video.

_____

While Viewing

A | Watch the video. Circle any words you wrote in exercise **B** of the Before Viewing section as you hear them.

Alwar's new reservoirs have made life better.

A man digging clay in Rajasthan, India.

B | Read the sentences. Watch the video again. Check (✔) the correct city or region for each sentence. Sometimes two places are correct.

	New Delhi	Alwar
1. It's a very large city.	❏	❏
2. Getting enough water has been a problem here.	❏	❏
3. Their water comes from a polluted river.	❏	❏
4. Small dams have given people more water.	❏	❏
5. Other places are learning from the ideas here.	❏	❏
6. Small dams don't work here.	❏	❏
7. This place needs to find a new idea for getting water.	❏	❏

C | Watch the video again and circle the word you hear in each sentence.

1. Every day, 50 million gallons of chemicals are put into the (river/water).
2. The people of New Delhi require about 1 billion (gallons/liters) of water a day.
3. The government says the answer is to build more big (reservoirs/dams).
4. They began collecting stone and rock and made (small/large) earthen dams.
5. Today, a village that was dry and lifeless is (green/wet) and healthy.
6. They provide water for more than (80/800) communities.

After Viewing

A | In your notebook, rewrite these sentences in the passive voice.

1. Factories put chemicals into the river. _Chemicals are put into the river by factories._
2. The people in New Delhi require a lot of water.
3. Trucks deliver water to people.
4. Rajendra Singh started an organization to help people.

B | **Critical Thinking.** Form a group with two or three other students and discuss the questions.

1. In Lesson A, you learned about the Three Gorges Dam, and in the video you learned about dams in India. What do you think are the advantages and disadvantages of dams?
2. In Lesson B, you will listen to students talking about a drought (a long period of time without rain). Do you think droughts are more difficult for people living in cities or for people living on farms? Explain.

A | **Meaning from Context.** Read and listen to the information. Notice the words in blue. These are words you will hear and use in Lesson B.

A man looks at the bottom of a dry dam in Leigh, Australia.

Australia's Water

Water is important in any country, but in Australia, it is the most important resource. Australia is the driest continent in the world, and water is very scarce in many regions. The normal amount of rain in some places is only one inch (25 millimeters) per year.

Several years ago, the rain stopped falling in Australia, and many parts of the country soon experienced a drought—a time of extremely dry weather. Children in some towns have never seen rain in their whole lives.

It was a crisis for the entire country, and many people were very worried. The government had to decide how to allocate water for different uses. Rules were made about domestic use of water for things such as gardens, swimming pools, and showers. Some water is also needed for industry because the country makes cars, ships, and machines. But Australians' main use of water is for agriculture. Farms produce rice, grapes, oranges, cattle, and many other foods, and these require a lot of water. Instead of rain, Australia uses water from rivers and underground reservoirs for farming.

Some parts of Australia have had more normal amounts of rain recently, but in many places there, the crisis continues. And with the earth's climate getting hotter, other countries will face urgent decisions about water use, like Australia has.

B | **Discussion.** With a partner, discuss the questions below.

1. Has your country ever had a drought? How did it affect people?
2. Are there any rules in your country about using water?

C | Complete each definition with the correct form of a word from the box. Use your dictionary to help you.

allocate (v.)	crisis (n.)	experience (v.)	industry (n.)	scarce (adj.)
agriculture (n.)	domestic (adj.)	extremely (adv.)	normal (adj.)	urgent (adj.)

1. If you _____ something, you make a decision about how to use it.
2. _____ is the work of making things in factories.
3. If something is _____, it is usual and people expect it.
4. _____ is raising plants and animals on farms.
5. If something is _____, you need to take care of it very soon.
6. A _____ is a large and serious problem.
7. _____ means related to the home and family.
8. If you _____ something, it happens to you.
9. _____ means to a very great degree.
10. If something is _____, there isn't very much of it for people to use.

A | **Self-Reflection.** Check (✔) your opinion for each statement in the survey below.

Opinion Survey: Water	I Agree.	I Disagree.	I'm Not Sure.
1. It's a bad idea to have **agriculture** in countries that don't have much water.	❏	❏	❏
2. Water might be **scarce** in my country in the future.	❏	❏	❏
3. We should **allocate** more water to factories.	❏	❏	❏
4. **Domestic** appliances like dishwashers waste too much water. Everyone should wash their dishes by hand.	❏	❏	❏
5. **Industry** uses too much water and pollutes it.	❏	❏	❏
6. When there is a water **crisis**, it's usually caused by people.	❏	❏	❏
7. When a country **experiences** a drought, other countries should send water.	❏	❏	❏
8. I use a **normal** amount of water for people in my country.	❏	❏	❏
9. It is **extremely** important to try to conserve water.	❏	❏	❏
10. Water is an **urgent** problem in my country today.	❏	❏	❏

 B | **Discussion.** Form a group with two or three other students and compare your answers with the group. Explain your reasons and talk about priorities.

> I don't think we should allocate more water for cities.

> Really? Why not?

> Because we need more water for agriculture.

 C | **Presentation.** Tell the class about some statements in exercise **A** that your group has the same opinion about, and some things that you have different opinions about.

> We all think that . . .

A man uses water from a nearby river to water his crops.

A woman in Bangladesh collects drinking water from a lake.

Before Listening

A | Understanding Visuals. The Murray-Darling Basin is an important agricultural region in Australia. Look at the map and answer the questions.

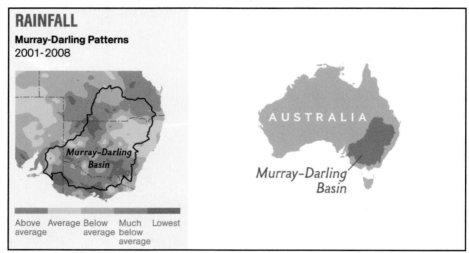

RAINFALL
Murray-Darling Patterns
2001-2008

Murray-Darling Basin

AUSTRALIA

Murray-Darling Basin

Above average Average Below average Much below average Lowest

1. What was the rainfall pattern in 2001–2008?

   _____

2. What does the chart tell you about the rain in that area?

   _____

3. What problems do you think farmers have there?

   _____

B | Discuss your answers from exercise **A** with a partner.

Listening: A Group Discussion

A | Listening for Main Ideas. Listen to the students' discussion and number the photos in the order you hear about them.

track 1-36

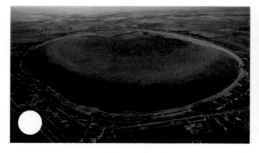

B | **Listening for Details.** Listen to the discussion again. Complete the statements with information about the drought and its effects.

1. In some places there it hasn't rained once in _____ years.

2. The Adlington farm used to have _____ cattle, and now they have only _____ because _____ is so scarce.

3. Lake Boga almost disappeared because all the water is used by _____.

4. Lake Boga used to be a _____ place, but now no one stays in the _____.

5. Australia used to grow _____ tons of rice a year—now they only grow _____ tons.

6. There are a lot of water rules and restrictions in Australian _____.

7. People have to save water from their showers to use in their _____.

C | **Note-Taking.** Listen to the conversation again. Choose and write down the three most important facts in your notebook that the students can use for their presentation on "How people are affected by drought."

After Listening

Critical Thinking. Compare your answers in exercise **C** of the Listening section with a partner's. Then discuss the questions.

1. Which uses of water did the students talk about?
2. In your opinion, what should be the main priorities? Explain.

Pronunciation

Suffixes and Syllable Stress

In some words, the syllable stress changes when a suffix (e.g., *-ion*) is added to the end. Paying attention to this can improve your listening comprehension and your pronunciation. Examples:

educate → edu**ca**tion   **all**ocate → allo**ca**tion

pres**ent** → presen**ta**tion   con**serve** → conser**va**tion

A | Listen to the words and sentences below. Circle the stressed syllable in each **bold** word.

1. industry   It's a big **in dus tri al** city.
2. agriculture   He studied at an **ag ri cul tur al** college.
3. government   She works for a **gov ern men tal** agency.
4. describe   The **de scrip tion** of Lake Boga was very interesting.

B | Take turns reading the words and sentences from exercise **A** to a partner.

Language Function

Expressing Opinions

In everyday conversations and class discussions, you need to ask for and give opinions. Here are some expressions you can use to ask for an opinion.

Do you think . . . ?   *What's your opinion of . . . ?*
What do you think about . . . ?   *How do you feel about . . . ?*

Here are some expressions you can use to give your opinion:

I think . . .   *I feel . . .*
I don't think . . .   *In my opinion, . . .*
If you ask me, . . .

If you ask me, *water for the cities is the top priority.*

A | Read the information in the chart.

How much water does it take to . . .

wash the dishes?   flush the toilet?   wash a load of clothes?   take a four-minute shower?

 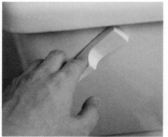  

8 gallons/30 liters   3.5 gallons/13 liters   22 gallons/85 liters   30 gallons/113 liters

 B | **Discussion.** Form a group with two or three other students. Read the situation. Then discuss the questions below.

Situation: Your family lives in a small house. A large water pipe in your city broke yesterday, so you will have less water until the pipe can be fixed. It will take the city two weeks to fix the pipe. Each person in your family can only use 13 gallons (50 liters) of water a day. Discuss what your family will do to reduce the amount of water you use.

1. What are your priorities for using water?
2. What will you do so you use only 13 gallons of water per person a day?

C | Make a list of your family's priorities. Talk about your priorities and make a list of your decisions.

D | **Presentation.** Share your ideas for exercise **B** with the class.

Grammar

Superlative Adjectives

We use superlative adjectives to compare three or more people, places, or things.
> Eva is the **shortest** person in our class.
> Brazil is the **largest** country in South America.

To form the superlative, we add *the –est* to one-syllable adjectives. For adjectives ending in *-y*, we change the *y* to *i* and add *the -est*.
> clean → the cleanest
> dirty → the dirtiest

We use *the most* to form the superlative of adjectives of two or more syllables.
> urgent → the most urgent
> significant → the most significant

Some superlative forms are irregular.
> good → the best
> bad → the worst

A | With a partner, complete the sentences with the superlative form of the adjectives in parentheses.

1. The Nile River in Egypt is the _____longest_____ (long) river in the world.
2. The _____ (poisonous) spiders live in Australia.
3. I think Moscow is the _____ (interesting) city in the world.
4. The Petronas Towers in Malaysia used to be the _____ (tall) in the world.
5. The _____ (old) city in the world is Damascus in Syria.
6. The _____ (good) food in the world comes from my country.

B | Write superlative sentences. Use the adjectives in parentheses and try to guess the correct facts.

1. (dry) Region in Australia: Murray-Darling Basin/Northern Queensland/Western Australia

   _____

2. (important) Crop in Australia: fruit/rice/wheat

   _____

3. (big) Ocean: the Pacific Ocean/the Indian Ocean/the Atlantic Ocean

   _____

4. (heavy) Land animal: elephant/rhinoceros/gorilla

   _____

C | **Discussion.** With a partner, discuss your opinions about the topics below. Use superlatives and expressions from the chart on page 78.

| good movie | delicious food | dangerous job | exciting sport to watch |

You will role-play a government meeting about how to allocate the local water supply. In the meeting you will try to decide how much water you should allocate to each of the different organizations.

 A | Form a group with three other students. Read the information below and the role cards. Assign a role to each member of your group.

Situation: The government built a new dam near a large city, and now the reservoir is getting full. Scientists determined the amount of water that the city can take from the reservoir every year. Now the government will have a meeting to decide how to use that water.

Role #1: Manager of the City Water Company

- The population of the city has increased by 200,000 people in the last 10 years.
- Now there are strict rules about using water for gardens and washing cars.
- The price of water is very high.

Requested allocation: 30 percent of the total amount

Role #2: President of the National Farmers' Association

- Most farms are very small, and farmers don't earn much money.
- With more water, farmers could start growing cotton to sell to other countries.
- Farmers have had problems with dry weather in the last few years.

Requested allocation: 60 percent of the total amount

Role #3: President of the International Aluminum Company

- The company wants to build a large aluminum factory next to the reservoir.
- The factory would provide new jobs for more than 1000 people.
- This would be the biggest factory in the region.

Requested allocation: 50 percent of the total amount

Role #4: Director of the National Parks Service

- Several kinds of rare fish and birds live in lakes that are connected to the reservoir.
- Foreign tourists often come to see and photograph these animals.
- If there isn't enough water, all the animals will die.

Requested allocation: 20 percent of the total amount

B | Read the information on your role card. Prepare a one-minute talk. Your talk should answer these questions:

1. Who are you? What organization or company do you work for?
2. How much water does your organization need?
3. Why does it need this amount of water?

Presentation Skills:
Speaking at the Right Volume

When you are speaking in front of the class, you need to make your voice a little louder than normal. This makes it easier for your audience to understand you. It also shows that you are confident.

 C | **Role-playing.** Role-play the meeting. Work together and decide how much water each organization will get. The amount must total 100 percent.

 D | **Presentation.** Present your group's decision to the class.

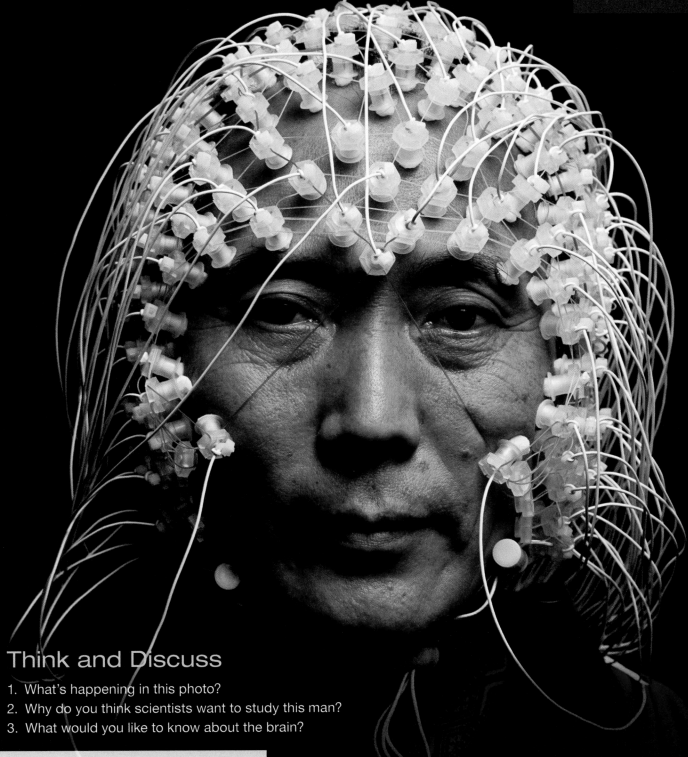

Inside the Brain

ACADEMIC PATHWAYS

Lesson A: Listening to a Documentary
Discussing Problems and Solutions

Lesson B: Listening to a Conversation between Students
Planning a Group Presentation

Think and Discuss

1. What's happening in this photo?
2. Why do you think scientists want to study this man?
3. What would you like to know about the brain?

The wires on Buddhist teacher and artist Dru-gu Choegyal
Rinpoche's head are measuring his brain activity.

Exploring the Theme:
Inside the Brain

Look at the photos and read the captions. Then discuss the questions.
1. What are some things your brain helps you do?
2. What happens to your brain when you learn something new?
3. What is your *hippocampus*?

How Does Learning Affect Our Brains?

Studies show that when we learn something new, it changes the structure of our brains.

How Do We Remember Information?

Glen McNeill spends six or seven hours a day riding his motor bike through the streets of London, England, so he can become a taxi driver. When he finishes his training, his *hippocampus*, the area of the brain used for memory, will be larger than most adults'.

A laurel maze at Glendurgal in Cornwall, England

track 2-2

A | **Meaning from Context.** Read and listen to the information. Notice the words in blue. These are words you will hear and use in Lesson A.

Facts to Make You Think about Your Brain

1. Every time you have a new thought or recall a memory, your brain creates a new **connection** or pathway.

2. Even without words, you can understand when someone is happy, sad, or angry. There is a small area in your brain called the *amygdala* that helps you "read" other people's faces and understand their **moods**.

3. The belief that we only use a **tiny** amount (10 percent) of our brains is false. Each part of the brain has a **function**, so we use 100 percent of our brains.

4. Learning something new can change the **structure** of the brain in just seven days. If you want to change your brain quickly, you should try learning a new skill like juggling or playing a musical instrument.

5. The things you do, eat, smell, and touch every day all **generate** thoughts. The average person experiences approximately 70,000 thoughts a day.

6. Your brain is an amazing, **complex** organ. It contains more than 100 billion neurons[1] that are always sending messages. But not all neurons are the same: different neurons send messages at different **speeds**.

7. Every time you think, laugh, or sneeze, it's because chemical **signals** are moving from neuron to neuron. Your brain is a very powerful organ. In fact, when you are awake, your brain generates between 10 and 23 watts of electricity—or enough power to power a light bulb.

8. The *hypothalamus* is the part of your brain that **controls** your body temperature. It knows your correct body temperature (98.6 degrees Farenheit/37 degrees Celsius). When you get too hot, it makes you sweat.[2] When you get too cold, it makes you shiver.[3]

Sources: http://www.nursingassistantcentral.com/blog/2008/100-fascinating-facts-you-never-knew-about-the-human-brain/, www.tastyhuman.com/30-interesting-facts-about-the-human-brain/

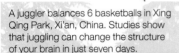

A juggler balances 6 basketballs in Xing Qing Park, Xi'an, China. Studies show that juggling can change the structure of your brain in just seven days.

[1]A **neuron** is a cell that is part of the nervous system.
[2]When you **sweat**, water or sweat comes through your skin.
[3]When you **shiver**, your body shakes slightly.

B | Write each word in blue from exercise **A** next to its definition.

1. _____ (v.) to produce

2. _____ (n.) things that carry information

3. _____ (v.) makes someone or something do what you want

4. _____ (adj.) having many parts

5. _____ (n.) the rates at which things move

6. _____ (n.) something that is made of parts that are connected

7. _____ (adj.) very small

8. _____ (n.) a use or purpose

9. _____ (n.) the ways you are feeling at a particular time

10. _____ (n.) the place where two things are joined together

A | Complete each sentence with the correct form of a word in **blue** from exercise **A** on page 84. Use each word only once.

1. The heart has a very important _____. It moves blood through the body.

2. The new art museum is a very interesting _____. It's made of glass and shaped like a pyramid.

3. Airplanes move at very high _____. Most planes fly at about 500 miles (805 kilometers) per hour.

4. It's amazing that water, wind, and our brains can all _____ electricity!

5. Brain cells are very _____. You can't see them without a microscope.

6. When you are driving and you see a red traffic light, it's a _____ to stop.

7. Allen seems like he's in a bad _____ today. I think it's because his team lost last night.

8. Our landlord _____ the heat in our apartment. We can't change it ourselves.

9. My hotel room doesn't have an Internet _____, so I can't send email.

10. Russian is a very _____ language. It has a different alphabet and the grammar and pronunciation are very difficult.

B | **Discussion.** With a partner, discuss the questions below.

1. Look at the facts on page 84. Which facts do you think are most interesting? Explain.
2. Your *amygdala* helps you "read" other people's faces and understand their **moods**. How can doing this be useful?
3. What things put you in a good **mood**? What things put you in a bad **mood**?
4. What are some **signals** you can give someone to show you're happy? To show you understand? To show you agree?

Your *amygdala* helps you "read" other people's faces and understand their moods.

Before Listening

  Predicting Content. Discuss the question with a partner.

You are going to listen to a documentary about the human brain. Which of these topics do you expect to hear about in the documentary? Circle your ideas.

exercise	learning	food
neurons	memory	intelligence

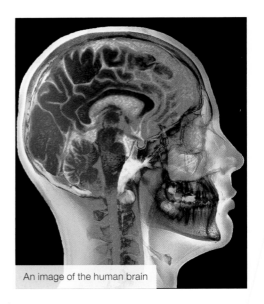

An image of the human brain

Listening: A Documentary

🎧 track 2-3 **A** | Listen to the documentary and check your predictions.

🎧 track 2-3 **B** | **Listening for Main Ideas.** Listen again and put a check (✔) next to the main ideas.

- ☐ Your brain is a very important and complex organ.
- ☐ Your brain tells your muscles what to do.
- ☐ Your brain is very powerful.
- ☐ You brain can send messages very quickly.
- ☐ Your brain helps you protect your pets.
- ☐ Learning changes your brain.
- ☐ Exercise helps you learn.

🎧 track 2-3 **C** | **Listening for Details.** Read the statements below. Then listen again and circle **T** for *true* or **F** for *false*.

1.	Your brain weighs five pounds.	T	F
2.	Computers can process information more quickly than our brains can.	T	F
3.	Your brain contains about 100 million neurons.	T	F
4.	Motor neurons can send information at 200 miles per hour.	T	F
5.	Exercise can improve your mood.	T	F
6.	Exercise produces chemicals that make it easier to learn.	T	F

After Listening

Discussion. With a partner, discuss the questions below.

1. What are some activities or skills that were difficult for you at first, but are easy for you now (e.g., riding a bicycle)?
2. Do you agree that exercise improves your mood? Explain.
3. Do you think that exercise helps you study or solve problems more easily? Explain.

Pronunciation

track **2-4**

Linking Sounds

When people speak quickly, they do not stop or pause after each word. In fact, you often hear words that are joined or linked together. Three common types of linking are:

Consonant sound → Vowel sound

It's a fascinating job.

Vowel sound → Vowel sound

I knew it was the right answer.

The book will certainly be interesting.

Consonant sound → Same consonant sound

What was your reason for being late?

Collaboration. Work with a partner. Listen to the sentences. Then take turns saying the sentences. Identify the types of linking used in each sentence. Write **C-V** for consonant-vowel, **V-V** for vowel-vowel, and **C-SC** for consonant-same consonant.

track **2-5**

1. Your brain <u>controls everything</u> you do. ___C-V___
2. Your brain <u>generates enough</u> energy to power a light bulb. _____
3. The activity in your <u>brain never</u> stops. _____
4. Your brain sends a message to your foot to shake the <u>bee off</u> quickly. _____
5. <u>Any exercise</u> that makes your heart beat faster can help your mood. _____
6. Your body produces a chemical that makes <u>it easier</u> to learn. _____

Grammar

Infinitives after Verbs

We can use infinitives after certain transitive verbs.
> I'll <u>try</u> **to study** more tonight.
> Last night I <u>needed</u> **to sleep**.
> I <u>forgot</u> **to bring** my notebook to class.

Note: Verbs cannot have other verbs as objects.
✗ Volkan and Begum **plan take** a vacation in August.
✔ Volkan and Begum **plan to take** a vacation in August.

A | Take turns asking and answering the questions with a partner. Notice the underlined words in each sentence.

1. What do you <u>want to do</u> next weekend?
2. What do you <u>need to do</u> tonight?
3. What do you always <u>remember to do</u> in the morning?

B | Complete each sentence with an appropriate infinitive.

1. I promise not _____*to spend*_____ too much money on my vacation.
2. Pablo tried _____ his friend John with his homework.
3. My daughter sometimes forgets _____ her teeth in the morning.
4. If you want _____ a new vocabulary word, you should write it down.
5. The Norton family decided _____ a new car.
6. Lee is pretending _____ sick so he can stay in bed all day.
7. Do you want _____ our presentation this afternoon?
8. I really hope _____ Amy next time she comes to New York.

C | **Discussion.** Practice asking and answering the questions with a partner.

1. What do you try to do every day?
2. What do you need to do tomorrow?
3. What do you want to do this weekend?
4. What do you hope to do this summer?

> What do you try to do every day?
>> I try to go to the gym every day.

D | Look at the photos and read the captions. Notice the verbs in **bold**.

They are **planning** to take a vacation.

She **learned** to play the violin.

They are **deciding** what to order.

You must **remember** to be on time for a job interview.

E | **Self-Reflection.** Finish the sentences about yourself. Then read your sentences to a partner.

1. I plan to _____.
2. In this class, I'm learning to _____.
3. I really want to _____.
4. Yesterday, I remembered to _____.
5. I've decided to _____.
6. In the future, I hope to _____.

F | Say any verb from the box below to your partner. Your partner must quickly say a correct sentence using that verb. Then switch roles. Repeat the process as many times as possible in two minutes.

remember	learn	plan	want	decide	need
choose	hope	prepare	promise	try	forget

forget

I forgot to bring my notebook to class today.

Language Function

Making Suggestions

We use the modal *could* to make suggestions.

You **could** talk to the professor and explain the problem.

Here are some other expressions we use to make suggestions.

(You) might want to take the exam again.
Let's study after class.
Why don't you/we do the worksheet at home?
You could try to imagine the situation in a different way.
Maybe you should study with a friend.

A | Work with a partner. Complete the conversation between two college students. Then practice the conversation. Switch roles and practice it again.

Mike: I have to pick my cousin up at the airport on Friday, so I can't go to class. Do you think Professor Harris will let me hand my paper in on Monday instead?

Eric: I'm not sure. (1) _____ you hand it in on Thursday instead?

Mike: I don't think I can finish it by then.

Eric: Well, you (2) _____ email it to her on Friday.

Mike: Good idea. I'm going to try to talk to her after class.

Eric: You (3) _____ want to tell her before class starts, because I think she has a class right after ours.

Mike: OK, thanks. (4) _____ stop at the Student Center before class and get something to eat.

Eric: Sounds good. I haven't eaten lunch yet.

B | Write three situations you need help with. Then take turns reading your situations and giving suggestions to your partner.

1. _____.
2. _____.
3. _____.

I missed class and don't have any notes to study for the test.

We could study together tomorrow.

Discussing Problems and Solutions

A | Read the information about the different problems people have.

Josh
"My wife and I are from different countries. We can't decide where to live after our children are born."

Maya
"I already speak English. Now I want to learn Japanese, but I don't have time to take classes because of my busy work schedule."

Toby
"I spend too much money on video games, music, and electronics. Every time I see a new game, I want to buy it. I'm spending too much money!"

Ken
"Every time I want to leave my apartment, I have to look for my keys. I never remember to put my keys in the same place so I can find them."

Renata
"I don't want to live alone in this house anymore. My husband died five years ago, and my son and daughter are married now and have their own houses and families. This house feels too big for me now."

B | **Brainstorming.** What should these people do? Brainstorm possible solutions to each person's problem in your notebook.

C | Form a group with four other students. Choose one of the people from exercise **A** to role-play. Take turns talking about your problems and making helpful suggestions. Use your own words and the expressions from page 90.

> My wife wants to be closer to her family when our children are born.

> You could spend a few years in one country and then move.

> Or try to convince your wife to live in your country.

MEMORY MAN

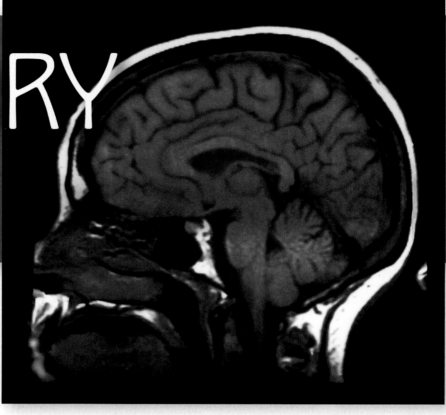

Before Viewing

A | Using a Dictionary. Look at the photos and read the captions. Use your dictionary to help you understand any words you do not know.

Nature vs. Nurture: Where do we get our abilities?

Heredity is a natural process. We inherit genes from both our parents. The genes contain DNA. This genetic information has a great effect on a child's body and health.

Children have an enormous capacity for learning. Their environment—the situation in which they grow and learn—has a great effect on them.

B | Self-Reflection. Discuss the questions below with a partner. Think about the information you learned about the brain in Lesson A and the information from page 92 as you discuss the questions.

1. What can you do very well (e.g., sing, write, draw pictures)?
2. Did you inherit this ability from your parents, or did you learn it?

While Viewing

A | Read the questions below. Then write the answers while you watch the video.

1. Where is Gianni Golfera from? _____
2. Golfera says, "It's a kind of memory that's connected to what I _____."
3. What are some examples of things Golfera remembers? _____
4. At what age did Golfera start trying to remember more and more? _____
5. What are some reasons for Golfera's excellent memory? _____

B | Read the statements below. Then watch the video again and circle **T** for *true* or **F** for *false*.

1. Golfera can remember 60 numbers after he hears them once.   **T**   **F**
2. Golfera says he can remember the days of his life in detail.   **T**   **F**
3. Dr. Antonio Malgaroli is a microbiologist.   **T**   **F**
4. Scientists understand why some people lose their memories.   **T**   **F**
5. Research shows that a great memory depends on DNA.   **T**   **F**
6. Golfera wrote a book to teach people to improve their memories.   **T**   **F**

After Viewing

A | Critical Thinking. Discuss the question below with a partner.

Did Golfera inherit a special kind of memory, or can any person have a memory like Golfera's?

B | To test your memory, follow the instructions below. Then switch roles.

1. Write down six numbers between 1 and 100 in any order across a piece of paper.
2. Show your partner the paper and read the numbers aloud.
3. Take the paper away and ask your partner to repeat the numbers.

C | Discussion. In Lesson B, you will learn about the mental versus emotional abilities of the brain. Discuss your opinions about the following statements with a group.

1. The brain is responsible for creating our emotions.
2. Our memory affects both our mental (thinking) and emotional abilities.

A | Prior Knowledge. Discuss the questions below with a partner.

1. Who are some of the people you love?
2. What do you think makes people fall in love?

track 2-6 **B | Meaning from Context.** Read and listen to the article about love. Notice the words in blue. These are words you will hear and use in Lesson B.

A newly married couple dances on Mendenhall Glacier.

Romantic Love vs. Long-Term Attachments

There are many different kinds of love. There is the strong emotion we feel when we fall in love. There is the attachment between parents and children, and the quiet feeling of security that develops slowly in long-term relationships, when couples are together for many years.

Your brain knows the difference between romantic love and other attachments. When we're in love, the amount of a brain chemical called *dopamine* increases. This increase in dopamine gives us the extra energy we feel when we're in love.

At the same time, this increase in dopamine can make the brains of people who are "lovesick" similar to the brains of people with OCD— Obsessive Compulsive Disorder.[1] People with OCD cannot stop thinking about something, and these thoughts can cause compulsive behaviors—actions the person cannot control, such as washing their hands again and again. Similarly, people who are in love often cannot stop thinking about the person they are in love with. Both people with OCD and people in love may sometimes find it difficult to function normally in their daily lives because of their thoughts.

Fortunately, this "lovesickness" is a short-term condition. With time, strong romantic feelings decrease, and we can concentrate on "real life" again. As time passes, couples have higher levels of oxytocin—a brain chemical connected with calm feelings of happiness and trust.

So is love only a matter of brain chemistry? In fact, while chemicals do affect the way we feel, psychological factors are also important. We might be attracted to someone who likes the same things we like, for example, or someone who makes us feel safe and secure.

[1]According to research by Donatella Marazziti at the University of Pisa in Italy

A | Read the information below. Then work with a partner to find the words in **blue** from the article on page 94 that have good context clues. Underline the context clues you find.

Critical Thinking Focus: Using Context Clues	
Context clues can help you understand the meanings of words you read or hear. Here are some clues from the article on page 94.	
Type of Context Clue	**Explanation**
A definition	Sometimes the text or the speaker gives a definition of a word or term. For example: . . . *and these thoughts can cause* **compulsive** *behaviors—*<u>actions the person cannot control</u>, . . .
Other words nearby	Sometimes other words nearby a new word or expression help explain its meaning. For example: . . ., *and the quiet feeling of security that develops slowly in* **long-term** *relationships, when couples are* <u>together for many years</u>. *long-term* = for many years
Your knowledge of the world	The article mentions the **attachment** <u>between parents and children</u>. I feel love for my parents, so I understand that *attachment* may be a kind of love.

B | Form a group with another pair of students. Compare the context clues you found from exercise **A**.

C | Fill in each blank with one of the words in **blue** from exercise **B** on page 94.

1. They have a _____ relationship. They've been married for 29 years.
2. They have _____ tastes in music: both like classical music.
3. My teenage daughter has a strong _____ to her best friend. They have been friends since they were three years old.
4. I can't _____ on my homework when you're talking loudly.
5. Couples can feel all types of _____ for each other—love, sadness, anger, and happiness.
6. Your brain and body cannot _____ well if you do not eat and sleep enough.
7. If something is _____, it involves thoughts.
8. Marc wanted to be _____, so he wrote a song and sent roses to Laura.
9. He got a _____ job in an office. It only lasts for six weeks.
10. Charlene likes living near the police department. She says it gives her a feeling of _____.

Oxytocin levels increase when a woman has a baby.

Before Listening

 track 2-7 A | Read and listen to part of a conversation. What are the classmates talking about?

> **Cathy:** Did you understand everything Professor Wong said yesterday about short-term memory?
>
> **Toshi:** Yeah, I think so.
>
> **Cathy:** I'm not sure that I did.
>
> **Toshi:** Well, here's what I got from the lecture. Your short-term memory only lasts a few seconds, right? Information enters the brain through the senses—things we taste, touch, smell, and so on… and we remember it long enough to function normally.
>
> **Cathy:** Sorry, but what do you mean by "function normally"?
>
> **Toshi:** Well, for example, if I ask you a question, you can remember the question long enough to answer it.
>
> **Liz:** Right, but you might not remember the question tomorrow.

B | **Understanding Visuals.** Look at the flow chart. Then discuss the questions below with a partner.

The Memory Process

Sensory Information

Information enters the brain through our senses (what we taste, smell, touch, see, and hear), and it is stored[1] for a very short time—less than a second.

Some of the information moves to our short-term memory.

Short-Term Memory

Only the information we need to use immediately moves to our short-term memory, such as a classmate's name or an email address.

Long-Term Memory

Only information that we try to remember or that the brain decides is important moves to our long-term memory. This information, such as the name of our first teacher or the lyrics to a song, can last a lifetime.

Memories become stronger when they are sent down the same pathway in the brain many times. These memory pathways or connections become our longest-lasting memories.

[1]When you **store** something, you keep it until you need to use it.

1. How does information enter the brain? What are some examples?
2. What information from short-term memory moves to long-term memory?
3. What are some things you have difficulty remembering (names, new vocabulary, etc.)?
4. In your opinion, what's the best way to remember something you want to remember?
   a. Repeat it to yourself.
   b. Write it down.
   c. Pay extra attention to it.
   d. Other

Listening: A Conversation between Students

A | **Listening for Main Ideas.** Listen to the conversation. What conclusions do the students make about short-term and long-term memory?

Short-term memory: _____

Long-term memory: _____

B | **Listening for Details.** Listen again and complete the sentences.

1. To create a long-term memory, your brain has to _____.

2. To learn new information, you have to _____.

3. To learn how to ride a bicycle, you have to _____.

After Listening

A | Take turns asking and answering the questions below with a partner.

1. In your own words, what's the difference between short-term and long-term memory?

2. What kinds of information can you remember easily (e.g., names, songs, directions, etc.)?

B | **Self-Reflection.** Read the statements below. Then circle the number that shows how much you agree with each statement.

1. It was easier to learn something new when I was younger.

   strongly disagree   1   2   3   4   5   strongly agree

2. Even with practice, there are some things I just can't learn how to do.

   strongly disagree   1   2   3   4   5   strongly agree

3. I learn from mistakes more quickly than I learn in other ways.

   strongly disagree   1   2   3   4   5   strongly agree

4. It's easier for me to learn how to do something new if someone shows me rather than tells me how to do it.

   strongly disagree   1   2   3   4   5   strongly agree

5. It's easier for me to remember information if I write it down.

   strongly disagree   1   2   3   4   5   strongly agree

C | **Discussion.** Compare and discuss your answers from exercise **B** with a partner.

A group of students works together on a project. Cooperative learning makes students an active part of their own education.

A | **Self-Reflection.** Look at the photo and read the caption. Then discuss the question below with a partner.

What experiences have you had with group projects?

B | **Brainstorming.** With your partner, brainstorm a list of the good things about doing group work and possible problems. Write your ideas in the T-chart below.

(+) Good Things	(−) Problems
more people to share ideas	some people don't do any work

C | **Critical Thinking.** With your partner, look at your list of problems from exercise **B**. Think of ways to solve each of the problems in your T-chart.

> If some people don't do any work, the group could give each person a role.

D | **Discussion.** Form a group with another pair of students. Share some of your ideas from exercise **C**. Use phrases from the Student to Student box below to help you explain your ideas.

Student to Student: Presenting Your Ideas in a Small Group

Here are some phrases you can use when sharing your ideas with the class or small group.

We believe that . . .   *Amy and I think that . . .*   *It seems to us that . . .*

Language Function

Making Suggestions during Group Work

Here are some expressions you can use to make polite suggestions during group work.
   Why don't we *write our ideas on the board?*
   Let's *make a list of possible ideas first.*
   I suggest we *talk about our ideas first, then write them down . . .*
   Can we *brainstorm some ideas for our topic?*

A | A group of students in a psychology class has to do a group project. Read their assignment.

Psychology 302: Professor Morgan

Group Project Assignment: (Due: October 23rd)

For the past two weeks we have studied attachment theory, beginning with Harry Harlow's experiments with monkeys. In those experiments, researchers took baby monkeys from their mothers. The monkeys had many emotional problems without their mothers' love. We also studied John Bowlby. His work showed us that human babies need a sense of security, too. Without this security from an adult, they have problems in future relationships. Finally, we looked at Phillip Shaver's recent ideas about attachment theory and romantic love.

Assignment: You will plan a class presentation of 10–15 minutes. First, select two of the researchers we studied. You will briefly summarize their research and then explain which scientist's work you think will have the greatest impact on people today. Be sure to support your opinion with reasons.

B | **Critical Thinking.** Form a group with two or three other students. Now that you know about the assignment, follow the steps below with your group.

1. Read the information about each group member. Discuss what each person would probably say about the assignment.
2. Complete each person's statement or question. Use expressions from the chart in the Language Function section on page 98 as well as the information about the assignment on this page.
3. Practice saying the group members' statements and questions.

Todd Olivier studies veterinary science and loves animals.

"I suggest doing the presentation about __Harlow__ and _____."

Dara Ebadi studies early childhood education and writes for the campus newspaper.

"_____ I do the summaries? I understand the research pretty well."

Robbie Chang prefers not to work very hard on school projects.

"I _____ we choose Rose to speak. She's very easy to understand."

Gloria Santos has an adopted daughter, Amy. Amy's parents died when she was only two years old.

"Why don't we talk about _____ and _____?"

James Day hopes that things work out with his girlfriend, Laurel. He wants to have a big family some day.

"_____ decide which scientist will have the greatest impact today. I think _____'s work is very interesting."

Rose Baldari loves to speak in front of the class.

"_____ we choose one person to do the talking?"

In this section, you are going to work in a group and plan a presentation that you will give during another class.

A | Form a group with three other students. Assign a role to each member of your group. Then read the assignment below. *(See pages 211–212 of the Independent Student Handbook for more information on doing group presentations and doing research.)*

Leader—Makes sure the assignment is done correctly and that all group members do their work.

Secretary—Takes notes on the group's ideas and plans.

Expert—Understands the topic well and checks the group's ideas.

Manager—Makes sure the work is done on time; chooses place and time to meet outside of class.

B | **Planning a Presentation.** As a group, choose one of the topics from the chart below for your presentation.

Brain Function	Brain Chemistry	Learning Styles and Strategies
What happens when parts of the brain are injured?	What happens when young children don't receive enough love?	What is the best way to measure intelligence?
How can people improve their brain function?	How does exercise affect brain chemistry?	What are some important study skills for language learners?

C | **Discussion.** With your group, discuss the following questions. The group's secretary should take notes.

1. Which topic did you choose? Why?
2. Where can you find easy-to-understand information about your topic?
3. Where and when can your group meet outside of class to do your research and practice your presentation?
4. What kind of visuals will you use to support your presentation?

D | **Organizing Ideas.** Prepare to present your group's plans for your presentation to the class. Use your notes from exercise **C**.

E | **Reporting to the Class.** Report your group's ideas to the rest of the class.

Presentation Skills: Pausing to Check Understanding

When you present ideas, it's important to check to make sure your audience understands you. You can do this by pausing occasionally and looking at your audience. If they look confused, ask them if they need you to repeat any information or give clarification. Stop occasionally and ask your audience if they have any questions.

F | **Presentation.** Your teacher will tell you when you will give your presentation to the class.

What We Eat

ACADEMIC PATHWAYS

Lesson A: Listening to a Seminar
Participating in a Mini-Debate
Lesson B: Listening to a Group Discussion
Using Visuals to Support a Presentation

Think and Discuss

1. Look at the photo. What is this man doing? Why?
2. What do you think you will learn about in this unit?

A Huichol farmer harvests corn in the Sierra
Madre Occidental Mountains in Mexico.

Exploring the Theme:
What We Eat

A | Look at the diagram and read the information. Then answer the questions.

1. According to the diagram, how many servings of vegetables should you eat every day? How many servings of dairy products?
2. Is your diet similar to the Portuguese diet? Explain.

B | Look at the photos and read the captions. Then discuss the questions.

1. Which of the families do you think has a healthier diet? Explain.
2. Why do you think the Canadian family spends so much more money on food than the Egyptian family?
3. Which family's diet would you rather eat? Explain.

Colorful rice field terraces in Yunnan, China

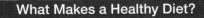

What Makes a Healthy Diet?

Fruits:
3 to 5 servings

Fat and oil:
1 to 3 servings

Dairy products:
2 to 3 servings

Meat, fish, and eggs:
1½ to 4 servings

Beans:
1 to 2 servings

Vegetables:
3 to 5 servings

Grains and potatoes:
4 to 11 servings

Many countries have produced guidelines for their citizens that recommend the best kinds of food to eat. These guidelines tell people how many servings of fat, dairy, vegetables, etc., they should eat every day. Usually these guidelines say that people should eat a lot of fruits and vegetables. They also say that a healthy diet can include a small amount of sugar and sweets. This chart shows Portugal's guidelines for a healthy diet.

Typical Diets around the World

The Ahmed family in **Egypt** (six adults, six children) spends about $68.53 a week on food.

The Melander family in **Canada** (two adults, three children) spends about $500.07 a week on food.

WHAT WE EAT | 103

A | **Using a Dictionary.** Work with a partner. Check (✔) the words you already know. Use your dictionary to help you with any words you don't know. These are words you will hear and use in Lesson A.

❏ vitamins	❏ source	❏ specific	❏ regional	❏ guidelines
❏ servings	❏ improve	❏ average	❏ recommend	❏ include

Fresh vegetables and fruits at a farmers' market

B | Complete each sentence with the correct form of one of the words from exercise **A**.

1. Today many countries have produced _____ to teach their citizens about healthy diets.

2. Most doctors _____ eating a lot of fruits and vegetables.

3. Fresh fruits such as oranges and bananas contain important _____.

4. You should eat a few _____ of protein every day. Fish, meat, and tofu all contain protein.

5. Cheese is an excellent _____ of calcium; so are milk and yogurt.

6. Scientists believe that the _____ food in Sardinia helps the people who live there live long, healthy lives.

7. It's OK to _____ some sweets such as chocolate in your diet, but not too many.

8. Some scientists believe that eating broccoli can _____ your memory. I'm going to eat some before the test next Friday!

9. Bananas only grow in _____ areas of the world. They can only grow in countries with warm, tropical climates such as Costa Rica.

10. On an _____ day I drink three cups of coffee, but yesterday I drank five.

C | Listen and check your answers from exercise **B**. *track 2-9*

D | Circle the word or phrase that has the most similar meaning to each word in blue.

1. **average**	normal	difficult	unusual
2. **guidelines**	habits	regions	rules
3. **improve**	make better	make worse	compare
4. **include**	conserve	contain	develop
5. **recommend**	select	locate	suggest
6. **regional**	local	gradual	international
7. **serving**	amount	diet	function
8. **source**	end	cause	region
9. **specific**	available	particular	efficient
10. **vitamins**	substances	causes	targets

A | **Self-Reflection.** Complete the diet quiz. Give an explanation or example for each of your answers.

How healthy is your diet?

	Usually	Sometimes	Never
1. I try to eat a healthy diet.	❑	❑	❑
Explanation/Example: _____			
2. I take vitamins.	❑	❑	❑
Explanation/Example: _____			
3. I eat 3–5 **servings** of fruits and vegetables every day.	❑	❑	❑
Explanation/Example: _____			
4. I know a lot about my country's diet **guidelines**.	❑	❑	❑
Explanation/Example: _____			
5. My diet **includes** meat.	❑	❑	❑
Explanation/Example: _____			
6. The **average** person in my country eats very little fast food.	❑	❑	❑
Explanation/Example: _____			
7. I drink the **recommended** amount of water (6–8 glasses per day).	❑	❑	❑
Explanation/Example: _____			
8. I eat foods that are good **sources** of calcium such as yogurt and cheese.	❑	❑	❑
Explanation/Example: _____			
9. I try to eat foods that are **specific** to my country.	❑	❑	❑
Explanation/Example: _____			
10. I think my diet is healthy.	❑	❑	❑
Explanation/Example: _____			

B | **Discussion.** Compare and discuss your answers from exercise **A** with a partner.

C | **Critical Thinking.** With your partner, discuss the questions below.

1. What do you know about the eating **guidelines** from your country? What do they **recommend**?
2. Some scientists say that broccoli can **improve** your memory. Do you know of any other foods that help **improve** your memory or help you think better? What are they?
3. Why do you think so many people take **vitamins** and other supplements nowadays?

Pronunciation

Intonation of Finished and Unfinished Sentences

The speaker's intonation goes down at the end of a statement when it is finished.

I have to go to the supermarket.

She lives in Tokyo.

If you don't hear falling intonation, the speaker hasn't finished the statement.

I saw Pam yesterday. . . .

Mike's brother called. . . .

track 2-11

A | Listen to the intonation for each statement. Then write **F** if the statement is *finished* or **U** if it is *unfinished*.

1. I really don't like milk _____
2. Rick has two brothers _____
3. For dinner, we had chicken _____
4. On my next vacation, I want to go to Chile _____
5. My mother is a teacher _____
6. On Saturdays, we usually go to the park _____

B | Work with a partner. Practice reading the pairs of sentences below. Use the correct intonation at the end of each sentence. Look at the punctuation to help you.

1. a. It's one of the most modern countries . . .
   b. It's one of the most modern countries in Asia.

2. a. We eat it three times . . .
   b. We eat it three times a day.

3. a. People were eating more . . .
   b. People were eating more of everything.

4. a. A lot of Koreans love yogurt . . .
   b. A lot of Koreans love yogurt and ice cream.

Before Listening

Discussion. With a partner, discuss the questions below.

1. Which countries in the world have modernized very quickly?
2. How does diet change when his or her country becomes more modern?

Listening: A Seminar

A seminar is a small-group class where students and a teacher share information about a subject. Often, the students give presentations about a research topic.

track 2-12 **A** | **Listening for Main Ideas.** Listen to the first part of a student's seminar presentation about changes in the Korean diet between 1969 and 1995. Then discuss the questions with a partner.

1. What is this presentation about?
2. What has happened to the Korean diet since 1969?
3. In which year did Koreans eat more food—1969 or 1995?

track 2-12 **B** | **Listening for Details.** Listen to the first part of the presentation again and complete the chart with the numbers you hear.

Korean *bulgogi* is a dish made with beef.

Change in Korean Eating Habits		
Kind of Food	**Ounces per Day in 1969**	**Ounces per Day in 1995**
Total Food	37	
Rice and Grain		
Vegetables		
Fruits		
Meat		
Milk and Dairy Products		

Sources: http://www.ajcn.org/cgi/reprint/71/1/44.pdf American Journal of Clinical Nutrition
http://www.nytimes.com/2009/12/23/world/asia/23seoul.html

Koreans make *kimchi* out of many kinds of vegetables.

track 2-13 **C** | Listen to the second part of the presentation. Then discuss the questions below with a partner.

1. According to Mi-Ran, what was the biggest change in the Korean diet?
2. How are young Koreans today physically different from their parents?
3. What conclusion does this fact support?
   a. The modern diet in Korea is healthier than the traditional diet.
   b. Changes in diet have made Korea a more modern country.
   c. People in Korea should go back to a more traditional diet.

Most people in Korea eat rice at every meal.

After Listening

Discussion. Form a group with two or three other students and discuss the questions below.

1. What information from Mi-Ran's presentation did you find most interesting? Explain.
2. Do you know other countries where the diet has changed a lot? How and why did it change? Is the people's health better or worse now?

Grammar

The Real Conditional with the Present

We use the real conditional with the simple present to talk about facts or things that usually occur in certain situations.

If children eat more protein, they grow up to be taller.

When can replace *if* in the present real conditional.

***If** people have more fruit in their diet, they get more vitamins.*

***When** people have more fruit in their diet, they get more vitamins*

The simple present is used in both the *if* clause and the main clause.

*If **I get** some money, **I spend** it.*

*If **I have** chocolate in the house, **I eat** it.*

The clause with *if* can come at the beginning or end of the sentence. If the clause is at the beginning, it is followed by a comma.

If I have time, I eat a big breakfast. / I eat a big breakfast if I have time.

A | Use the words and phrases below and your own ideas to write real conditional sentences.

feel tired	play	die	save money	feel thirsty	get sick

1. you dial my cell phone number

   If you dial my cell phone number, it plays my favorite song.

2. you don't sleep enough

   _____

3. you use less electricity

   _____

4. you don't eat a healthy diet

   _____

5. you don't water a plant

   _____

6. you don't drink enough water on a hot day

   _____

If I drink coffee late at night, I can't sleep.

B | Work with a partner. Read the situations. Then take turns talking about the results for each situation. Use real conditional sentences.

1. you eat a lot of sugar
2. you drink coffee at 10 o'clock at night
3. you eat a lot of fast food
4. you don't have breakfast
5. you are allergic to chocolate and strawberries
6. you don't eat enough fruits and vegetables
7. you don't get enough sleep
8. you eat a very big lunch
9. you don't drink coffee or tea in the morning

C | Self-Reflection. Complete each sentence using the real conditional and information about yourself.

1. <u>If I can't sleep</u>_____, I watch TV.
2. _____, I feel nervous.
3. _____, I can't sleep.
4. _____, I ask the teacher.
5. _____, I fall asleep.
6. _____, I go to the doctor.
7. _____, I say "Hello."
8. _____, I call my best friend.
9. _____, I cry.
10. _____, I go shopping.

 D | Discussion. Work with a partner. Compare and explain your sentences from exercise **C**.

Language Function

Interrupting and Returning to Topic

In English, it is polite to let the other person finish speaking before you start; however, in a group situation, sometimes another speaker needs to interrupt, or break in to make a point or ask a quick question. Here are some polite expressions you can use to do this.
Can/Could/May I . . .

. . . interrupt?   . . . stop you for a second?   . . . say something here?   . . . ask a question?

If you are the speaker and someone has interrupted you, here are some expressions you can use to return to your topic.

Anyway, . . .   Moving on, . . .   As I was saying, . . .   To continue, . . .

A | Read the sentences and questions from the listening section on page 107. Identify and write the polite expressions.

1. Mi-Ran, may I say something here?
2. Moving on . . . when we compare the kinds of food people ate, we see a significant difference.
3. Could I ask a question, Mi-Ran?
4. To continue—as the country developed, instead of just eating a lot of rice and vegetables, Koreans started including many other kinds of foods in their diets, . . .

B | Complete the chart with the polite expressions from page 109. Add any other expressions you know.

Stopping a Speaker	Going Back to the Topic
Can/Could/May I interrupt?	Anyway, . . .

C | **Role-Playing.** Form a group with three other students. Read the situation and follow the steps below.

Situation: You are members of your school's Health and Nutrition Committee. The director of your school has asked you to create some eating guidelines for the students at your school. You are having a meeting to discuss the guidelines.

1. Think of your own ideas and write them down in your notebook. Don't share your ideas with your group yet. Wait until you begin your discussion.

   Example: *Students should only eat sweets once or twice a week.*

2. When everyone has finished writing their own ideas, begin your group discussion. Decide who in your group will begin your discussion.
3. Politely interrupt to share your ideas with the group. Use expressions from the chart in exercise **B** to interrupt and return to the topic.
4. As a group, try to agree on five guidelines.

So, as I was saying, I think we should recommend that students eat a lot of fruits and vegetables every day—

Can I ask a question? How many servings of fruits and vegetables should students eat every day?

D | **Presentation.** As a group, present your five guidelines to the rest of class.

E | **Discussion.** With a partner, discuss the questions below.

1. In your culture, is it polite to interrupt a speaker? Who? When?
2. Do Americans interrupt more or less than people in your culture? Explain.

Participating in a Mini-Debate

 A | Planning a Presentation. Work with a partner. Read the information below and follow the steps.

> You are going to have a mini-debate with other students about traditional versus modern diets. Your teacher will assign you an opinion. You will either agree or disagree with the statement below. (This might not be your real opinion!)
>
> A modern diet is healthier than a traditional one.

B | Brainstorming. With your partner, brainstorm a list of ideas that support your opinion. Write your ideas in your notebook.

Critical Thinking Focus: Supporting Reasons with Examples

When you are presenting an argument, giving specific examples to support your reasons will help make your argument stronger.

The modern diet is healthier because we can get a lot of different kinds of food. (Reason)
And some foods come from other countries such as pineapples and bananas. (Example)

C | Choose your best ideas from exercise **B** and complete the chart below.

Mini-Debate: Opinion: _____

Reason 1:
Explanation/Examples:

Reason 2:
Explanation/Examples:

Reason 3:
Explanation/Examples:

 D | Note-Taking. Form a group with another pair of students that discussed the opposite opinion. Tell them your reasons, explanations, and examples. Listen to the other pair of students and take notes on their explanations and examples.

 E | Critical Thinking. Work with your original partner. Look at your notes and discuss the other students' reasons. Think of arguments against their opinion. Make notes on your ideas in your notebook.

 F | Form a group with the other pair of students again and take turns giving your arguments against their opinion.

The Food and Culture of OAXACA

Oaxaca is a very popular city for visitors to Mexico.

Foreigners come to Oaxaca to take classes in Mexican cooking.

Before Viewing

A | **Prior Knowledge.** In Lesson A, you learned about the Korean diet. In this video you will learn about food from Oaxaca, Mexico. What are some foods from Mexico you know about? Tell a partner.

B | **Predicting Content.** Look at the photos. Write five food words that you think you will hear in the video.

_____

Oaxaca, Mexico

While Viewing

A | **Checking Predictions.** Watch the video and circle the words in exercise **B** in the Before Viewing section that you heard.

B | **Note-Taking.** Then watch the video again. Take notes on the other food words you hear.

_____

_____

C | Compare your notes from exercise **B** with a partner's.

D | Read the statements. Then watch the video again and circle **T** for *true* or **F** for *false*. Correct the false sentences.

		T	F
1.	Oaxaca is famous for its traditional culture.	T	F
2.	Oaxaca is one of the richest states in Mexico.	T	F
3.	Susana Trilling went to Oaxaca to start her own restaurant.	T	F
4.	*Mole* is a sauce made with chili peppers and spices.	T	F
5.	People eat *mole* on chicken and meat.	T	F
6.	The *Guelaguetza* is a new dance from Oaxaca.	T	F

E | Watch the video again and then complete the sentences.

1. When you come to Oaxaca, beautiful _____ and wonderful _____ are all around you.

2. Oaxacan food is _____ around the world.

3. Susanna Trilling _____ the chilies in Oaxacan food.

4. Many foreigners come here to _____ how to make real Oaxacan *mole* and other _____.

5. Susanna's students _____ about Oaxacan food in their own _____.

6. Susanna thinks Oaxacan food is as _____ and _____ to make as Thai food, or French food.

7. Oaxacan people say that a healthy person is _____ and loves to work and _____.

One of the most famous Oaxacan foods is a sauce called *mole*.

After Viewing

A | Form a group with two or three other students and discuss the questions.

1. Which ideas in exercise **E** above do you agree with? Why?
2. Do you think the Oaxacan diet is healthy? Explain.
3. Which place in your country has the best food? Give examples.
4. Have you ever taken a cooking class? If yes, what kind of food did you learn to make? If no, are you interested in taking a cooking class? Why, or why not?

B | **Conditional Sentences.** Match the beginning of each conditional sentence with the correct ending.

1. Oaxacans think if a person is healthy, _____
2. If you go to Oaxaca, _____
3. If you feel cold in winter, _____
4. If you want to make *mole*, _____

a. beautiful colors and wonderful smells surround you.
b. you have to use chili peppers and spices.
c. you can warm up in Oaxaca.
d. he/she loves to work and eat.

C | **Using a Graphic Organizer.** In Lesson B you will hear students discussing fast food. With a partner discuss the differences between traditional food, such as the food from Oaxaca, and the fast food you know about. Write your ideas in the T-chart below.

Oaxaca is also famous for its old buildings and its dances.

Traditional Food	Fast Food
It's healthy.	It's unhealthy.

A | **Meaning from Context.** Read and listen to the descriptions. Then match each
description with the correct visual below. Notice the words in blue. These are words you
will hear and use in Lesson B.

track 2-14

1. This **bar graph** shows how much fruit people eat in one country. The *y* **axis**
   represents the number of servings of fruit. The *x* axis represents age groups. Each
   apple **represents** one serving. You can see that teenagers don't eat very much fruit.
   _____

2. This **line graph** shows how the amount of sugar people eat in one country has
   changed. The numbers are the yearly amounts of all kinds of sugar eaten by one
   person. The **line** illustrates how much the use of sugar has increased. The last **point**
   shows that in 2000, each person ate almost 152 pounds (69 kilograms) of sugar! _____

3. This **pie chart** shows how the average family in one country spends the money in
   its food budget. The biggest **section**, or slice, is for meat and fish, and the smallest
   section is for "others"—things such as salt and cooking oil. _____

4. This **diagram** explains what people should eat for a healthy diet. The **labels** tell you
   how many servings of each type of food people should eat every day. _____

a.
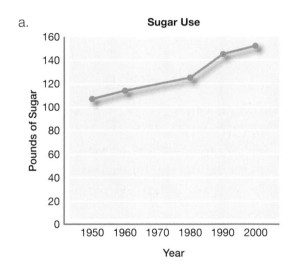
Sugar Use

b.
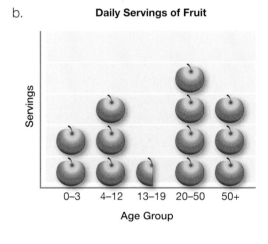
Daily Servings of Fruit

c.
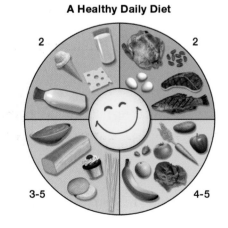
A Healthy Daily Diet

d.
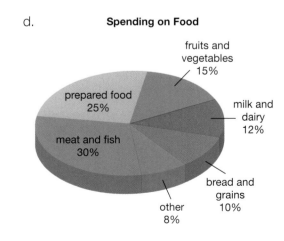
Spending on Food

B | **Self-Reflection.** Do you think these charts, graphs, and diagrams describe how people
eat and spend money on food in your country? Why, or why not? Discuss with a partner.

A | Label each visual with the correct form of a word in **blue** from exercise **A** on page 114.

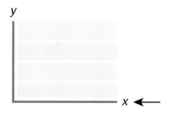

1. _____   3. _____   5. _____   7. _____   9. _____

DAIRY PRODUCTS

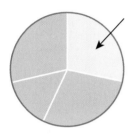

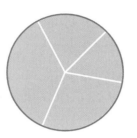

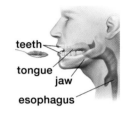

2. _____   4. _____   6. _____   8. _____   10. _____

B | **Understanding Visuals.** Match the type of visual with its function.

1. A pie chart ____
2. A diagram ____
3. A line graph ____
4. A bar graph ____

a. shows percents of a whole.
b. shows change over time.
c. explains the parts of something, or shows how something works.
d. compares amounts or numbers.

C | Read the information below. With a partner, decide which kind of visual you should use to show each kind of information.

1. You want to show how much meat people in different countries eat.
   Type of visual: ___bar graph___
2. You want to show how the number of restaurants in your city has increased every year in the last 20 years.
   Type of visual: _____
3. You did a survey of what students at your school had for breakfast today. You want to show what percent of students had a large breakfast, a small breakfast, only coffee, or no breakfast.
   Type of visual: _____
4. You want to show the number of your classmates who eat fast food every day, every week, every month, or almost never.
   Type of visual: _____

(See page 216 of the Independent Student Handbook for more information on understanding maps, graphs, and diagrams.)

Before Listening

👥 **A** | **Discussion.** With a partner, discuss the questions below. Then number the pictures.

1. How often do you eat fast food? What do you usually eat? Where?
2. In your opinion, how healthy are these fast food items? Work with your partner to rank them from healthiest (1) to unhealthiest (5).

| ⃝ **Vegetable pizza** | ⃝ **Fish sandwich** | ⃝ **Cheeseburger** | ⃝ **Frozen yogurt** | ⃝ **French fries** |

👥 **B** | Read the assignment and answer the questions with your partner.

Health and Nutrition: 101

Assignment: Group Presentation

For this assignment, you will create and present health guidelines for eating fast food. Work with two or three other students and follow these steps.

Step 1: Create guidelines for eating fast food. Your guidelines should include the following information:
   • How often people should eat fast food
   • Suggestions on other foods people should eat

Step 2: Create visuals to support your guidelines.

Step 3: Write guidelines on the board, a large sheet of paper, or on PowerPoint® slides.

Step 4: Present your group's guidelines to the class. Everyone in your group should present!

1. Do you think the assignment is easy or difficult? Explain. _____
   _____

2. How would you complete the assignment? _____
   _____

Listening: A Group Discussion

A | **Listening for Main Ideas.** Listen to the first part of a group discussion. Check (✓) the ideas that the students talk about. Circle the idea that they decide to use.

_____ make a list of fast food restaurants that have healthy choices

_____ tell people to eat healthy food in fast food restaurants

_____ tell people how often it's OK to eat fast food

_____ ask fast food restaurants to sell healthier food

B | **Listening for Details.** Read the statements. Then listen to the second part of the discussion and circle **T** for *true* and **F** for *false*.

1.	The students only have 10 minutes left.	**T**	**F**
2.	They learned that fast food usually is not healthy because it has too much salt and fat.	**T**	**F**
3.	They looked at bar graphs in class.	**T**	**F**
4.	They agreed that people should only eat fast food once a month.	**T**	**F**
5.	They are going to use a line graph to present their guidelines.	**T**	**F**
6.	They are going to write their guidelines on the board.	**T**	**F**

C | Listen to the intonation in these sentences from the discussion. Did the speaker finish the sentence? Circle *Yes* or *No*.

1.	I think we should just talk about regular fast food, like fried chicken	**Yes**	**No**
2.	Maybe our guidelines should tell people how often it's OK to eat fast food	**Yes**	**No**
3.	But if we say that people should never eat fast food, they won't listen	**Yes**	**No**
4.	If people usually eat a healthy diet, one fast food meal in a month won't be a problem	**Yes**	**No**
5.	Next we need to write our guidelines on the board	**Yes**	**No**

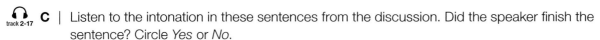

D | With a partner, practice repeating the sentences from exercise **C** with the same intonation.

After Listening

Form a group with two or three other students. Create your own health guidelines about eating in fast food restaurants. Then share your guidelines with the class.

Language Function

Managing a Discussion

When working in a group on an assignment, it is important to manage the discussion so that you can complete the assignment correctly and on time. Here are some things you may need to do when having a group discussion.

- get the discussion started
- bring other people into the discussion
- ask students for their ideas
- keep the discussion moving
- summarize the group's ideas

A | Read the statements and questions from the students' discussion in the Listening section. Then match each sentence or question with its function (why we use it).

1. OK, ready? __e__
2. So, who has a suggestion for our guidelines? _____
3. We only have five minutes left, so we'd better hurry. _____
4. Omar, what do you think? _____
5. So, in summary, we've decided . . . _____
6. Well, what does everyone think about that? _____

a. Asking one person's ideas
b. Keeping the discussion moving
c. Asking the group for ideas
d. Bringing other people into the discussion
e. Getting the discussion started
f. Ending and summarizing the group's ideas

B | Form a group with two or three other students. Discuss the three diagrams of guidelines for a healthy diet below. Choose the diagram you think is the best. Each group member should take a turn leading part of the discussion. Use expressions from exercise **A** to help you manage your group discussion.

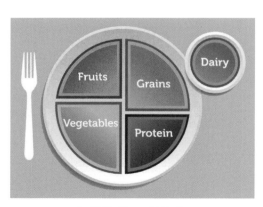

1. U.S. Food Plate

2. Japanese Nutritional Guide

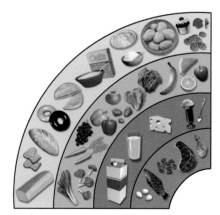

3. Canada's Food Guide

Grammar

The Real Conditional with the Future

We use the real conditional with the future to talk about situations that are real or possible and have results in the future.

> *If you eat too much fast food, you will gain weight.*
> *If I don't have time to cook tonight, I'll have a sandwich for dinner.*

The clause with *if* can be at the beginning or end of the sentence. If the clause is at the beginning, it is followed by a comma.

> *If I eat all this fried food tonight, I'll feel sick tomorrow. / I'll feel sick tomorrow if I eat all this fried food tonight.*

A | Complete the real conditional sentences with the correct form of the verb in parentheses.

1. If I _____ (eat) this second serving, I _____ (be able to, not) eat dessert.

2. If you _____ (exercise) every day for 30 minutes or more, you _____ (lose) weight.

3. If you _____ (get, not) enough sleep tonight, you _____ (be) tired tomorrow.

4. The children _____ (be, not) hungry for dinner if they _____ (have) a big snack after school.

5. If I _____ (have, not) enough time, I _____ (be able to, not) prepare a healthy dinner tonight.

6. If you _____ (eat, not) breakfast, you _____ (feel) tired and hungry in class.

B | **Discussion.** Work with a partner. Read the situations below. Then discuss what will happen in each situation. Think of as many possible results as you can. Use real conditional sentences.

1. people change to a more traditional diet
2. people eat chocolate every day
3. fruits and vegetables are cheaper
4. children learn how to cook in school
5. the government puts a tax on fast food

> If people change to a more traditional diet, they'll spend less money on food.

You are going to work with a group to prepare visuals to support a presentation about healthy eating guidelines for children.

A | Form a group with two or three other students. Read the information and follow the steps below.

Situation: The government of your country has asked your group to prepare a presentation about daily diet guidelines for children who are four to eight years old. Your presentation should include visuals that children can understand, and also written information for parents.

1. Read the information in the chart and think about what kind of visual you can use to present and explain the information to children. Use expressions from pages 110, 118, and the Student to Student box on this page as you discuss your ideas.

Student to Student: Expressing Thanks and Appreciation

When you are collaborating on a group project, you can use these expressions to thank members of your group.

Thanks for finding those photos online. I really appreciate your making that chart.
I really appreciate your help.

Diet Recommendations for Children Ages Four to Eight

Kind of Food	Number of servings daily (Note: use smaller serving sizes for younger children)
Grains	4
Vegetables	3
Fruits	2
Dairy	2–3
Protein (Meat, Fish, or Eggs)	2

2. Plan the written guidelines that you will include in your presentation for parents.
3. Work together to create visuals to support your presentation.

B | **Planning a Presentation.** Decide how your group will explain your visuals and guidelines to the class. Plan your presentation so that each member of your group presents some information.

C | **Presentation.** Present your guidelines and visuals to the class. Every member of the group should take a turn speaking.

Presentation Skills: Talking about Visuals

Here are some phrases you can use in talking about any kind of visual.

This graph/diagram shows/explains _____.
The line/box represents _____.
The main point is that _____.

Our Active Earth

ACADEMIC PATHWAYS

Lesson A: Listening to an Earth Science Lecture
Giving a News Report
Lesson B: Listening to a Group Discussion
Giving a Group Presentation

Think and Discuss

1. What are some similarities between earthquakes and volcanoes?

2. What are some countries that have volcanoes?

3. What are some topics you think you will discuss in this unit?

Mount Merapi, Java Island, Indonesia

Exploring the Theme:
Our Active Earth

A | Look at the diagrams and read the information. Then discuss the questions.

    1. What causes earthquakes?

    2. How do volcanoes form?

B | Look at the map and discuss the questions.

    1. What do the colors on the map mean?

    2. In which parts of the world are earthquakes most likely to occur?

    3. What information does this map show about your country?

What Causes Earthquakes and Volcanoes?

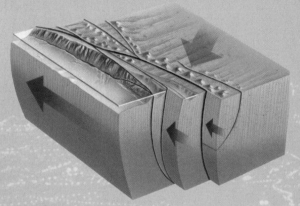

Volcanoes

Volcanoes form when a very hot material called lava escapes through cracks in the earth's surface. Some volcanoes occur when one of the earth's plates pushes against another.

Earthquakes

The crust is the thin, outer surface of the earth. The earth's surface is broken into very large pieces called plates. When the plates move, one result of their movement is earthquakes.

Our Active Earth

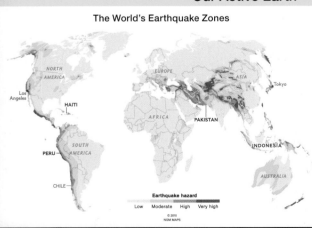

The World's Earthquake Zones

This map shows the world's earthquake zones, or areas of the world where earthquakes are most likely to occur.

An eruption of Mount Piano de Lago, Catania, Italy

A | **Meaning from Context.** Read and listen to the article. Notice the words in blue. These are words you will hear and use in Lesson A.

track 2-18

Inexpensive Buildings for Earthquake Zones

The earth's crust **consists** of several different pieces called tectonic plates. These plates are always moving. The places where the earth's plates meet are called boundaries. When the plates **push** together, they can form mountains. Some of the plates jump as they move. When these plates jump, they can cause earthquakes.

Places where earthquakes are more likely to occur are called earthquake zones. Haiti and Chile are examples of countries in earthquake zones.

In 2010, strong earthquakes occurred in Haiti and Chile. The earthquake in Haiti **killed** more than 200,000 people, but in Chile, fewer than 1000 people died. So why did more people **survive** the Chilean earthquake?

One difference is the buildings. In Chile and in other developed countries, buildings are **constructed** from stronger **materials**—for example concrete[1] walls are **reinforced** with steel[2] rods.

In countries such as Haiti, heavy walls and roofs are usually not reinforced. This is **dangerous** because in an earthquake, buildings **shake**, and they can **collapse** on top of the people inside.

Engineers in several countries are working to solve the problem. Better buildings can be constructed cheaply. The engineers hope that in the future, more people will survive earthquakes.

[1]**Concrete** is a hard material made from sand, water, and cement.
[2]**Steel** is a strong, hard metal.

1. Pakistan   **2. Haiti**

Light walls: Lightweight walls are less affected by earthquakes and are less likely to fall when the ground **shakes**. In Pakistan, a **material** called plaster is used to help **reinforce** the inside and outside of straw walls.

Light roofs: Metal roofs are lighter than concrete and won't **collapse** when an earthquake occurs.

Small windows: Small windows mean that walls are stronger.

B | **Discussion.** Work with a partner. Look at the diagrams at the bottom of this page and page 124 and read the information. Then discuss the questions below.

1. Which house do you think is the safest during an earthquake? Explain.
2. Which kind of house might be the cheapest to **construct**? Explain.

C | Fill in each blank with the correct form of a word in **blue** from the article on page 124. There are two extra words.

1. Why do some buildings and houses _____ during an earthquake?
2. In Peru, people use plastic to _____ their walls.
3. What are some things people can do to _____ an earthquake?
4. When the earth _____, you can feel it. It's very scary!
5. Why are buildings with large windows more _____ than buildings with small windows?
6. In some places, people use natural _____ such as bamboo to make their walls stronger.
7. What happens when the earth's plates move and _____ against each other?
8. In what countries are people likely to be _____ by earthquakes?

D | **Critical Thinking.** With a partner, take turns asking and answering questions 1, 3, 5, 7, and 8 from exercise **C**.

3. Peru   **4. Indonesia**

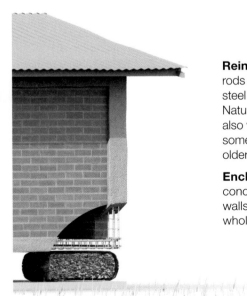

Reinforced walls: The **reinforcing** rods don't have to be made from steel or other kinds of metal. Natural **materials** such as bamboo also work well. In Peru, plastic is sometimes used to **reinforce** walls in older houses.

Enclosed materials: In Indonesia, concrete and metal rods hold brick walls together. In an earthquake, the whole wall moves as one piece.

Before Listening

Read the information below and label the places in the photo.

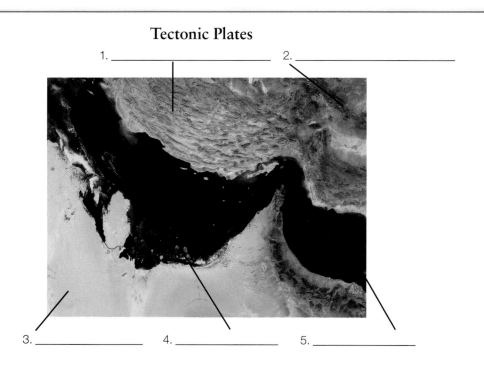

Tectonic Plates

1. _____   2. _____

3. _____   4. _____   5. _____

   The Persian Gulf (top left) and the Gulf of Oman (bottom right) were formed when two tectonic plates pulled apart. Now, the Arabian Plate (bottom left) is pushing against the Eurasian Plate (top right) and sliding underneath it. The mountains in Iran (top) are one result of this process. Earthquakes are another result.

   In plate tectonics, an area like this one in the Persian Gulf region is called a boundary. A boundary between two plates is the line that separates one plate from another.

Source: http://visibleearth.nasa.gov/view_rec.php?id=2363

Listening: An Earth Science Lecture

track 2-19   **A** | **Listening for Main ideas.** Listen to part of an earth science lecture and answer the following questions.

1. What is the lecture about? _____
2. How many major tectonic plates does the earth have? _____
3. What kind of boundary is in the Persian Gulf region? _____
4. Is the movement at transform boundaries smooth or rough? _____

Listening for Specific Information

When we listen to a lecture, we often have questions about the topic. It's important to be able to listen for the specific information we need to answer those questions.

B | Study the chart below. Which information do you need in order to complete the chart?

Border Type	Convergent		Transform
Movement	Plates come together; one plate can move under or over another.	Plates move apart.	
Results		A body of water can form between the two plates.	

In California, USA, the Pacific and North American plates slide past each other along the San Andreas Fault.

🎧 **C** | **Note-Taking.** Listen again and complete the chart from exercise **B**.

track 2-19

After Listening

Critical Thinking Focus: Predicting Exam Questions

Imagine that you are taking an earth science course. After listening to the lecture on plate tectonics and taking notes, what's next? For many students, thinking about possible exam questions is helpful.

👥 **A** | Look at the information from the exercises on page 126 and exercise **B** on this page. With a partner, think of at least five questions that might be on an exam. Some questions could be quite general, and others more specific.

1. _____
2. _____
3. _____
4. _____
5. _____

👥 **B** | Form a group with another pair of students and take turns answering each other's exam questions.

👥 **C** | **Self-Reflection.** Discuss the questions with your group.

1. What are some things you typically do to prepare for an exam?
2. Did you find asking yourself questions before completing the chart from exercise **B** above helpful? Explain.
3. What experience have you had with earthquakes?

Language Function

	Using Transitions
	Transitions show relationships between ideas. When you are speaking, transitions help your listeners understand you and follow your train of thought.

A | With a partner, discuss the meaning of each pair of sentences in the chart below.

Relationship	Expressions	
addition	in addition furthermore	(1) There will be two exams this semester. **In addition,** we'll have three quizzes. (2) Walls with smaller windows are safer. **Furthermore,** they're cheaper to build.
contrast	however on the other hand	(3) Steel reinforcing rods are very strong. **However,** they're too expensive for us to buy. (4) Living near volcanoes isn't always safe. **On the other hand,** the land near volcanoes is excellent for farming.
example	for example for instance	(5) There are other ways to communicate. **For example,** you can mail a letter if you don't have a computer. (6) Buildings can be constructed with lighter materials. **For instance,** straw weighs much less than concrete.
result	therefore as a result	(7) The prime minister has a serious illness. **Therefore,** he has cancelled the trip. (8) One plate can move under another plate. **As a result,** the mountains are pushed up even higher.

B | Fill in each blank with an appropriate transition.

1. I didn't sleep much last night. _____ , I'm very tired today.

2. The food at that restaurant isn't very good. _____ , it's near my house, so I go there often.

3. You should give your mother a nice gift. _____ , you could give her some roses.

4. That grocery store has a large selection of foods. _____ , the prices are high, so we don't go there often.

5. This house has enough space for our whole family. _____ , it would be safe during an earthquake.

Grammar

Imperatives

We use imperatives to give instructions.
> ***Close*** *the windows during a rainstorm.*
> ***Don't drive*** *during a snowstorm.*

We also use imperatives to give commands.
> ***Call*** *for help!*
> ***Don't go*** *outside!*

A | Read the instructions for keeping safe during an earthquake. <u>Underline</u> the imperatives.

Keep Yourself and Your Family Safe

Before an Earthquake

- In each room of your house, find a safe place where nothing is likely to fall on you.
- Have enough canned food and water in the house for each member of your family.
- Plan where you will meet if an earthquake occurs when you are not home.

During an Earthquake

- Get under a desk or table.
- Stay away from windows and furniture that might fall on you.
- If you're outside, get to an open place away from buildings.

After an Earthquake

- Help injured people or call for help if someone is seriously hurt.
- Know that smaller earthquakes, called aftershocks, are likely.
- Listen to a radio or TV for emergency information.

B | **Collaboration.** With a partner, choose one of the situations below. Then in your notebook, write four sentences giving instructions on what to do (and not do) in that situation. Use imperatives.

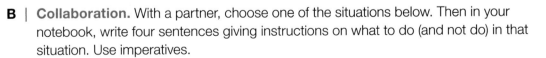

a snowstorm	a thunderstorm	a trip to another country
an important exam	a flood	your idea

C | **Discussion.** Form a group with another pair of students. Take turns explaining the instructions you wrote for the situation you chose in exercise **B**.

D | **Role-Playing.** Read the situation. Then follow the instructions below.

In earthquake-prone Japan, schoolchildren learn how to protect themselves from falling objects.

Situation: You are in an earthquake zone. You have just heard on the news that there might be an earthquake. You and your partner are neighbors. You are going to role-play a conversation about your earthquake safety plans.

1. One of you will be Student A, and the other will be Student B.
2. Complete the conversation below.
3. Practice your conversation.

Student A:	I heard there might be an earthquake, but I have not had time to go to the store. _____.
Student B:	Don't worry! I have a lot of canned food at my house. For example, I have _____. I'll give you some.
Student A:	Thank you! I also need to think of a safe place in my house. _____, a place where nothing will fall.
Student B:	Good idea. We should also think of a meeting place in our neighborhood, for instance _____ or _____.
Student A:	Right. I want to watch the news for information about the earthquake, but I don't have a TV.
Student B:	I have a TV at my house. However, _____.
Student A:	That's OK. I can listen to it on the radio or read about it online.

E | Form a group with another pair of students and perform your role-play from exercise **D**.

F | **Critical Thinking.** Talk about the questions with your group.

1. Do you think the neighbors in exercise **D** are well prepared for an earthquake? Why, or why not?
2. How do you think the neighbors in exercise **D** feel about the situation? For example, are they confident, afraid, excited, or something else? Explain.

Giving a News Report

 A | Work with a partner. Read the information. Then complete the exercises below.

> **Situation:** You are a team of television news reporters. There has just been an earthquake. Your assignment is to prepare and give a news report with the most important information about the earthquake.

 B | **Planning a Presentation.** Use the chart below to help you plan your news report. Write short notes, not full sentences.

Questions	Notes
1. Where did the earthquake occur?	
2. How strong was the earthquake?	
3. How many people were killed?	
4. What happened to the city? Did bridges or buildings collapse? Are any roads, airports, etc., closed?	
5. What safety instructions will you give people?	
6. What are rescue workers doing to help people?	
7. How can people get more information?	

C | Decide which topics you and your partner will each report on. Then practice your news report using transitions and the imperative as needed.

D | **Presentation.** Give your news report for another pair of students or for the rest of the class. Use your notes to help you. Remember to look at the "TV camera" while you're speaking.

In 1906, fires and falling buildings killed thousands of people and nearly destroyed the city of San Francisco, California.

Volcano Trek

In the video, two geologists and a team of researchers study Ethiopia's Erta Ale volcano.

Before Viewing

Look at the diagram below. Use the words from the diagram to complete the information.

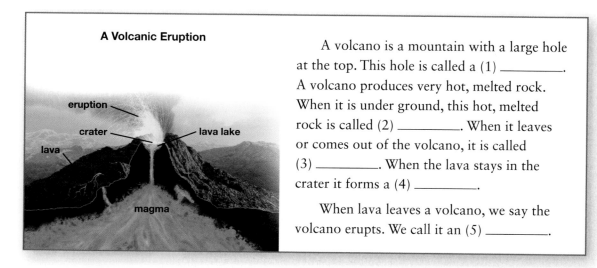

A Volcanic Eruption

eruption

crater

lava

lava lake

magma

A volcano is a mountain with a large hole at the top. This hole is called a (1) _____. A volcano produces very hot, melted rock. When it is under ground, this hot, melted rock is called (2) _____. When it leaves or comes out of the volcano, it is called (3) _____. When the lava stays in the crater it forms a (4) _____.

When lava leaves a volcano, we say the volcano erupts. We call it an (5) _____.

While Viewing

A | Watch the video and circle each vocabulary word from the Before Viewing section when you hear it.

B | Read the statements. Then watch the video again. Circle **T** for *true* and **F** for *false*.

1. The temperature of the lava from Erta Ale is more than 2000 degrees Fahrenheit.   **T**   **F**
2. The explorer's trek was easy.   **T**   **F**
3. The geologists are from the University of Paris.   **T**   **F**
4. Erta Ale is in the Afar area of Ethiopia.   **T**   **F**
5. Erta Ale has the oldest lava lake in the world.   **T**   **F**
6. As lava cools, it becomes red.   **T**   **F**

C | **Making Inferences.** Watch the video again and answer the question. In your notebook, write notes on the information you see or hear that helps you answer the question below.

Do Dr. Franck Tessier and Dr. Irene Margaritis enjoy their work as geologists?

After Viewing

A | **Self-Reflection.** Watch again and write two questions you'd like to ask the geologists Dr. Franck Tessier and Dr. Irene Margaritis.

1. _____

2. _____

B | **Discussion.** Form a group with two or three other students. Share the questions you wrote for the geologists in exercise **A**.

C | **Using a Graphic Organizer.** With your group, brainstorm some of the pros (advantages) and cons (disadvantages) of a career as a geologist. Write your ideas in the T-chart below.

Pros	Cons
interesting	dangerous

A scientist wearing a protective suit collects volcanic samples.

D | Use ideas from your T-chart to write sentences in your notebook. Use transitions.

Example: *A career as a geologist is interesting. However, it can be dangerous.*

E | **Critical Thinking.** Discuss the questions with a partner.

1. How do you think volcanoes and earthquakes are similar?
2. Do you think volcanoes or earthquakes are more dangerous? Explain.
3. Do you find earthquakes or volcanoes more interesting? Explain.

A | **Prior Knowledge.** Discuss the questions with a partner.

1. What do you think are some advantages of living near a volcano?
2. Can you think of any famous volcanic eruptions?
3. Are there any volcanoes in your country? What are their names?

B | **Meaning from Context.** Read and listen to the information about an unusual job. Notice the words and phrases in blue. These are words and phrases you will hear and use in Lesson B.

track **2-20**

The Gatekeeper of Merapi

1 Mbah Marijan has a very unusual job. He's the Gatekeeper of Merapi, an **active** volcano on the island of Java in Indonesia. **According to** traditional stories, an ogre[1] named Sapu Jagat lives inside Merapi. The Gatekeeper knows the mountain better than anyone, and his job is to keep the ogre quiet, or else tell people when the volcano will become dangerous so that they can **evacuate**.

Mbah Marijan (second from right) and his followers carry gifts for Mount Merapi.

2 It's an important job because many people live near Merapi. Marijan's own village of Kinarejo is only three miles (five kilometers) from the volcano, and the city of Yogyakarta, where 500,000 people live, is just 20 miles (32 kilometers) away. In fact, more people live near active volcanoes in Indonesia than in any other place in the world. On the island of Java alone, there are 30 volcanoes and 120 million people.

3 One of the world's best-known **natural disasters** occurred in Indonesia in 1883. The eruption of Mount Krakatau, a volcanic island near Java, caused a tsunami[2] that killed more than 36,000 people. In addition, there was enough volcanic ash[3] from the **eruption** to **affect** the earth's weather for several months.

4 Active volcanoes are dangerous; however, people live near them because volcanic **soil** is very rich. In Kinarejo, most people are farmers. For them, living near Merapi means **making a living.** Evacuating means leaving behind their homes, animals, and lives—at least for a while. So as long as the Gatekeeper says it's safe to stay, the **villagers** of Kinarejo won't leave.

[1]An **ogre** is a frightening spirit or monster.
[2]A **tsunami** is an enormous ocean wave.
[3]**Ash** is burnt material.

C | Match each word and phrase in **blue** from exercise **B** on page 134 with its definition.

1. according (to) (phrase) ____
2. active (adj.) ____
3. affect (v.) ____
4. disaster (n.) ____
5. eruption (n.) ____
6. evacuate (v.) ____
7. make a living (v.) ____
8. natural (adj.) ____
9. soil (n.) ____
10. villagers (n.) ____

a. people who live in a small town in the country
b. something that has a very bad effect or result
c. having to do with nature; not man-made
d. phrase that tells us where information comes from
e. to leave an area because of some danger
f. to earn the money that you need
g. a sudden explosion of rocks, ash, and lava
h. the material on the earth's surface in which plants grow
i. with volcanoes, having recently erupted or likely to erupt
j. to influence or change something

Volcanoes such as Semeru and Bromo in East Java have affected Indonesia's land as well as its culture.

D | **Critical Thinking.** Discuss the question below with a partner.

Who knows more about a volcano—scientists with modern equipment, or a person such as Marijan who lives nearby? Explain.

E | Complete each sentence with your own ideas. Then take turns saying your sentences to your partner.

1. Volcanic **eruptions** are dangerous because _____.
2. Many **villagers** don't have _____.
3. **According to** my parents, _____.
4. If we ever need to **evacuate** this building, I'll _____.
5. The worst **natural disaster** that I remember was _____.
6. The **soil** near here is _____.
7. **Active** volcanoes are _____.
8. Teachers **make a living** by _____.
9. _____ **affects** my life every day.
10. My favorite **natural** food is _____.

F | Read the article on page 134 again. Then use the vocabulary words in **blue** and the outline below to talk about the article. Try not to look back at the article. One partner will talk about paragraphs one and three. The other partner will talk about paragraphs two and four.

Paragraph 1.	Mbah Marijan's job
Paragraph 2.	People living near volcanoes in Indonesia
Paragraph 3.	The eruption of Mount Krakatau
Paragraph 4.	Reasons for living and staying near a volcano

Pronunciation

Syllable Stress Review and Syllable Number

In Unit 4, you learned that putting the stress on the correct syllable of a word is very important. When you stress a syllable, you say it longer and more loudly than other syllables. In addition, saying the correct number of syllables will help your listeners understand you.

Examples:

col **lapse**	*sur* **vive**	**dan** *ger ous*	*ma* **te** *ri als*
2 syllables	2 syllables	3 syllables	4 syllables

 A | Listen and <u>underline</u> each syllable in the words below. Then write the number of syllables next to each word.

1. <u>ac</u> <u>cord</u> ing (to)
2. active
3. affect
4. disaster
5. eruption
6. evacuate
7. make a living
8. natural
9. villager

 B | Listen again and repeat the words as you hear them. Then circle the syllable with the most stress.

 C | Work with a partner. Practice your pronunciation. Say the words or sentences for either *a* or *b* below. Your partner will listen and tell you which one you said. Then switch roles.

1. a. You can return it.
   b. You can turn it.
2. a. We demand a change.
   b. We demanded a change.
3. a. common
   b. Come in.
4. a. It's likely.
   b. It's unlikely.
5. a. no mail
   b. normal
6. a. allocate the food
   b. I'll locate the food.
7. a. We need a research team.
   b. We need a search team.

Before Listening

 Self-Reflection. You are going to listen to a group of students studying together. Discuss the questions with a partner.

1. When you study for a test, do you prefer to study alone or with a group? Explain.
2. What are the pros and cons of studying with a group?

Listening: A Group Discussion

track 2-23 **A | Listening for Main Ideas.** Listen to part of a study group discussion. Answer the following questions:

1. What are the students discussing? _____

2. Why are they doing this? _____

Mount St. Helens, United States

track 2-23 **B | Listening for Details.** Listen again and complete each sentence with the information you hear.

1. When melted rock is _____ the earth, it's called magma.
2. When _____ comes *out* of the earth, it's called _____.
3. According to Professor Lopez, lava can kill people and _____.
4. The U.S. government told everyone to _____ before Mount St. Helens erupted.
5. _____ people were killed when Mount St. Helens erupted.
6. The Gatekeeper is an important part of village _____.

After Listening

 Discussion. Take turns asking and answering the questions below with a partner.

1. In your own words, why is a volcanic eruption dangerous?
2. What do you think people who live near volcanoes can do to stay safe?

Grammar

Gerunds as Subjects and Objects

We often use gerunds as the subjects of sentences. A gerund subject is always singular.

> **Walking** is my favorite form of exercise.
> **Mountain climbing** can be very dangerous.

We also use gerunds as the objects of verbs or prepositions.

> I enjoyed **learning** about volcanoes.
> Lisa is interested in **studying** geology.

A | Fill in each blank with the gerund form of the verb in parentheses.

1. _____ (farm) is a common way of life in Kinarejo.
2. I never worry about _____ (be) killed by a volcano.
3. _____ (jog) is good for your heart.
4. _____ (have) an earthquake safety plan is very important.
5. She is afraid of _____ (lose) her job.
6. Are you interested in _____ (get) a degree in science?

B | **Note-Taking.** How does the natural world affect our lives? Listen and take notes to complete the chart below.

track 2-24

Name: Hasan
Country: Bangladesh
Occupation: _____
Other notes: _____
_____
_____
_____
_____

Name: Margaret
Country: _____
Occupation: Dairy farmer
Other notes: _____
_____
_____
_____
_____

Name: Cecilia
Country: Cuba
Occupation: _____
Other notes: _____
_____
_____
_____
_____

C | Work with a partner. Use your notes from exercise **B** to retell your partner what you remember about each person. Use gerunds.

D | Work with your partner. Take turns interviewing each other using the questions in the chart below. Take notes on your partner's answers to the questions in the chart or in your notebook.

Interview Question	Notes
1. What are some things you enjoy doing in your free time? Why?	
2. What are some things you are planning to do in the future? Why?	
3. What are some things you worry about? Why?	

E | **Presentation.** Form a group with another pair of students. Take turns telling the group about your partner. Try to use gerunds.

> Sherry enjoys gardening in her free time. She grows flowers and vegetables. She also enjoys singing. . . .

Presentation Skills: Speaking Slowly

When you talk to a group or give a presentation in front of the class, it's important not to speak too quickly. When you speak too quickly, your audience may not understand everything you are saying. Try to slow down, and even pause sometimes so that your audience has time to think about what you are saying. People often speak quickly when they are nervous. Taking a deep breath can help you feel less nervous and help you slow down.

Student to Student: Polite Refusals

Sometimes someone asks or invites you to do something that you cannot do, or do not want to do. There are several ways you can politely refuse an invitation or request. Here are some phrases you can use.

Thank you, but (I have other plans/ I'm busy tonight/I'd rather not/etc.). I wish I could, but (I don't have a car/ I have a class at that time/etc.). I'm sorry, I can't. Maybe some other time.

(See pages 210–211 of the Independent Student Handbook for more information on useful phrases.)

Language Function: Refusing Politely

 Discussion. Read the information about polite refusals in the Student to Student box. Then follow the steps below with a partner.

1. Write three invitations or requests for a classmate. For example,

   Would you like to have a cup of coffee with me after class? or Could you lend me a dollar?

2. Take turns making your requests and invitations. Each time, you or your partner will politely refuse.

3. When you and your partner have finished, repeat the exercise with a new partner.

You are going to give a group presentation about a natural disaster. You will choose a topic and present it to the class.

 A | **Planning a Presentation.** Form a group with two or three other students. Discuss the natural disasters below. Choose a topic for your presentation.

avalanche	drought	ice storm	landslide	tsunami
tornado	flood	heat wave	hurricane	forest fire

 B | Research more information about your topic if you need to. You can use the Internet, a dictionary, other books, or ask your teacher for information.

 C | Use the outline below to help you organize the information about your topic. *(See pages 211–213 of the Independent Student Handbook for more information on doing group projects, presentations, and research.)*

Topic: _____

1. What's the definition of this natural disaster? _____
_____

2. Where and when does this kind of natural disaster usually occur (in cold places, warm places, certain countries or parts of the world, during certain times of year, etc.)?
_____
_____

3. What are some causes of this kind of natural disaster?
_____
_____

4. What happens when this kind of disaster occurs?
_____
_____

5. What are some things people should do or not do when this kind of natural disaster occurs?
_____
_____
_____
_____

A tornado

An avalanche

A flood

 D | Create a visual (a drawing, diagram, chart, or map) on paper or on PowerPoint to support your ideas.

E | Decide what information each member of your group will present. Each member of your group should speak.

 F | **Presentation.** Present your topic to the class. Do not read directly from the notes or your slides. Just use them to help you remember ideas. Remember to speak slowly.

Ancient Peoples and Places

Think and Discuss

1. Look at the photo. Which ancient people built this pyramid?
2. Why do you think they built it?
3. Which other ancient peoples built pyramids?

The Temple of Great Jaguar, Tikal, Guatemala

Exploring the Theme:
Ancient Peoples and Places

A | Look at the photos and read the captions. Then discuss the questions.

1. Which of these ancient peoples or places do you find most interesting? Explain.
2. What ancient sites are shown in these photos?

B | Look at the map and the map key. Then answer the questions.

1. What does the color red show on the map? the color green? the color brown?
2. In which countries did the Incas live?
3. Which ancient peoples and sites were in Africa? Central America?
4. Which of these ancient peoples or places are from your area of the world?

The Mayans

The Temple of Great Jaguar at Tikal, a historical site in modern-day Guatemala, was part of the ancient Mayan civilization. Tikal was a very large city with several tall pyramids. Many other cities were built by the Mayans—not only in Guatemala, but also in modern-day Mexico, Honduras, and Belize.

Map Key
- Ancient Egypt
- Inca Empire
- Mayan Civilization
- Great Zimbabwe
- Mohenjo Daro
- Thang Long

The Incas

The center of the Inca culture was the Cuzco region of Peru. One of the most famous Inca sites is Machu Picchu. According to archaeologists, Machu Picchu was built for an Inca emperor named Pachacuti. This illustration shows an Inca emperor and his army.

The Egyptians

The ancient Egyptians lived mostly along the Nile River in north Africa in what is now Egypt. This wooden statue was found in the tomb of Amenhotep II, the 7th pharaoh, or king of the 18th dynasty of Egypt.

The Thang Long Citadel

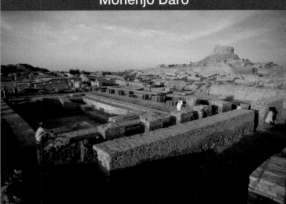

The Thang Long Citadel in Hanoi, Vietnam, was a cultural center for the Thang Long Imperial City. *Citadel* means "safe place for royalty." The 1300-year-old site was uncovered in 2002 and became a UNESCO World Heritage site in 2010.

Great Zimbabwe

Great Zimbabwe was the royal palace of the Zimbawean king and the capital of the Kingdom of Zimbabwe (AD 1100–1450). The site's enormous stone walls are one of its most interesting features.

Mohenjo Daro

The city of Mohenjo Daro was built by the Indus Valley Civilization around 4500 years ago in what is now Pakistan. At that time, some 40,000 people lived in Mohenjo Daro.

🎧 track 3-2 **A** | **Meaning from Context.** Look at the diagram and photos and read the captions. Notice the words in blue. These are words you will hear and use in Lesson A.

It's not often that the vice president of Guatemala visits an archaeological **site**, but that's what happened when William Saturno, an archaeologist, found a very old Mayan **mural**. The mural showed the beauty of Mayan painting. Saturno discovered the mural inside a room that was once next to a **pyramid**. The mural room and pyramid were later covered by a larger pyramid —part of the **ancient** Mayan city known as San Bartolo.

At first, Saturno could only see a small part of the mural. He had to **dig** through earth and stone in order to **reveal** the rest. Then, instead of using a camera, Saturno used his scanner to take digital **images** of the mural. He took about 350 scans!

The mural wasn't the only important find at San Bartolo. The archaeologists also uncovered a **royal tomb**. There, the bones of a Mayan king were **buried**, with objects such as a bowl in the shape of a frog and an image of the Mayan rain god Chac.

B | Write each word in blue from the captions in exercise **A** next to its definition below.

1. _____ (n.) a place that contains the body of a dead person

2. _____ (n.) pictures of someone or something

3. _____ (v.) to use the hands or a tool to make a hole in the ground

4. _____ (v.) put into the ground and covered with earth or stone

5. _____ (n.) a picture painted on a wall

6. _____ (adj.) having to do with kings, queens, princesses, or their families

7. _____ (adj.) extremely old

8. _____ (n.) a place where a particular thing happens

9. _____ (v.) to show or uncover something so that people can see it

10. _____ (n.) large stone structure with a flat base and triangular sides

A | Fill in each blank with the correct form of a word in **blue** from exercise **A** on page 144.

San Bartolo

San Bartolo in Guatemala is an important archaeological (1) _____. The most (2) _____ part of the site dates to around 300 BC. At San Bartolo, a newer (3) _____ was built over an older one. A beautiful (4) _____ was found in a room next to the pyramid. The second major discovery at San Bartolo was a (5) _____. The dead person in the tomb had been a member of a Mayan (6) _____ family. Several objects were (7) _____ with the person in the tomb. The mural room was buried under earth and stone. Saturno had to (8) _____ in order to uncover the mural. The mural (9) _____ a lot about Mayan culture. Saturno took about 350 digital (10) _____ of the mural, so now other people can see them, too.

A green stone figure was found with other items in the Mayan royal tomb at San Bartolo.

B | Take turns asking and answering the following questions with a partner.

1. Where in the world can you see **pyramids**?
2. What **ancient** cultures have you studied? What do you remember about them?
3. What are some ways people **reveal** their emotions?
4. Which countries have **royal** families?
5. What kinds of objects do you think were **buried** with Mayan kings?
6. Have you seen any famous **murals**? Which one? What kinds of **images** did it show?
7. What famous archaeological **site** would you like to visit? Why?
8. What kinds of things do archaeologists **dig** for? What do they hope to find?
9. Are there any **ancient tombs** in your country? What did archaeologists find in them?

C | **Discussion.** Form a group with two or three other students and discuss the questions.

1. What ancient civilizations are there in your part of the world?
2. Where did those people live?
3. How do we know about them now?

The temples, pyramids, and palace of Palenque, Chiapas, Mexico.

Pronunciation

Question Intonation

In *yes/no* questions, the speaker's voice rises on the last content word. Content words (*nouns, verbs, adjectives,* and *adverbs*) are words that carry meaning.

*Did you see the **tomb**?*

*Is the professor going to **meet** with him?*

In questions with *wh-* words, the speaker's voice rises on the stressed syllable of the last content word then falls.

*Where is the **pyramid**?*

*How many people went on the **trip**?*

The Taj Mahal was built in the 17th century AD.

A | Listen to the questions from the chart above. [track 3-3]

B | Listen again and repeat. [track 3-3]

C | Write five new questions that you would like to ask your partner. Then practice asking the questions with the correct intonation.

1. Why _____?
2. Are _____?
3. Does _____?
4. Which _____?
5. How much _____?

Before Listening

Prior Knowledge. With a partner, take turns asking and answering the questions below. Use the correct question intonation.

1. Which Mayan sites do you know about?
2. What do you know about them?
3. Have you visited any Mayan sites?
4. Do you enjoy visiting archaeological or historical sites?

Listening: A Guided Tour

🎧 track 3-4 **A** | **Listening for Main Ideas.** Listen to the guided tour and circle the correct answer.

1. Which Mayan site are the tourists visiting?
   a. Tulum
   b. Palenque
   c. Uxmal

2. Why is this one of the most popular Mayan historical sites?
   a. It has several pyramids and other structures.
   b. It has a ball court.
   c. It's easy to get to.

3. Why is the Magician's Pyramid unusual?
   a. It has rounded sides.
   b. It has triangular sides.
   c. It has steep sides.

The Magician's Pyramid

🎧 track 3-4 **B** | **Listening for Details.** Listen again and answer the questions below.

1. From which period of Mayan history is this site? _____

2. Where does the name for the Magician's Pyramid come from? _____

3. In how many stages was the pyramid built? _____

4. Where does the group go after seeing the pyramid? _____

5. What is in front of the Governor's Palace? _____

6. What is a jaguar? _____

After Listening

👥 **Collaboration.** Work with a partner. Imagine that you want to find out more about the Mayan civilization. Write three questions to ask the tour guide. These questions can be about any part of Mayan life (for example, food, clothing, housing, etc.).

1. _____?
2. _____?
3. _____?

Grammar

A | **Prior Knowledge.** Look at the sentences below. How are they similar? How are they different?

1. They buried the king in a tomb.
2. The king was buried in a tomb.

The pyramids of Giza in Egypt are among the original Seven Wonders of the Ancient World.

The Passive Voice with the Past

We use the passive voice when the agent (the doer) of an action is unknown or unimportant. When the action happened in the past, the verb *to be* is in the past.

> Beautiful images **were painted** on the walls.
> The pyramids **were built** thousands of years ago.

We also use the passive voice with past tenses to emphasize the direct object of a past action.

> Archaeologists **discovered** a beautiful mural. *(active)*
> A beautiful mural **was discovered** by archaeologists. *(passive)*

The *by* phrase can be used to indicate the agent in a passive sentence.

> A royal tomb was uncovered **by hikers**.

B | Complete each sentence in the past tense with the passive form of the verb in parentheses.

1. The Temple of Artemis at Ephesus _____ (build) to honor a Greek goddess.
2. The Hanging Gardens of Babylon _____ (plant) by King Nebuchadnezzar II.
3. The Lighthouse of Alexandria _____ (construct) in the third century BC.
4. The Colossus of Rhodes _____ (destroy) by an earthquake.
5. The Statue of Zeus at Olympia _____ (keep) inside its own temple.
6. Eight hundred tons of stone _____ (carry) every day to build the Great Pyramid of Giza.
7. The Mausoleum of Mausollos at Halicarnassus _____ (design) by Greek architects.

The Temple of Artemis in Ephesus, Turkey

 C | **Discussion.** With a partner, discuss any other facts you know about the Seven Wonders of the Ancient World.

D | Read and listen to the information below and <u>underline</u> each use of the passive voice.

track 3-5

The New Seven Wonders

Bernard Weber wanted to use modern technology to bring the people of the world closer together. He knew that the original Seven Wonders of the Ancient World were chosen by one person. Six of the wonders don't exist anymore. So he created a way to let the world determine the New Seven Wonders: an open election using the Internet and text messaging. Anyone could nominate[1] a special site, and anyone could vote.

The Taj Mahal in Agra, India

The Treasury in Petra, Jordan

Naturally, many people voted for sites in their own countries. In some places, people were encouraged[2] by their government to vote. On the other hand, sites in 220 countries were nominated, so there were plenty of wonders to vote for.

The Great Wall in China

Millions of votes were registered, and on July 7, 2007, the seven winners were announced in Lisbon, Portugal. Fourteen finalists were also announced—perhaps because it was difficult to limit the Wonders of the World to only seven.

[1]If someone or something is **nominated** for a position or prize, their name is formally suggested for it.
[2]If you **encourage** someone, you suggest they do something.

E | **Critical Thinking.** Discuss the questions with a partner.

1. What do you think about Weber's idea?
2. Did the old list of wonders need modernizing?
3. Was this a good way to bring people around the world together?

F | **Discussion.** Work with your partner. Look at the chart on page 150 and discuss your ideas about the New Seven Wonders of the World. Why do you think each site was chosen? Can you think of other sites that should be on the list instead?

Language Function

Using the Passive Voice to Talk about Famous Sites

We often use the passive voice when asking for information about and discussing famous or historical places.

When **was** Tikal **built?**   It **was built** around the fourth century BC.
By whom **was** it **built?**   It **was built** by the Mayans.

A | **Discussion.** Look at the information in the chart below. Then with a partner, discuss which information you already knew about and which information was new to you.

The New Seven Wonders of the World

Wonder	Location	Facts
Chichén Itza	Yucatán, Mexico	Chichén Itza is a group of pyramids and other structures that were built by the Mayans. The land under the site was purchased by the state of Yucatán on March 29, 2010.
The "Christ the Redeemer" Statue	Rio de Janeiro, Brazil	The "Christ the Redeemer" Statue was built in the 1920s. It is made of soapstone and concrete and is a symbol of the city of Rio de Janeiro.
The Colosseum	Rome, Italy	The Colosseum is an enormous amphitheater constructed by the ancient Romans. It was completed in less than eight years.
The Great Wall of China	People's Republic of China	The Great Wall of China was built to defend the Chinese Empire. It actually consists of several sections of wall—not just one.
Machu Picchu	Cuzco, Perú	Machu Picchu is a very well-known historical site. It is often called "The Lost City of the Incas" and was built in the 15th century AD during the time of the Inca emperor Pachacuti.
Petra	Jordan-Ancient City	The historical city of Petra, Jordan, is known for buildings that were cut into the rock. It was not seen by the modern Western world until 1812, when a Swiss explorer went there.
The Taj Mahal	Agra, India	The Taj Mahal is located in Agra, India. It was built by an emperor named Shah Jahan, who wanted to remember his beloved wife, Mumtaz Mahal.

B | With your partner, write some quiz questions about the information in the chart.

C | Form a group with another pair of students. Close your books. Take turns asking the other pair your quiz questions. Give a point for every correct answer. See which pair gets the most points.

Presenting an Ancient Artifact

A | Look at the photos and read the captions about three ancient artifacts.

1.

This artifact is either a spoon or a shovel made from the **horn**[1] of an animal. It may have been used for cooking or digging by the Anasazi people. The Anasazi lived in the southwestern United States where this artifact was found.

2.

This Mayan mask was found in Mexico. It was the death mask of a Mayan king named Pakal. It's made of jade, which is a smooth green stone.

3.

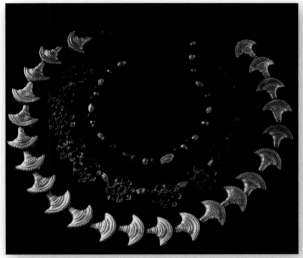

This beautiful necklace was found on the Island of Crete, Greece. It was buried with an ancient Greek woman. It's made of glass and gold.

B | Form a group with two other students. Discuss the questions below about each artifact.

1. Where was the artifact found?
2. When was it made?
3. What material was it made from?
4. What do you think it was used for?

C | **Planning a Presentation.** With your group, prepare a short presentation about the artifacts from exercise **A**. Write notes on your ideas in your notebook. Your presentation should include the following:

1. Information that answers the questions from exercise **B**.
2. Some additional details from your own ideas. Use your imagination. (What words describe the artifact? Who do you think found it? What other artifacts do you think were found with it? Why did you choose this artifact?)

D | Practice your presentation with your group. Each student in your group should present one artifact.

E | **Presentation.** Get together with another group. Take turns presenting your artifacts.

[1]The horns of an animal such as a cow are the hard pointed things that grow from its head.

THE LOST CITY OF MACHU PICCHU

Peru

Before Viewing

A | **Discussion.** With a partner, discuss the questions below.

1. What are some tourist attractions near you?
2. What draws visitors to those places?
3. What are some of the advantages and disadvantages of tourism?

B | Look at the words in the box. Check (✔) the words you know. Use a dictionary to help you with the words you don't know.

❏ tourism   ❏ damage   ❏ civilization   ❏ mountains   ❏ explorer

track 3-6 **C** | Read the information and fill in each blank with a word from the box above. Then listen and check your answers.

Machu Picchu

The city of Machu Picchu was built by the Incas high in the Andes (1) _____ in what is now Peru. The Inca (2) _____ lasted from around AD 1100 to around AD 1500, when the Spanish *conquistadors* arrived in South America.

After the Incas were defeated by the Spanish, few people knew about Machu Picchu. Then in 1911, an American (3) _____ named Hiram Bingham found the city. At that time, it was a very quiet place.

Today, Machu Picchu is a popular destination for tourists. Some people worry that the visitors will (4) _____ the historical site. Other people say that (5) _____ brings money into an area that very much needs it.

While Viewing

A | Watch the video. Then describe the places below to a partner. Practice using the passive voice.

1. Machu Picchu
2. Aguas Calientes, Peru

B | Read the statements. Then watch the video again and circle **T** for *true* and **F** for *false*.

1. Machu Picchu is over 1500 years old.	**T**	**F**
2. Hiram Bingham found Machu Picchu again in 1911.	**T**	**F**
3. The conservationists don't think more visitors will be good for Machu Picchu.	**T**	**F**
4. Aguas Calientes grew quickly because of tourists.	**T**	**F**

Critical Thinking Focus: Making Inferences

When you make an inference, you draw conclusions using information that is not directly stated.

C | **Making Inferences.** Watch again and listen for the following quotations from the video. Then answer the questions below.

> **Narrator:** Jose, a local hotel owner, says that Peru and Machu Picchu can take a few more visitors.
>
> **Jose:** Why not be like the rest of the world? Why not expose and show Machu Picchu to the rest of the world? It's such a wonderful place. Why keep it to a few?

1. How do you think Jose feels when he sees a lot of tourists visiting Machu Picchu?

_____

2. Do you think the people who live near Machu Picchu agree with Jose? Explain.

_____

3. Do you think the conservationists agree with Jose? Explain.

_____

After Viewing

A | **Collaboration.** What would you like to know about Machu Picchu? Work with a partner to write three questions in your notebook for a local tour guide.

B | **Discussion.** Form a group with two or three other students and discuss the questions below.

1. Which of the ancient cultures or places that you have learned about so far in this unit do you find most interesting? Explain.
2. In Lesson B, you are going to learn about two other ancient civilizations. What do you think we can learn from ancient civilizations?

The Inca ruins of Machu Picchu

A | **Meaning from Context.** Look at the photos and read and listen to the information. Notice the words in **blue**. These are words you will hear and use in Lesson B.

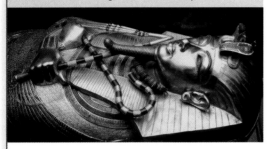

Inside Tutankhamen's tomb, a detailed gold death mask covered the king's mummified body.

Archaeologist Dr. Zahi Hawass prepares the Tutankhamen mummy for a CT scan.

New Clues about Tutankhamen: His Life and Death

In 1922, Howard Carter found the remains[1] of a young man in a tomb filled with royal treasures from ancient Egypt. Newspapers around the world reported the discovery and described the gold jewelry, precious stones, and beautiful art found in the tomb. Everyone wanted to know who this important man was.

We now know Tutankhamen was the son of Akhenaten, and he ruled Egypt from 1332–1322 BC. He became pharaoh as a child, and he died young. On the other hand, many questions are still unanswered. Was "Tut" ill? Was he murdered? What did he look like when he was alive?

In 2005, scientists began to analyze Tut's remains with computer tomography (CT) and modern forensic medicine—a science usually used to solve murder cases. Tut's remains were scanned in a CT machine, which created 3-D[2] images. Using this technology, scientists were able to determine that Tut was probably not murdered and was about 19 when he died.

Scientists also worked with an artist to create a life-like model of Tut. Not everyone likes the result, however. People disagree about his race, but according to the CT scans, he probably looked a lot like modern Egyptians.

[1]The **remains** of a person or animal are the parts of it left after it dies.
[2]A **3-D** image is an image that shows the three dimensions of an object: height, width, and depth.

B | Write each vocabulary word in the correct column below. Use the context of the article and your dictionary to help you.

Noun	Verb	Adjective

C | Write each word in **blue** from exercise **A** on page 154 next to its definition.

1. _____ (n.) valuable objects
2. _____ (v.) to look at something carefully in order to understand it
3. _____ (adj.) very valuable
4. _____ (v.) to find the solution or answer to a problem or question
5. _____ (v.) told people about something that happened
6. _____ (v.) to be killed by someone
7. _____ (v.) controlled (e.g., a country)
8. _____ (adj.) living, not dead
9. _____ (n.) one of the major groups people can be divided into because of physical features
10. _____ (v.) to discover a fact as a result of research or investigation

D | Complete each sentence with the correct form of a word in **blue** from exercise **A** on page 154.

1. She's a hydrologist. She _____ river water.
2. Our country's most important _____ are in our National Museum.
3. Tutankhamen _____ Egypt for a very short time before he died.
4. Your bike was stolen? You should _____ it to the police.
5. Brazil is an interesting country. Its population is made up of people from many different cultures and _____.

E | **Discussion.** With a partner, discuss the questions below.

1. When you have a problem, do you prefer to ask someone for help, or **solve** it yourself? Explain.
2. What are some things you own that are **precious** to you?
3. What do you think King Tut probably looked like when he was **alive**?
4. What factors or things help you **determine** where to live?
5. Name a famous person who was **murdered**. What happened?

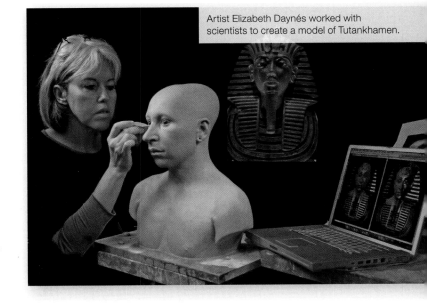
Artist Elizabeth Daynés worked with scientists to create a model of Tutankhamen.

Before Listening

A | Read the notes Silvio, a college student, wrote while watching a documentary on TV.

> Documentary Title: Uncovering the Past in Hanoi
>
> - 2002, government plan — a new building in Hanoi
>
> - They started construction, then found: ancient palaces & meeting halls / dishes /wells for water / figures of dragons / coins / weapons / etc. (1000's of artifacts)
>
> - Name: Thang Long Citadel — (citadel a safe place for royalty)
>
> - Archaeologists dug down more than 12 feet (4 meters) (layers from diff time periods)
>
> - oldest things: the wells (7th century AD) until 18th c (French begin to arrive; later they occupy Vietnam)
>
> - Gov't chose new site for its building; Thang Long now a historical site

B | With a partner, use Silvio's notes to talk about the documentary he watched. Use complete sentences.

A plan to construct a new government building in Hanoi resulted in the richest archaeological find in Vietnam's history.

> The documentary was about the discovery of an important historical site in Hanoi.

Listening: A Conversation between Students

A | **Listening for Main Ideas.** Listen to a conversation about a class assignment. Then answer the questions below. *(track 3-8)*

1. Which class is the assignment for? _____

2. What is the assignment? _____

3. What is Silvio's problem with the assignment? _____

B | Listening for Details. Listen again and choose the best phrase to complete each sentence.

1. Laura told Silvio that _____

   a. he should have taken a lot more notes.

   b. his notes were not very helpful.

   c. he had already begun to summarize the information.

2. Laura suggests that Silvio _____

   a. write out his notes as complete sentences.

   b. ask himself questions about the documentary he watched.

   c. talk to some of the archaeologists on campus.

3. Laura says including a few smaller details _____

   a. can make a summary very confusing.

   b. can help support the main ideas.

   c. can take too much time in a presentation.

The newly restored pavillion inside the former imperial citadel of Thang Long in Hanoi, Vietnam

C | Making Inferences. Read the statements. Then listen again and circle **T** for *true* or **F** for *false*.

1. Laura would probably not enjoy the documentary.	T	F
2. Laura is good at note-taking.	T	F
3. Laura thinks newspaper reporters are good at note-taking.	T	F
4. Silvio feels unhappy at the end of the conversation.	T	F

After Listening

A | Planning a Presentation. Use Silvio's notes on page 156 and what you understood from the conversation to answer the *wh-* questions below and prepare to give a short summary.

What was the documentary about? _The documentary was about the discovery of an important historical site in Hanoi._

Who was involved? _____

When was the site discovered? _____

How was the site discovered? _____

Why is the site important? _____

B | Presentation. With a partner, take turns summarizing the information about the discovery of the Thang Long Citadel. Use Silvio's notes from page 156 and your answers from exercise **A** to help you.

Grammar

Phrasal Verbs

Phrasal verbs are formed with a verb + particle. Some examples of particles are *up, down, in, out,* and *at.*

> She **gets up** at five thirty every morning.

Phrasal verbs have their own meanings that are different from the usual meaning of the verb and particle.

> She went outside and **looked** up at the sky. (She looked in the direction of the sky.) (verb)
> She **looked up** the meaning of the word in her dictionary. (She found information using a dictionary.) (phrasal verb)

Like regular verbs, some phrasal verbs are transitive (they take objects).

> Victor **wrote down** the information.

Other phrasal verbs are intransitive (they do not take objects).

> Steve **showed up** late for class today.

A | Work with a partner. Complete each sentence or question with the correct phrasal verb from the box below. Use your dictionary to help you as needed.

hand in	leave out	pay back	get together	close down	help out

1. He borrowed money from me. Now he needs to _____ me _____.
2. That store is going to _____ next month. That makes me sad.
3. You need to work on this summary. You can't _____ the most important information.
4. Let's _____ after class to practice our presentation.
5. Lyle, I don't have your paper. Did you forget to _____ it _____?
6. I want to _____. Is there something I can do?

Language Function: Discussing Problems

Student to Student: Voicing a Small Problem

Not every problem is serious, but having a small problem and saying nothing can sometimes create bigger problems in your relationships with other people. Here are some ways you can voice a small problem politely.

It's no big deal, but . . .   *I hate to say it, but . . .*
Actually, that's a problem for me because . . .   *I feel I need to say something about . . .*

A | Practice the conversation with a partner. Then switch roles and practice it again.

Yoko: I'm going to have a few friends over tonight. Everyone has finished exams, and we just want to relax a little.

Pamela: Actually, that's a problem for me because I still need to study. I have an exam tomorrow, and I have to hand in a report on Tuesday.

Yoko: Oh, I'm sorry. I didn't know. Maybe I can get together with them tomorrow night instead.

Pamela: I'd really appreciate that. Also, it's no big deal, but do you remember that 10 dollars you borrowed last week?

Yoko: Oh, of course! I'm so sorry. I completely forgot. I can stop by an ATM after class and pay you back tonight.

Pamela: That's great. Thanks.

B | **Role-Playing.** Role-play the situation below with your partner. One of you will be Student A and one of you will be Student B.

Student A	Student B
You are working on an assignment with a classmate. Your assignment is to write a summary about an archaeological site. You want to do the research for the assignment, and have your partner write the summary. Have a conversation about this with your partner.	You are working on an assignment with a classmate. Your assignment is to write a summary about an archaeological site. You want to write the summary together because you think it is difficult and will take a lot of time. Have a conversation about this with your partner.

C | **Discussion.** With your partner, discuss the questions below.

1. In your language or culture, is it polite or impolite to voice a problem?
2. What are the advantages and disadvantages of voicing a problem? (What could happen if you don't say anything?)

You are going to research information about one of the New Seven Wonders of the World or another archaeological site that interests you and give a summary about it to the class.

A | Read the Presentation Skills box about oral summaries. Then look at the list of topics below and choose a topic for your summary.

The Colosseum in Rome is one of the New Seven Wonders of the World.

Presentation Skills: Oral Summaries

When you give a summary, you should only include the most important information—information that answers the questions, *Who*, *What*, *When*, *Where*, *How*, and *Why*. You should not include your own opinion in a summary, just the facts.

Chichén Itza   Machu Picchu
The "Christ the Redeemer" Statue   Petra
The Colosseum   The Taj Mahal
The Great Wall of China   An archaeological site that interests you

B | **Using a Graphic Organizer.** Use the chart below (or make one in your notebook) to help you organize the information for your summary. Do not write out your summary. Add a few interesting details to support the main ideas.

Summary Topic: _____

Who?	*What?*	*When?*

Where?	*How?*	*Why?*

C | **Planning a Presentation.** Practice giving your summary in front of a mirror or in front of friends. Are your ideas clear? Are you speaking too fast or too slowly? *(See page 218 of the Independent Student Handbook for a Presentation Checklist.)*

D | **Presentation.** When you give your presentation, remember to:

- Look at your notes or slides only occasionally.
- Look up and make eye contact with your audience.
- Ask your audience if they have any questions.

Species Survival

ACADEMIC PATHWAYS

Lesson A: Listening to a Biologist's Talk about Birds
Discussing Endangered Species

Lesson B: Listening to a Conversation about a Science Experiment
Planning and Presenting a Research Proposal

Think and Discuss

1. Look at the photo and read the information on this page.
   What topics do you think you will discuss in this unit?

2. Over time, giraffes have developed very long necks. Why do you
   think this happened? How are long necks helpful to giraffes?

Giraffes in South Africa

Exploring the Theme:
Species Survival

Look at the photos and the map and read the captions. Then discuss the questions.

1. What did Darwin do in the Galápagos? What is his theory called?
2. What are two examples of useful traits that help animals survive?
3. What are scientists doing to help species survive?
4. Do you think it is important to help endangered species survive? Explain.

Sullivan Bay, Bartolome Island, Galápagos Islands

The Galápagos Islands and Natural Selection

Charles Darwin, an English naturalist, visited the Galápagos Islands where he studied many interesting species of animals and developed his theory called natural selection. According to his theory, animals of the same species have slightly different traits. Animals that have helpful traits are more likely to survive and reproduce. The offspring of these animals inherit the helpful traits from their parents, and over time, all of the members of a species have this helpful trait.

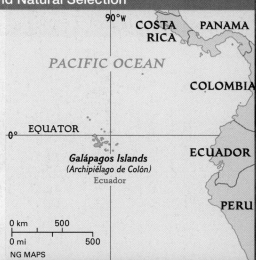

How Nature and Science Help Species Survive

Darwin studied how small differences in certain traits within each species of animal could be helpful for its survival. For example, the shells of the giant tortoises in the Galápagos were different sizes and shapes depending on which island they lived on and what they ate.

Over time the Arctic hare has developed a very useful trait—a thick white coat, which keeps it warm in the winter. The hare's white coat also makes it difficult for its predators (animals that eat it) to see it against the snow and ice.

Scientists and researchers are traveling to places like the Congo Basin in Africa and making notes and keeping track of all of the different species they find. They are doing this in order to help prevent the species there from becoming extinct.

A | **Meaning from Context.** Look at the map. Read and listen to the information. Notice the words in blue. These are words you will hear and use in Lesson A.

The *Beagle* in South America: The *Beagle* expedition's priority was to map the harbors and coastlines of South America. Charles Darwin spent a lot of his time on land, exploring parts of Argentine Pampas, the Atacama Desert, and the Andes mountains.

① **Argentina, 1832:** At both Punta Alta and Monte Hermoso, Darwin found many fossils of large prehistoric animals. He could not **identify** the fossils, but they were similar to modern animal **species** from the area. This might have been the beginning of the idea that modern species could change over time from earlier species.

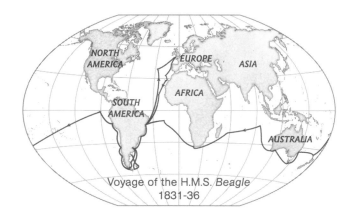

Voyage of the H.M.S. *Beagle* 1831-36

③ **Galápagos Islands, Ecuador, 1835:** Here, Darwin began to develop his ideas about why and how the diversity of species occurred. In a **process** he called natural selection, an animal with a useful trait was more likely to survive, and therefore, more likely to **reproduce**. The animal's **offspring** would then **inherit** the useful trait. In contrast, animals of that same species with a different trait might die and not reproduce. In this way, a species would **adapt** to its environment and change over time.

② **Chile, 1833:** In South America, the men on the *Beagle* sometimes ate a South American bird called a *rhea*. In Patagonia, Darwin heard about a smaller type of *rhea*. It lived mostly in southern Patagonia, while the larger *rhea* lived in northern Patagonia. The two species were separated by the Rio Negro. At this time, Darwin became interested in the **diversity** of animal life. Could an animal's **environment** affect **traits** such as size?

B | Write each word in blue from exercise **A** next to its definition below.

1. _____ (n.) the air, land, and water that people, animals, and plants live in
2. _____ (v.) to recognize someone or something
3. _____ (n.) a person's children or an animal's young
4. _____ (n.) a variety of things that are different from each other
5. _____ (n.) things one gets from one's parents, such as eye color
6. _____ (v.) to produce young animals or plants
7. _____ (v.) to change in order to be successful in a new situation
8. _____ (n.) a certain kind of animal or plant
9. _____ (v.) an action or event that leads to a certain result
10. _____ (v.) to be born with something because one's parents also had it

A | Read the article below and fill in each blank with the correct word from the box.

diversity	inherited	process	reproduced	traits

Out of Africa

Anthropologists, scientists who study human beings, have long said that modern humans first lived in Africa, and then moved east toward Asia, north across the Mediterranean, and later throughout the world.

Now, a very large genetic[1] study supports that theory. The study looked at nearly 1000 people in 51 places around the world. It found the most genetic _____ in Africa and less genetic diversity farther away from Africa. How did this happen? When small groups of people moved away, they took only a small amount of all the possible genetic information with them. People in the small groups _____ . Their offspring _____ their parents' more limited set of genes. Their _____ were very similar to those of their parents. This _____ continued as small groups of people continued to move farther from Africa.

Human Migration

☐ Fossil or artifact site   40,000 years ago Migration date   → Generalized route

SOURCES: SUSAN ANTÓN, NEW YORK UNIVERSITY; ALISON BROOKS, GEORGE WASHINGTON UNIVERSITY; PETER FORSTER, UNIVERSITY OF CAMBRIDGE; JAMES F. O'CONNELL, UNIVERSITY OF UTAH; STEPHEN OPPENHEIMER, OXFORD UNIVERSITY; SPENCER WELLS, NATIONAL GEOGRAPHIC SOCIETY; OFER BAR-YOSEF, HARVARD UNIVERSITY

NGM MAPS

Anthropological evidence shows that human beings first lived in Africa and then moved to different places around the world.

[1]**Genetic** means related to genes (small pieces of DNA) and heredity.

B | **Discussion.** With a partner, discuss the questions below.

1. How can the **environment** you live in affect your health and happiness?
2. Can you **identify** many **species** of birds? of plants? Explain.
3. What are some **species** of animals that live in your country?
4. What are some of the **traits** you **inherited** from your parents and grandparents?
5. What parts of the world have a large **diversity** of plant and animal **species**?

Before Listening

How did these giraffes get their long necks and beautiful markings? Geneticist Sean Carroll wants to find out how genes make nature's diversity possible.

Taking Brief Notes

When you take notes while you are listening, you often have to write down important information quickly. Here are some note-taking strategies you can use to help you do this.

Strategy #1: Write Only Key Words

Listen for the content (*nouns, verbs, adjectives,* and *adverbs*) words that will be stressed. These words will help you remember the talk. Don't write function words. Function words (e.g., *that, so, from, actually, those*) are necessary for correct grammar, but you don't need them in your notes.

You hear: *Many people know the story of Charles Darwin and the voyage of the Beagle. But some of the story is—in fact—legend.*
You write: *People know Darwin and Beagle. Story part legend*

 A | **Note-Taking.** Listen to a talk about Charles Darwin and the voyage of the *Beagle.* In your notebook, make a list of some of the key words you hear. Don't worry about writing complete ideas yet.

track 3-10

 B | **Note-Taking.** Listen to the talk again and take notes in your notebook. This time, write complete ideas, but do not write down function words.

track 3-10

Strategy #2: Use Abbreviations

Use shortened forms and symbols. You can use any abbreviation system that works for you. Here are some examples:

s/t (something)	*yr.* (year)	*w/* (with)	*diff.* (different)
s/o (someone)	*govt.* (government)	→ (leads to or causes)	*dept.* (department)

You hear: *First of all, it was a long voyage. It lasted for over five years.*
You write: Beagle *voyage long, >5 yrs.*

 C | **Note-Taking.** Listen again and take new notes in your notebook. Write complete ideas using only key words, abbreviations, and symbols.

track 3-10

D | Compare your notes with a partner's. Did you identify the same main ideas and use the same key words? Did you leave out function words? Did you use similar abbreviations? *(See pages 206–207 of the Independent Student Handbook for more information on note-taking.)*

Listening: A Biologist's Talk about Birds

A | **Predicting Content.** Look at the photo on the right and read the caption. You are going to listen to a biologist in the U.K. lead a bird-watching trip. What topics do you expect to hear and learn about? Discuss your ideas with a partner.

An adult finch (with red beak) teaches its songs to a chick. The chick has a gene that makes it able to learn singing.

Critical Thinking Focus: Using a Graphic Organizer to Take Notes

A graphic organizer can help you to take notes in situations when you can predict the content of a talk or lecture. You can also transfer notes from your notebook to a graphic organizer after a talk to help you review and organize the ideas. *(See pages 214–215 of the Independent Student Handbook for more information on using graphic organizers.)*

track 3-11

B | **Using a Graphic Organizer.** Listen to the talk and complete the notes in the graphic organizer below.

Type of Finch	goldfinch	
Where It Lives		Most of Europe + NW Africa and Turkey
Special Traits		
What It Eats	Male: seeds from inside flower Female: other seeds	
Other Habits		Lives diff. places in diff. seasons. Summer: parks & forests Winter: gardens and farm fields

track 3-11

C | **Critical Thinking.** Compare your notes with a partner's. Did either of you miss any information? Listen again and complete your notes.

After Listening

A | **Collaboration.** Work with a partner. Choose a species of animal you are familiar with and prepare a short, informal presentation about it. Use the questions below to help you plan your presentation.

What is the name of this species?   Where does it live?
What are some of its habits?   What does it look like?
What are its special traits?   What does it eat?

A bird's **beak** is the hard structure on its face—a bird's mouth.

A **seed** is the small object that grows into a plant when placed in the ground that many species of birds eat. This Eurasian nuthatch is holding a sunflower seed in its beak.

B | **Presentation.** Form a group with another pair of students. Take turns presenting your species of animal to the other pair. Ask for and give clarification as needed.

Pronunciation

A | Listen to the following words. Then answer the questions below.

banana	demand	answer

1. How many syllables are in each word?
2. Which is the stressed syllable in each word?
3. How many different vowel sounds are in each word?

Full and Reduced Vowel Sounds and Secondary Stress

In English, unstressed syllables are shorter (in time) than stressed syllables. In addition, the vowel sound in many unstressed syllables is *reduced* to /ə/, or schwa.

Examples:

    ba **na** na   de **vel** op   a **wake**
    /ə/   /ə/   /ə/   /ə/   /ə/

Stressed syllables in English are pronounced with a *full* vowel sound.

Examples:

    lo cal   **fac** tor   **sea** son
    /o/   /æ/   /iy/

Some syllables in English have secondary stress. Like unstressed syllables, they are shorter than the syllables with the main (primary) stress. However, they are pronounced with a full vowel sound.

Example: The main stress in *analyze* is on the first syllable, but the third syllable has secondary stress. It is pronounced with the full vowel sound /ay/.

B | Listen to the words below. <u>Underline</u> the stressed syllables in each word. Then practice saying the words with a partner.

    1. practical   2. attachment   3. proportion   4. compare   5. available   6. support

C | Listen to the words below. <u>Underline</u> the syllable with the most stress in each word. Circle the syllables with secondary stress. Then practice saying the words with your partner.

    1. recommend   2. atmosphere   3. romantic   4. classify   5. quantity   6. disappear

D | Work with your partner to analyze your name or the name of a famous person.

1. How many syllables are there?
2. Which syllables have primary or secondary stress?
3. Which syllables are unstressed?
4. Which vowel sounds are full, and which are reduced (schwa) sounds?

Grammar

As Darwin noticed, the Galápagos giant tortoise differs from island to island.

The Simple Present with Facts

We use the simple present to talk about facts.

*The Galápagos giant tortoise **differs** from island to island.*
*The male goldfinch **has** a very long beak.*
*Goldfinches **fly** to warmer parts of Europe in September and October.*
*The male goldfinch **eats** the seeds inside flowers.*

A | Complete each of the statements about animals below. Use the simple present form of the verb in parentheses. Then read each statement and circle **T** for *true* or **F** for *false*.

1. Penguins _____ (live) in Alaska.   **T**   **F**

2. The average giraffe _____ (sleep)   **T**   **F**
   less than four hours a day.

3. Like humans, bears _____ (have) 32 teeth.   **T**   **F**

4. A baby hippopotamus, or "calf" _____   **T**   **F**
   (weigh) between 50 and 100 pounds (23 and 45 kilograms) when
   it is born.

5. Elephants _____ (use) their large   **T**   **F**
   ears to help them stay cool.

B | Compare your answers with a partner's. Then check your answers at the bottom of the page.

A hippopotamus and her calf, Serengeti, Tanzania, Africa

Answers: 1. F, 2. T, 3. F Bears have 42 teeth, 4. T, 5. T

Language Function

Three male goldfinches

Explaining Causes and Effects

We often use certain words or phrases to signal causes and effects. We use *because* and *since* to signal a cause.

Because *finches need to eat hard seeds, they have developed large, strong beaks over time.*

Since *polar bears live in snowy places, they have developed white fur to help hide them from their prey, or the animals that they kill for food.*

We use *As a result (of this)* and *Therefore* to signal a result or effect.

Over time, finches' beaks have become very strong. **As a result**, *they can eat hard seeds.*

Polar bears have white fur. **Therefore**, *their prey doesn't always notice them.*

Polar bears' white fur is helpful to them because it makes it difficult for their prey (the animals they eat) to see them in the snow.

This polar bear cub has inherited his mother's thick white fur.

 track 3-16 **A** | Read and listen to the information about the process of natural selection. Write down the words and phrases you hear that signal causes and effects.

1. The environment affects animals in some way.
2. Animals with helpful traits do well in their environment.
3. These animals survive.
4. These animals reproduce.
5. The offspring of these animals inherit the helpful trait.
6. Most of the animals in the species have this helpful trait.

 B | With a partner, explain the process of natural selection using the sentences and signal words you wrote down in exercise **A**.

> Because the environment affects animals in some way, species develop certain helpful traits . . .

Discussing Endangered Species

 A | **Prior Knowledge.** Look at the picture and read the caption. Then discuss the questions below with a partner.

An endangered lynx, protected in Spain's Andújar Natural Park, jumps over a fence into a feeding area. The fence keeps other animals out and rabbits in.

1. What are some endangered species you know about?
2. Why are those species endangered?
3. Do you think we should try to protect endangered species? Explain.

B | Read the information below about the Iberian lynx.

The Iberian lynx is native to Spain and Portugal. It is the most endangered cat species in the world. Its diet consists mostly of rabbits and not much else. This is beneficial because rabbits can have a negative impact on the ecosystem when there are too many of them. As a result of hunting, loss of habitat, and cars, the lynx population has decreased significantly. About 10 years ago there were approximately 400 Iberian lynx; now there are only 100. There are only two small, protected areas in Spain where these beautiful animals live.

 C | **Brainstorming.** Work with a partner. Imagine that you must decide whether or not to continue protecting the Iberian lynx. Brainstorm a list of the pros and cons of protecting the lynx in the T-chart below. Two examples are given.

Pros	Cons
—The lynx is helpful to the ecosystem (eats rabbits).	—Lynx can eat people's chickens or pets in rural areas.

 D | Form a group with another pair of students for an informal debate. Follow the steps below.

1. Choose which pair will argue the *pros* and which pair will argue the *cons* of lynx protection.
2. With your partner, review your notes from exercise **C**. You may want to add more ideas or examples to help make your argument stronger.
3. Take turns presenting your argument to the other pair.
4. As a group, decide which argument was stronger, the *pros* or the *cons*.
5. Discuss your real opinion about the situation. Do you think it is important to protect the Iberian lynx?

Presentation Skills: Choosing Information to Support Your Topic

When planning a presentation, it is important to carefully choose information that best supports your topic. You should include reasons and examples that support your main idea and avoid information that does not support it. This is particularly important when you are presenting one side of an argument (for example, in a debate).

A Disappearing World

The Sangha River divides the border between Cameroon, Central African Republic, and Republic of the Congo.

Nouabale-Ndoki National Park, Republic of the Congo

Before Viewing

A | **Using a Dictionary.** You will hear these words in the video. Work with a partner and match each word with its definition. Use your dictionary to help you.

Congo Basin

1. extinct (adj.) ___
2. extinction (n.) ___
3. logging (n.) ___
4. rainforest (n.) ___
5. expedition (n.) ___
6. wildlife (n.) ___
7. record (n.) ___

a. the activity of cutting down trees to sell the wood
b. written information about something
c. no longer having any living members of a species
d. an organized trip made for a specific purpose
e. a forest that receives 160 inches (405 centimeters) of rain a year
f. the death of all living members of a species
g. animals and other living things that live in the wild, not in zoos

B | **Prior Knowledge.** You are going to watch a video about a team of scientists who travel to the Congo Basin—an area in central Africa. The purpose of their expedition is to make a record of all of the wildlife they find. They hope that if people know more about the species there, they will do more to protect the area and to help prevent the wildlife there from becoming extinct. What do *you* know about the causes of extinction? Take the quiz below to find out. Read the statements. Then circle **T** for *true* or **F** for *false*. Use your dictionary to help you with any words you don't know.

QUIZ: THE CAUSES OF EXTINCTION

1.	Genetic diversity is reduced when species become extinct.	**T**	**F**
2.	Modern extinctions occur when a species loses its place to live.	**T**	**F**
3.	Logging increases the area where rainforest species can live.	**T**	**F**
4.	Knowledge about a species can help prevent its extinction.	**T**	**F**

Answers: 1.T, 2.T, 3.F, 4.T

C | Predicting Content. Work with a partner. Look at the photos on these pages and read the captions. Then discuss the questions below.

1. What kind of wildlife do you think Fay and his team will probably find in the Congo Basin?
2. What might be difficult about walking across the Congo Basin?

While Viewing

A | Watch the video and fill in each blank with the number you hear.

1. The Congo Basin contains almost _____ of the world's rainforests.
2. It may have up to _____ of all of the wild plants and animals found in all of Africa.
3. After _____ months of traveling, the team is now in Gabon.
4. "We can see a long way here, you know . . . _____ or _____ kilometers in every direction."
5. "We can see _____ degrees around."
6. "We'd been walking in the woods in our own little world for _____ months and now it was over."

The Ituri Forest in the Congo Basin

B | Note-Taking. Watch the video again. In your notebook, take notes on the topic below. Use the note-taking strategies you learned on page 166 of Lesson A.

Reasons why the Congo Basin is important

C | Compare your notes with a partner's. Then take turns retelling the information about the Congo Basin using your notes.

After Viewing

Critical Thinking. Form a group with two or three other students and discuss the questions.

1. Fay's expedition was long and difficult. Do you think it was valuable? Explain.
2. Would you prefer to go on a bird-watching trip like the one from Lesson A, or an expedition like Fay's? Explain.
3. In Lesson B, you will listen to some students discussing an experiment they are doing with fish. Is there some kind of animal you are interested in learning more about? Which species of animal? What would you like to learn about it?

A western lowland gorilla

A | **Meaning from Context.** Check (✔) the words you already know. Then read and listen to the article below. Notice the words in blue. Use context clues to help you understand the words you don't know. These are words you will hear and use in Lesson B.

❏ argue   ❏ classify   ❏ gene   ❏ sequence   ❏ technique
❏ aware (of)   ❏ controversial   ❏ sample   ❏ substance   ❏ variation

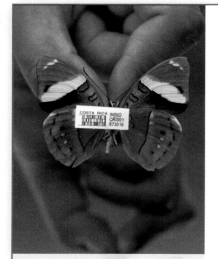

A barcoded olive wing butterfly,
San Jose, Costa Rica

Bar Coding Life on Earth

Paul Hebert is a biologist at the University of Guelph in Canada. But as a young man back in the 1970s, part of his job was to classify thousands of different species of moth[1]. Finding tiny variations in the moths in order to describe each species scientifically was not easy, however.

Then, in 2003, Hebert suggested something a bit controversial. Instead of using descriptions to identify different species, why not use their DNA?

Hebert argued that a bar code—similar to the bar codes on products in a store—could be created for every living thing on earth. Hebert suggested using a part of a gene called *CO1* to create bar codes. This gene is made up of four chemical substances known as *G, T, C,* and *A.* Nearly every form of life has the *CO1* gene, but the sequence of the *G, T, C* and *A* substances differs for each species. Using bar codes, scientists can identify or classify a plant or animal by testing a sample of its DNA.

Not everyone agrees with Hebert's ideas. Some people argue that research money should be used in other ways. Hebert says the bar code technique is a good way to identify species because it is making the public more aware of biodiversity. Some people have even sent him samples of plants and animals to identify from their own backyards!

Like all animals, this armadillo's DNA consists of four parts: *G, T, C,* and *A.* The sequence of these parts can be shown as a bar code.

[1]A **moth** is a winged insect similar to a butterfly.

B | Complete each sentence with the correct form of a word in blue from exercise **A**.

1. Most people aren't _____ of the number of species on earth.

2. Paul Hebert thinks it's difficult to _____ all the species using descriptions.

3. In some cases, there are only very small _____ between one species and another.

4. A different _____ for classifying species is to use their DNA.

5. Some people don't agree with Hebert's _____ idea of using DNA.

6. DNA can be taken from a small blood _____ .

7. The _____ that researchers are using is called *CO1.*

8. *G, T, C,* and *A* are the _____ that make up DNA.

9. Different _____ of *G, T, C,* and *A* carry different genetic information.

10. Hebert _____ that all species on earth should be bar coded.

A | Replace each <u>underlined</u> word with one of the words in **blue** from exercise **A** on page 174.

1. The food here is always the same. There's little <u>change</u> _____ from one day to the next.

2. This page shouldn't come before that one. They're in the wrong <u>order</u> _____ .

3. Are plants <u>categorized</u> _____ in the same way as animals?

4. This recipe for making bread is quite difficult. There must be an easier <u>way</u> _____ .

5. The moth ate some kind of sweet <u>stuff</u> _____ .

B | Take turns asking and answering the questions below with a partner.

1. What's one **technique** you use for learning new vocabulary words?
2. Would you rather **argue** for or against protecting endangered animals?
3. Which **genes** do you think you inherited from your mother or from your father? For example, if your father is tall and you're tall, then maybe you inherited his gene for being tall.
4. What's a **controversial** topic in your country or in the news today?
5. What do you think scientists can do to make people more **aware** of endangered species?
6. Do you think it's a good idea for companies to give away free **samples** of their products? Explain.
7. What would you do if you saw a strange green **substance** on your kitchen floor?
8. Put the following in the correct **sequence**: middle age, infancy, old age, youth.

C | Read the statistics below about bar coding life on earth. Then discuss the questions with your partner.

1. What information about these statistics surprises you? Explain.
2. Do you think bar coding species is useful? Explain.

Bar Coding Statistics

- There are about 1.7 million named species on earth.
- Scientists in 25 countries are working to bar code species.
- Their goal is to bar code 500,000 species by 2015.
- 40,000 species of moth and butterfly have already been bar coded.
- Hebert thinks most species will be bar coded by 2025.

Eyelash Viper
(*Bothriechis Schlegelii*)

African Pygmy Hedgehog (*Atelerix Albiventris*)

Scientists collaborate on a laboratory experiment.

Before Listening

 A | **Discussion.** Form a group with two or three other students. Look at the picture and read the caption. Then discuss the questions.

1. What do you like about working on a school assignment or other project with other people? What do you dislike about it?
2. When you work with a group, what can you do to make sure everyone gets along well? What can you do to make sure everyone does their fair share of the work?

Polite Expressions for Collaborating

The word *collaborate* means "work together." We need to collaborate in a variety of different academic and professional situations, such as planning a group presentation, or working on a project or experiment. Here are some common polite expressions you can use when working with a group.

Making Polite Requests

Would you mind *helping me with this?*
Could you please *hand me that notebook?*

Checking for Agreement

This is quite good; ***don't you agree****?*
I'd like to begin tomorrow. ***Is that all right****?*

Disagreeing Politely

I see your point, but *there are millions of species to classify.*
I'm afraid I don't agree with *that idea.*

Other Polite Expressions

Oh, sorry.   *No problem.*   *That's a great idea!*   *Thanks.*

---

track 3-18 **B** | Listen to part of a conversation in a laboratory. As you listen, put a check (✔) next to the polite expressions you hear.

❏ *Would you mind . . . ?*   ❏ *I'm afraid I don't agree with . . .*
❏ *Could you please . . . ?*   ❏ *Oh, sorry.*
❏ *. . . ; don't you agree?*   ❏ *That's a great idea!*
❏ *. . . Is that all right?*   ❏ *Thanks.*
❏ *I see your point, but . . .*

Listening: A Conversation about a Science Experiment

track 3-19 **A** | **Listening for Main Ideas.** Listen to the entire conversation and choose the answer that best completes each statement below.

1. The speakers are doing research on _____ .
   a. fish color and water temperature
   b. feeding fresh fruit to fish
   c. nighttime fish reproduction
2. The woman thinks they will get _____ .
   a. a good grade
   b. a clear result
   c. a new book
3. The man thinks they should write their lab report _____ .
   a. in a few days
   b. in the evening
   c. as soon as possible

track 3-19 **B** | **Listening for Details.** Listen again. In your notebook, write the answers to the following questions.

1. How are the fish in the experiment different from one another?
2. What happens to the experiment at night?
3. Why does the man say, "Thanks"?
4. What does the woman want to copy?
5. What does the man ask the woman to do tomorrow?

After Listening

 A | **Collaboration.** Imagine that you and your partner must do research together for a laboratory experiment. Follow the steps below.

1. Choose one of the experiments below.

Experiment #1	Experiment #2	Experiment #3
What causes birds to lay more eggs or fewer eggs than usual?	Do different kinds of music affect the growth of plants?	Which substances attract the most mosquitoes?

2. Imagine a situation and a conversation you might have in a laboratory. What are you doing? Why are you doing it? What are you talking about?
3. Practice the conversation and be sure to use polite expressions from page 176.

B | **Role-Playing.** Form a group with another pair of students. Take turns role-playing your conversations. As you listen, notice the polite expressions your classmates use.

Grammar

Phrasal Verbs: Review

Phrasal verbs are formed from a verb and a particle. Examples:

get <u>up</u>   write <u>down</u>   put <u>on</u>

You may want to look back at the information about phrasal verbs on page 158.

In the Foja Mountains of New Guinea, entomologis[t] Hari Sutrisno collects moths at night.

The meaning of a phrasal verb is usually very different from the base verb, so phrasal verbs need to be learned separately—almost like new vocabulary words.

Verb:	*I need to **leave** class early today.* (go away from)
Phrasal Verb:	*Don't **leave out** that information. It's very important.* (not include)

A | Meaning from Context. Read and listen to the telephone conversation. Notice the <u>underlined</u> phrasal verbs. Try to guess their meanings using context clues.

A tree frog from New Guinea's Foja Mountains

Matt:	Jessica? It's me!
Jessica:	Matt! It's great to hear your voice! Are you back in Australia now?
Matt:	Yes, and I really missed you, but I'm so happy you <u>talked</u> me <u>into</u> going on the expedition! I can't believe I almost <u>turned down</u> such a great opportunity.
Jessica:	Tell me all about it!
Matt:	Well, we were high up in the Foja Mountains. No human beings have ever lived there!
Jessica:	How exciting! Did you get a lot of work done?
Matt:	We did! We <u>set up</u> a tent as our laboratory. It was small but fine.
Jessica:	Did it rain a lot?
Matt:	Every day. Well—one afternoon the sky <u>cleared up</u> for a while, but the clouds were back by that evening. It was OK, though. The frogs didn't mind the rain.
Jessica:	Oh, tell me about the frogs!
Matt:	Can you believe there are 350 frog species in New Guinea? The best time to find them is at night. When I <u>turned on</u> my flashlight, I could see them easily and <u>pick</u> them <u>up</u> with my hands.
Jessica:	That sounds great! But wasn't it scary in the forest at night?
Matt:	Not really. It was fun and very interesting.
Jessica:	It sounds like a good trip.
Matt:	It was, and the lead scientist was really happy with my work.
Jessica:	That's great! Congratulations, Matt!

B | Work with a partner. Look back at the telephone conversation. Then write each <u>underlined</u> phrasal verb next to its definition.

1. _____ to say no to an invitation or opportunity
2. _____ to arrange
3. _____ to convince
4. _____ to cause light, sound, water, etc. to come from something by adjusting the controls
5. _____ to take with one's hands
6. _____ to become sunny

C | Practice the conversation from exercise **A** on page 178 with your partner. Then switch roles and practice it again.

D | Complete each sentence with the correct form of a phrasal verb from exercise **B**.

1. I didn't want to do it, but my friend _____ me _____ it.
2. Your bag is on the floor. You should _____ it _____ . The floor in here is very dirty!
3. Let's _____ the laboratory for our experiment tomorrow.
4. It was raining this morning, but now the sky has _____ .
5. When I get home, I always _____ the stereo and listen to some music.
6. I _____ Lara's invitation to go to the movies tonight, because I have to study for the test tomorrow.

Language Function: Congratulating

A | In the telephone conversation on page 178, Jessica congratulates Matt for doing well with his frog research. Look back at the conversation and notice the expressions she uses.

Student to Student: Congratulating

You can use informal expressions like these when you want to congratulate other students on their accomplishments.

That sounds great!	*Congratulations!*	*Way to go!*
Well done!	*Good for you!*	*Great job!*

In Kansas City in the U.S., a rancher is congratulated for his prize-winning steer.

B | Think of three or four things you have done well recently or are happy about. Write them in your notebook.

C | With a partner, take turns talking about the things you have done well and congratulating each other.

You are going to collaborate with a group to plan a research proposal. You will then present your proposal to the class.

 A | Form a group with two or three other students. Read the information and follow the steps below.

> **Situation:** Your group is going on a scientific research field trip! And the best news is that you have received a government research grant, so you have plenty of travel money. However, before you actually receive the grant money, you must submit your research proposal.

1. Brainstorm a list of several interesting places you might go to do your research. What could you research in those places? You can choose one of the places and one of the species from this unit or choose one of your own ideas.

Torres del Paine National Park in Patagonia, Chile

Research Proposal

A. Destination: _____

B. Research Topic(s): _____

2. Think about what you will need in order to travel to your destination and do your research. Will you need plane tickets? How many? Will you need tents, canoes, or binoculars? What other equipment will you need?

C. Travel Plans: _____

_____

D. Equipment Requests: _____

_____

3. Because you're getting a government grant, you'll be expected to do something with your research after you return home. How will you use your research? Will you write an article or create a documentary film about it? Will you use it as part of a larger study? How could your knowledge be useful to the world?

E. Follow-Up Plans: _____

_____

 B | **Planning a Presentation.** Decide which topics from your research proposal each member of your group will present. Practice your presentation.

 C | **Presentation.** Present your research plan to the class. Use your notes to help you remember your ideas.

Entrepreneurs and New Businesses

ACADEMIC PATHWAYS

Lesson A: Listening to a PowerPoint Lecture
Discussing New Business Ideas

Lesson B: Listening to a Case Study and a Conversation
Creating a Commercial

Think and Discuss

1. Look at the photo and read the caption. What are these men doing?
2. Do you think these men work for themselves or for someone else? Explain.
3. Do you think they enjoy their work? Explain.

Maasai men selling *tanga*, or saris, and beaded objects on a Mombasa beach in front of five-star hotels

181

Exploring the Theme:
Entrepreneurs and New Businesses

Look at the photos and read the captions and statistics. Then discuss the questions.

1. What is an entrepreneur?
2. How many people around the world want to start a business?
3. How many of these businesses will actually be started?
4. Would you like to own your own business? Explain.

Becoming an Entrepreneur

Starting a new business is always a risk, and most people don't earn much income in their first years in business. For one thing, it's always difficult to compete with older businesses. To succeed, a business owner must learn to adapt very quickly when conditions change. This young woman from Cappadocia, Turkey, makes and sells dolls.

Around the world, many people dream of having their own business and being their own boss. These people are called **entrepreneurs**, and they want to use their skills and interests to make money. Don Tabor, the leading kite designer and entrepreneur in the United States, holds his Chevron 15 rainbow kite.

Tulip fields in Lisse, Holland, create a rainbow of colors. Millions of tulips are grown in Holland every year. Most of these are exported to other parts of the world.

Statistics about Entrepreneurs and Small Businesses

Statistics from an organization called Global Entrepreneurship Monitor:

- 12 percent of working people around the world are starting or running a new business.
- Worldwide, there are about 300 million people who want to start their own businesses.
- Of these ideas for new businesses, about 30 percent will actually be started. That's 137,000 new small businesses a day around the world!

Source: http://www.moyak.com/papers/business-startups-entrepreneurs.html

track **3-21** **A** | **Meaning from Context.** Read and listen to the article. Notice the words in blue. These are words you will hear and use in Lesson A.

INJAZ and Entrepreneurs

For university graduates in Egypt, finding their first job is a serious problem—it usually takes five years. Students say that there aren't enough jobs. But employers say that university graduates don't have the right skills to work in business or government offices.

A group called INJAZ is working to change this situation. Every year, INJAZ has a competition that teaches Egyptian students how to run a business. Teams of students make plans, start their own small companies as entrepreneurs, and try to earn a profit. At the end of the competition, a group of Egypt's top business leaders choose the best company. INJAZ was adapted from an American program called Junior Achievement.

Last year, nine teams in Cairo competed in the program. Some teams decided to sell a service. For example, Ahmed Youssry's company collected and recycled paper and glass from large businesses. Other teams developed a product. Nour Rafaat's company created a magazine for teenagers called *Did you know?* And Abdulhameed Ahmed's company created a special bag for carrying laptop computers. The back of the bag is hard, so you can also use it as a "lap desk" for your computer.

Starting a business always means taking a risk. The students must borrow money to start their companies and pay it back from the company's income. And only one team can win the prize. Last year, the judges chose Abdulhameed Ahmed's computer bags—they even bought some of the bags. But every INJAZ team is a winner because they learn the skills they need to succeed in business.

Source: http://www.pbs.org/frontlineworld/stories/egypt804/video/video_index.html

B | Work with a partner. Answer the questions below.

1. What do students do in this competition?
2. What do they learn?
3. Would a competition like this be popular in your country? Explain.

C | Write each word in blue from exercise **A** next to its definition. Use your dictionary to help you.

1. _____ (v.) made something new
2. _____ (n.) a chance that something bad will happen
3. _____ (n.) money that you earn
4. _____ (n.) people who start their own businesses
5. _____ (n.) an event where people try to win or get something
6. _____ (n.) money that you get when you sell something for more than it cost you
7. _____ (n.) useful abilities
8. _____ (n.) help or work that is sold by a company
9. _____ (v.) to get the result that you wanted
10. _____ (n.) something that is produced and sold

A | Read the information below and try to guess the correct answers.

What makes a successful entrepreneur?

We asked top business leaders for their opinions about successful entrepreneurs. Circle the numbers of the statements you think describe a successful entrepreneur. Be careful—the business leaders disagreed with three of these statements!

A successful entrepreneur . . .

1. has ideas for services that people need.

2. always enjoys taking risks.

3. expects his or her income to increase every year.

4. thinks that hard work is more important than good luck for success in business.

5. often has ideas for improving products.

6. enjoys competing with other people in business, sports, and all kinds of other activities.

7. thinks making a profit is always the most important thing in business.

8. has good "people skills" (such as listening, communicating, and understanding people).

9. adapts quickly to a new place or situation.

10. likes to create unusual solutions for problems.

B | Compare your answers from exercise **A** with a partner's. Then compare your answers to those of business experts at the bottom of page 187.

C | **Self-Reflection.** Underline the statements in the article in exercise **A** that are true about you.

D | **Discussion.** With a partner, discuss your answers in exercise **C**. Do you think you would be a successful entrepreneur? Explain.

Before Listening

A | **Using a Dictionary.** With a partner, guess the definitions of the words below. Then use your dictionary to check if your ideas were correct. Write the correct definition for each word.

florist (n.) _____   trade (v.) _____   wholesale (adj.) _____

B | **Predicting Content.** Listen to the first part of a PowerPoint lecture and complete the notes. What do you think the professor will talk about in the rest of the lecture? Share your ideas with your partner.

track 3-22

1. Disadvantages of small business:
   More difficult to _____
   Attitudes and personality _____
   can make a business fail.

   Advantage of small business:
   They can _____
   in the world and in the
   _____.

Listening: A PowerPoint Lecture

A | **Listening for Main Ideas.** Listen to the rest of the lecture. Check (✔) the main idea of the lecture.

track 3-23

❏ The Zappettinis' business has been successful because they could adapt to changes.
❏ Old businesses have more problems when business conditions change.
❏ The Zappettini family has one of the oldest flower businesses in California.

B | **Listening for Details.** Listen again and complete the notes for each slide.

track 3-23

2. The San Francisco Flower Mart opened in _____.
   Bill Zappettini is a _____ trader here.

3. In the year _____: Zappettini's father started the first family business- a flower _____.

4. 1926: The Zappettinis helped start the San Francisco Flower _____ Association to work for better _____.

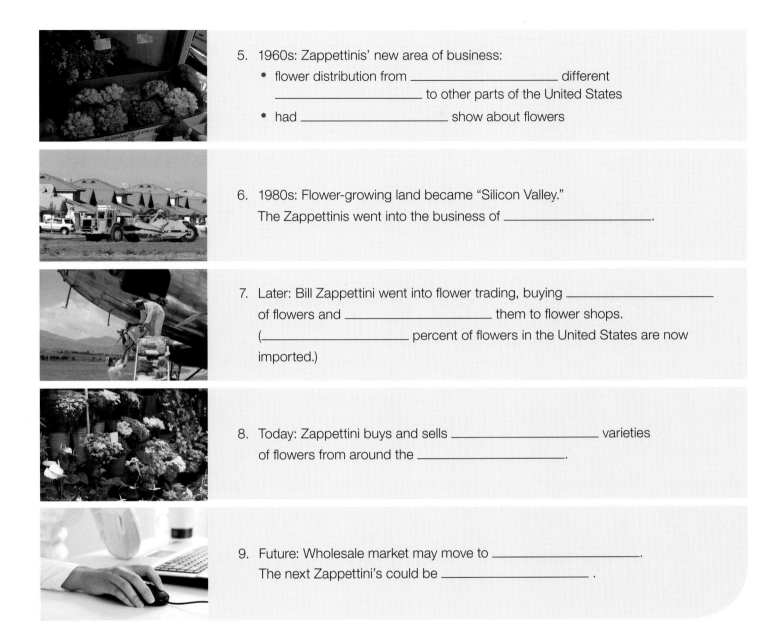

5. 1960s: Zappettinis' new area of business:
   * flower distribution from _____ different _____ to other parts of the United States
   * had _____ show about flowers

6. 1980s: Flower-growing land became "Silicon Valley." The Zappettinis went into the business of _____.

7. Later: Bill Zappettini went into flower trading, buying _____ of flowers and _____ them to flower shops. (_____ percent of flowers in the United States are now imported.)

8. Today: Zappettini buys and sells _____ varieties of flowers from around the _____.

9. Future: Wholesale market may move to _____. The next Zappettini's could be _____ .

After Listening

Critical Thinking. Discuss the questions with a partner. Then compare answers with the class.

1. In your opinion, what was the biggest change in the Zappettini family's business?
2. What are the pros and cons of working in a business with family members?
3. Would you like to own a business with your family? Explain.

Answers for exercise A on page 185: The business experts disagreed with 2, 3, and 7.

Grammar

A | **Prior Knowledge.** Read the sentences. Then <u>underline</u> the reasons why the Zappettinis did each thing.

1. The Zappettinis joined with other flower growers and formed the San Francisco Flower Growers Association in 1926 to work for better profits.

2. Mr. Zappettini talked about flowers as a part of everyday life in order to persuade people to buy more flowers from California.

The Infinitive of Purpose

We use the infinitive of purpose to give a reason for doing something.
> *Elias borrowed a lot of money* **to start** *his new business.*
> *You can watch American movies* **to improve** *your English.*

We also use the phrase *in order to* as an infinitive of purpose.
> **In order to get** *a good grade, John studied three hours for his test.*

An infinitive of purpose can come at the beginning or end of a sentence.
If it's at the beginning, it's followed by a comma.
> *They used signs on buses* **to advertise** *their products.*
> **To advertise** *their products, they used signs on buses.*

B | Rewrite the sentences in your notebook with the infinitive of purpose. Change the order.

1. To learn vocabulary words, I keep a notebook.
   I keep a notebook to learn vocabulary words.

2. In order to get to work by nine, I have to leave my house at eight fifteen.

3. To lose weight, I eat only fruit for breakfast.

4. I exercise three times a week to stay fit.

5. Ed took three computer classes to get a better job.

6. To improve your health, you should drink more water.

Flower fields near
Carlsbad, California, USA.

C | Self-Reflection. Write answers to the questions using the infinitive of purpose and your own reasons.

1. Why are you studying English? _I'm studying English to . . ._____ .
2. What is something you read recently? Why did you read it?_____ .
3. What kind of store did you go to most recently? What did you buy? _____ .
4. Where did you go on your last vacation or trip? Why did you go there?

   _____ .

5. Who have you called recently? Why did you call them? _____ .

D | Share your answers from exercise **C** with a partner. Ask questions to get more information and keep the conversation going.

> I went to Tokyo on my last vacation to visit my family.

> Really? How long were you there?

Language Function

Speculating about the Future

We use *may*, *might*, and *could* to talk about situations that are possible in the future.
> Latasha **may start** her own business after graduation.
> She **might sell** her T-shirt designs in stores.
> She **could be** very successful.

We use *may not* and *might not* (but not *could not*) to talk about things that will possibly not happen.
> ✔ Martin **may not/might not** go to college next year.
> ✗ Martin **could not** go to college next year.

A | What do you think these things will be like 10 years from now? Complete the sentences with your own ideas.

1. Computers might _____ .
2. Stores may _____ .
3. Cars might not _____ .
4. Businesses could _____ .
5. _____ may not _____ .
6. I might _____ .

B | Compare your ideas from exercise **A** with a partner's.

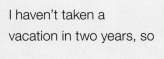 **C** | Listen to four people talk about future possibilities in their lives. Complete the missing information.

track 3-24

Brad

I haven't taken a vacation in two years, so _____, I _____. I'd really like to go to Rome and see the Colosseum.

Yumiko

_____ for a big company in Kyoto, but _____, I _____ with my brother.

Carlos

I don't know what I want to do _____ yet. I _____, or I _____ stay home _____.

Paula

I'm trying to decide what to do this summer. I'm a teacher, so I have three months off. I may take _____, or I _____ in Australia for a few weeks.

D | **Discussion.** Compare your answers from exercise **C** with a partner's. Notice the time expression each person uses to talk about the future. Discuss which possibilities you think are the most interesting.

E | **Self-Reflection.** Write some possibilities for your future using each of the time expressions below.

next fall: *Next fall, I might go to Brazil to visit my friend, Gabriella.*

next year: _____

in a few years: _____

Friday night: _____

this summer: _____

F | Share your sentences from exercise **E** with a partner. Ask questions to get more information about your partner's future possibilities.

> This summer, I may go to Montreal.

> Really? Have you ever been?

G | **Discussion.** Form a group with another pair of students. Take turns telling each other about your partner's most interesting future possibilities.

> Nelson might take a karate class this summer.

Discussing New Business Ideas

Critical Thinking Focus: Using Questions to Evaluate Information

One helpful way to evaluate information is to think of a list of questions about the topic. This will help you think about different aspects of the information.

 A | Form a group with two or three other students. Read the information about each new business below. Then discuss the questions below for each idea.

1. Is this a new idea, or are other companies already doing the same thing?
2. Would you buy this service or product? Explain.
3. What kind of people would use this product or service (e.g., men, women, high school students)?
4. Which of these businesses do you think will be most successful?

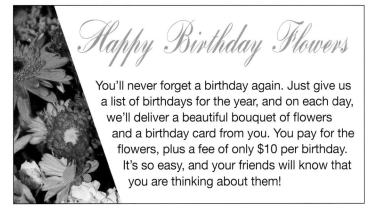

Happy Birthday Flowers

You'll never forget a birthday again. Just give us a list of birthdays for the year, and on each day, we'll deliver a beautiful bouquet of flowers and a birthday card from you. You pay for the flowers, plus a fee of only $10 per birthday. It's so easy, and your friends will know that you are thinking about them!

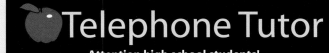

Telephone Tutor

Attention high school students!
Are you having trouble with your classes—especially math, science, or English?

We can help!

Call our special phone number, and our tutors will answer all your questions and explain your homework. Our tutors are all university students with top grades, and they're available every night from 8 p.m. to 2 a.m. Only $25 per hour, or try our special package: 10 hours for just $200.

Sun Showers
All-Natural Soap

You eat healthy, all-natural food—but do you use bath products that are full of chemicals? Our grandmothers used plants and flowers to make pure soap that smelled wonderful. We've found their old secret recipes, and we make our all-natural soap with plants from the mountains and forests of our country. We make five different kinds of soap—all good for your skin. A small luxury—only $20!

Restaurant Express

You're at home. It's late. You're hungry.
You want pizza, but your friend wants Chinese food, and you both want ice cream. What can you do?

Call us! We deliver food from 12 different restaurants, so you can eat exactly what you want. We'll be at your door in less than one hour. Pay a delivery fee of $1 for each menu item, plus $2 per restaurant. Service 6 p.m. until midnight, seven days a week.

 B | **Reporting to the Class.** As a group, tell the class about your answer to question 4 from exercise **A**. Give reasons for your answer.

Making a Deal in Fes

Shopkeepers and customers talk about prices.

The *souk* in the city of Fes is Morocco's oldest market.

Before Viewing

A | **Self-Reflection.** Read the statements below. Then check (✔) the statements that are true for your country.

1. All customers pay the same price for the same product. ❑
2. Shop owners spend a lot of time with their customers. ❑
3. You have to bargain to get a good price for a product. ❑
4. Most of the businesses are very small shops owned by families. ❑
5. Buyers and sellers don't talk very much together. ❑

B | **Discussion.** Compare your answers from exercise **A** with a partner's. Explain your answers.

While Viewing

A | Watch the video. Which of the statements from exercise **A** in the Before Viewing section are true for the *souk* in Fes? Underline them.

B | Watch the video again. Circle the words you hear.

1. Sales in the *souk* happen face-to-face; it's all very personal and very (slow/busy)!
2. In the *souk*, there really is something for (you/everyone).
3. In the *souk*, shopping is an exercise in (bargaining/business).
4. The carpet shop is where the sellers really pressure (customers/shoppers) to buy something.
5. There is one thing that all tourists should (look/watch) out for.
6. They shouldn't (pay/buy) too much!

C | Read the statements below. Then watch the video again and circle **T** for *true* or **F** for *false*.

1. In the *souk,* only the business owners decide   **T**   **F**
   the prices of the products.

2. Different customers might pay different prices   **T**   **F**
   for the same products.

3. Tourists are more successful at bargaining   **T**   **F**
   than Moroccans are.

4. Business owners and tourists think   **T**   **F**
   that bargaining is like a game.

5. Tourists sometimes buy too many things in the   **T**   **F**
   souk because they think the prices are cheap.

Many vendors in the *souk* serve their customers tea.

After Viewing

Critical Thinking. Form a group with two or three other students and discuss the questions.

1. What do you think the pros and cons of bargaining are?
2. What kinds of things do you think people should bargain for?
3. Think about the businesses you learned about in Lesson A. Do you think that bargaining could be a good way to sell any of those products or services? Explain.
4. If you were the owner of a small store, would you use bargaining in your store? Explain.
5. Do you think the vendors at the *souk* are successful entrepreneurs? Look back at the information on page 185. Which of the sentences do you think are probably true for the vendors at the *souk*? Explain.
6. In Lesson B, you are going to hear about a woman who started her own business selling beauty products. Do you think she uses bargaining to sell her products? Explain.

The shops in the *souk* sell everything a shopper could want.

A | **Meaning from Context.** Read and listen to the information. Notice the words in blue. These are words you will hear and use in Lesson B.

Why YOU need a business plan!

A business plan is your map to success. In it, you write down what you hope to achieve in your new business and how you will do it.

Your business plan should answer the following questions:

Your New Business

1. How big is the market for your service or product? How many people might be interested in it?

2. Who will your customers be? teenagers? young families? people who use computers?

3. How will you advertise your business and products to reach these people? Will you advertise online? in newspapers? on TV?

Your Money

4. What is your budget for your new business? How much money will you need for a store or office, a Web site, a computer, and other equipment?

5. How much is the potential income from your business? How much money do you expect to earn in the first three years?

6. Do you have enough money to start your business, or will you have to borrow money? Who might lend you this money? a bank? family or friends?

Your First Year

7. What do you want to achieve in your first year? For example, is your goal to sell 1000 pizzas or to have 10 new customers every week?

8. What problems do you predict in the first year? What action can you take to solve or prevent these problems?

B | Match each word in blue from exercise **A** with its definition. Use your dictionary to help you.

1. customer (n.) ___   a. to tell people about something in newspapers, TV, Web sites, etc.
2. advertise (v.) ___   b. a person who wants to buy something
3. borrow (n.) ___   c. to get money that you have to give back later
4. lend (v.) ___   d. possible in the future
5. predict (v.) ___   e. the number of people who want to buy a product
6. achieve (v.) ___   f. something that you hope to do
7. budget (n.) ___   g. to succeed in doing something after working hard
8. goal (n.) ___   h. to give money that you will get back later
9. market (n.) ___   i. a plan for spending money
10. potential (adj.) ___   j. to guess what will happen in the future

C | **Discussion.** With a partner, discuss the questions below.

1. Who is this brochure for?
2. What does it tell them to do?
3. Which questions would be the most difficult to answer? Why?

A | Complete the interview. Fill in each blank with the correct form of a word in **blue** from exercise **A** on page 194.

New Entrepreneur Interview: Andreas, from Germany

Interviewer: Tell us a little about your business.

Andreas: My brother and I are going to have an online store. We're going to sell soccer jerseys from national teams around the world—Brazil, Italy, Argentina . . .

Interviewer: Have you already started?

Andreas: No, because we don't have enough money yet. We need to _____ about 5000 Euros. I made a _____ so we know how much money we need for jerseys and a really good Web site.

Interviewer: Where are you going to get 5000 Euros?

Andreas: Our uncle is going to _____ us the money. We'll pay him back every month.

Interviewer: How will people find out about your products?

Andreas: We're going to _____ on the most popular sports news Web sites.

Interviewer: Do you think people will buy a jersey after they see only a small picture of it?

Andreas: Oh, I think there is definitely a big _____ for sports clothes. And soccer is the world's most popular sport. Our _____ will be young men and women who love soccer.

Interviewer: What do you hope to do with your business?

Andreas: Our _____ for the first year is to sell 5000 Euros of jerseys. I know that sounds like a lot, but we can _____ it if we really try. People buy a lot of things online. Jerseys aren't heavy, so they're easy to send in the mail. We have _____ customers all around the world!

Interviewer: Can you _____ any problems you might have in your business?

Andreas: Actually, I don't expect any problems!

B | Practice the interview from exercise **A** with a partner. Then switch roles and practice it again.

C | With your partner, look back at the information on business plans on page 194. Which questions did the entrepreneur answer? Which step didn't he do?

Before Listening

 Prior Knowledge. Look at the photo. Then discuss the questions below with a partner.

1. What is the woman in the photo doing? Why?
2. Do you think that businesses that sell beauty products make good profits? Explain.

Listening: A Case Study and a Conversation

🎧 track 3-26 **A** | **Listening for Main Ideas.** Listen to the case study and take notes to answer the questions. You do not have to write complete sentences.

1. What kind of business does Jie En run? _____
2. Who are her customers? _____
3. Why is her business successful? _____
4. Why is her experience important? _____

🎧 track 3-26 **B** | **Listening for Details.** Read the statements. Then listen again and circle **T** for *true* or **F** for *false*. Then correct the false statements to make them true.

1. The article is about a ~~17~~ 16 year-old-girl in Malaysia.	T	F
2. Jie En is a high school student.	T	F
3. Her profits are up to $150 a month.	T	F
4. She did surveys of all of her family members.	T	F
5. She recently hired an assistant.	T	F
6. In the future, she wants to study overseas.	T	F

👥 **C** | **Discussion.** With a partner, discuss the questions below.

1. What surprised you about Jie En?
2. Why do you think the professor told the class about this business?

🎧 track 3-27 **D** | Listen to two students talking about the case study. Complete the sentences.

1. I think she might ask about the _____ she talked about and how things are _____ in each place.
2. She may ask us about the names of all those _____ and their owners.
3. I think she'll ask about things the different companies did to be _____.
4. She could ask us to write a _____ _____.

🎧 track 3-27 **E** | Listen to the conversation again. Circle the sentence in exercise **D** that the students agree about.

After Listening

A | Form a group with two or three other students. Discuss the situation and question below.

> **Situation:** Imagine you are students in a business class and you are going to take a test on the different businesses you have learned about in this unit. What kinds of questions do you think a professor might include on the test? Write your ideas in your notebook.

B | Share your group's ideas with the rest of the class.

Pronunciation

track 3-28

> ### Thought Groups
>
> In English, we use thought groups when we speak. Thought groups are groups of words that form an idea or thought. Thought groups are marked by very small pauses. Usually there is one stressed word in each thought group. Using thought groups makes it easier for listeners to understand information.
>
> Here are some examples with slashes (/) to show the thought groups and **bold** to show the stressed words.
>
> Our **neighbor** next door / has a **big** brown dog.
>
> After my **class** / I'm going **grocery** shopping.
>
> Finally, after an **hour** / the **bus** arrived.
>
> On **Sundays** / we usually go **hiking** / in the **park** near our house.

track 3-29

A | Listen to the sentences. Mark the thought groups with slashes /.

1. My oldest friend/has been living in my neighborhood/for 15 years.
2. Josh and I are going home after lunch.
3. She started a business last year when she graduated from technical college.
4. You have to speak in English for five minutes to pass the test.
5. There's a beautiful red bird singing in the tree.
6. There's an article in the newspaper about the 16-year-old girl in Malaysia.
7. Her experiences can teach us a lot about business success.
8. She might study business when she goes to college.

B | Practice reading the sentences in exercise **A** to a partner.

Grammar

The Present Perfect Tense

We form the present perfect with *have* or *has* + the past participle of a verb.
> They **have owned** that store for ten years.

We use the present perfect to talk about:

- actions or situations that began in the past and continue until now.
  > Lydia **has worked** since she was 15 years old. (She works now.)
- actions or situations that have happened several times already.
  > I **have sold** the new model four times.
- actions or situations that happened at some time in the past and are connected with the present.
  > We **have** never **gone** to a small business convention before, so we want to go to one.

We use the present perfect with *just* and *already* to talk about actions that happened recently.
> I've **just** found the order form. Frank has **already** completed it.

We use the present perfect with *yet* to talk about actions we expect to happen very soon.
> But the boss hasn't approved it **yet**.

A | Complete the sentences below with the present perfect using the verb in parentheses.

1. My class ___has ended___ (end), so I can talk to you now.
2. Susan _____ (be) to Istanbul. She says it's a very interesting city.
3. My family _____ (live) in this city for three years.
4. The instructor _____ (give) us three quizzes and one exam this month.
5. We _____ (be) best friends since the day we met.
6. I _____ (have) lunch already, but I'd like some tea, please.

B | Match each question or statement with the correct response.

Questions/Statements	Responses
1. Has anyone seen the order form? ____	a. Yes. I've already told her.
2. Have you cleaned out the warehouse? ____	b. No, I haven't. I'm going to do it this afternoon before the shipment arrives.
3. I haven't placed the new order yet. ____	c. It was here two minutes ago.
4. Have you had lunch? ____	d. Well, ask the new assistant to do it today.
5. You look really tired. ____	e. No, I haven't. Let's order some sandwiches.
6. Does our boss know about the accident? ____	f. Yes, I am. I've been working double shifts for days.

Language Function

Using the Present Perfect to Start Conversations

We often use questions in the present perfect when we want to start
a conversation or help keep a conversation going.

Sue: So, **have** you **seen** any good movies lately?

Bob: Yes, I saw a great one last week.

Kim: How long **have** you **known** Sandy?

Nadia: Oh, we**'ve known** each other since we were six.

Greg: **Have** you ever **been** to this restaurant before?

Ana: No, but I hear the food is delicious.

 A | **Brainstorming.** With a partner, brainstorm a list of topics you can use to start a
conversation (e.g., English class, books, movies, sports games, etc.). Write your ideas in
your notebook.

B | **Discussion.** Stand up. Find a student you do not talk to very often. Practice starting a
conversation using a question in the present perfect and the topics you brainstormed in
exercise **A**. Then find another student and start a new conversation. Continue until your
teacher tells you to stop.

C | **Reporting to the Class.** Tell the class some interesting information you learned about
your classmates.

> Marco has been to the movies
> three times this week.

Student to Student: Giving Compliments

We often want to say something nice to someone, but giving compliments can be
difficult. Shy people may not accept compliments easily. Other people might not think
your compliments are sincere.

Here are some tips for giving compliments.

1. Tell the person what they did and why you liked it.
   I was very interested to hear that small businesses can be very successful.

2. Give specific examples or reasons.
   I liked the way you compared the two kinds of businesses in your presentation.
   It was easy to follow and very interesting.

 D | Form a group with two or three other students. Read the information in the Student to
Student box. Then practice giving compliments to your classmates.

You are going to create a commercial to advertise a new product. Then you will role-play your commercial to the class.

 A | Collaboration. Form a group with two or three other students. Read the information. Then follow the steps below.

> **Situation:** You are a team of entrepreneurs. You are working together to create a TV commercial to advertise your new product.

1. Decide what your new product is. Use one of the ideas below or your own idea.
   - a housecleaning product (dishwashing soap, laundry detergent, etc.)
   - a new kind of food or drink (tea, coffee, breakfast cereal, an energy drink, etc.)
   - a new kind of technology (a new phone, computer, etc.)
   - a beauty or personal care product (shampoo, skin cream, make up, toothpaste, etc.)
   - a health product (vitamins, running shoes, a health club, etc.)
2. Choose a name for your product.
3. Brainstorm the benefits of your product. Why is it better than other similar products? How will it help people? Why should people buy it?
4. Look at your list of benefits from step 3 and choose your best ideas.
5. Plan your TV commercial. All the members of your group should be involved. Use the example below to help you. Practice role-playing your commercial.

> **Mike:** Hey! What are you doing?
>
> **Miriam:** I'm cleaning my apartment.
>
> **Mike:** But why? Aren't we going out?
>
> **Miriam:** I bought this new product, Jiffy Clean. And I just can't stop cleaning. I've used it in the kitchen, in the bathroom, on my TV, and bookshelves. Even in the refrigerator!
>
> **Mike:** Well, that's good. Your apartment was getting dirty.
>
> **Miriam:** I know, but now I have Jiffy Clean, so it will never be dirty again.
>
> **Mike:** But are we going out . . . ?

 B | Role-Playing. Role-play your commercial for the class.

 C | Practice giving your classmates compliments using the information from page 199.

Presentation Skills: Showing Enthusiasm for Your Topic

If you have *enthusiasm* for something, it means you are interested and excited about it. When you show enthusiasm for the topic you are presenting or role-playing, your audience will be more interested in your topic, too. You can show enthusiasm with facial expressions, body language, and intonation.

Overview

The *Independent Student Handbook* is a resource that you can use at different points and in different ways during this course. You may want to read the entire handbook at the beginning of the class as an introduction to the skills and strategies you will develop and practice throughout the book. Reading it at the beginning will provide you with another tool to understand the material.

Use the *Independent Student Handbook* throughout the course in the following ways:

Additional instruction: You can use the *Independent Student Handbook* to provide a little more instruction on a particular skill that you are practicing in the units. In addition to putting all the skills instruction in one place, the *Independent Student Handbook* includes additional suggestions and strategies. For example, if you find you're having trouble following academic lectures, you can refer to the Improving Your Listening Skills section to review signal phrases that help you to understand the speaker's flow of ideas.

Independent work: You can use the *Independent Student Handbook* to help you when you are working on your own. For example, if you want to improve your vocabulary, you can follow some of the suggestions in the Building Your Vocabulary section.

Source of specific tools: A third way to use the *Independent Student Handbook* is as a source of specific tools, such as outlines, graphic organizers, and checklists. For example, if you are preparing a presentation, you might want to use the Research Checklist as you research your topic. Then you might want to complete the Presentation Outline to organize your information. Finally, you might want to use the Presentation Checklist to help you be a more effective speaker.

Table of Contents

Formal Listening Skills

Predicting

Speakers giving formal talks or lectures usually begin by introducing themselves and then introducing their topic. Listen carefully to the introduction of the topic, and try to anticipate what you will hear.

Strategies:

- Use visual information including titles on the board, on slides, or in a PowerPoint presentation.
- Think about what you already know about the topic.
- Ask questions that you think the speaker might answer.
- Listen for specific phrases.

Identifying the Topic:

Today, I'm going to talk about . . .
Our topic today is . . .
Let's look at . . .
Tonight we're talking about . . .

Understanding the Structure of the Presentation

An organized speaker will use certain expressions to alert you to the important information that will follow. Notice the signal words and phrases that tell you how the presentation is organized and the relationship between the main ideas.

Introduction

A good introduction includes something like a thesis statement, which identifies the topic and gives an idea of how the lecture or presentation will be organized.

Introduction (Topic + Organization):

I'll be talking about . . .   *My topic is . . .*
There are basically two groups . . .   *There are three reasons . . .*
Several factors contribute to this . . .   *There are five steps in this process . . .*

Body

In the body of the lecture, the speaker will usually expand upon the topic presented in the introduction. The speaker will use phrases that tell you the order of events or subtopics and their relationship to each other. For example, the speaker may discuss several examples or reasons.

Following the Flow of Ideas in the Body:

The first/next/final (point) is . . .   *First/next/finally, let's look at . . .*
Another reason is . . .   *However, . . .*
As a result, . . .   *For example, . . .*

Conclusion

In a conclusion, the speaker often summarizes what has already been said and may discuss what it means or make predictions or suggestions. For example, if a speaker is talking about an environmental problem, he or she may end by suggesting what might happen if we don't solve the problem, or by adding his or her own opinion. Sometimes speakers ask a question in the conclusion to get the audience to think more about the topic.

> **Restating/Concluding:**
>
> *As you can see, . . .*   *In conclusion, . . .*
> *In summary, . . .*   *To sum up, . . .*
> *At the end, . . .*

Listening for Main Ideas

It's important to tell the difference between a speaker's main ideas and the supporting details. In school, a professor often will test a student's understanding of the main ideas more than of specific details. Often a speaker has one main idea, just like a writer does, and several examples and details that support the main idea.

Strategies:

- Listen for a statement of a main idea at the end of the introduction.
- Listen for rhetorical questions, or questions that the speaker asks, and then answers. Often the answer is the statement of the main idea.
- Notice ideas that are repeated or rephrased.

> **Repetition/Rephrasing:**
>
> *I'll say this again . . .*   *So again, let me repeat . . .*
> *What you need to know is . . .*   *The most important point is . . .*
> *Let me say it in another way . . .*

Listening for Details (Examples)

A speaker will often provide examples that support a main idea. A good example can help you understand and remember the main idea better.

Strategies:

- Listen for specific phrases that introduce an example.
- Notice if an example comes after a general statement the speaker has given or is leading into a general statement.
- If there are several examples, decide if they all support the same idea or are different parts of the idea.

Giving Examples:

The first example is . . .

Here's an example of what I mean . . .

For instance, . . .

Let me give you an example . . .

For example, . . .

. . . such as . . .

Listening for Details (Reasons)

Speakers often give reasons or list causes and/or effects to support their ideas.

Strategies:

- Notice nouns that might signal causes/reasons (e.g., *factors, influences, causes, reasons*) or effects/results (e.g., *effects, results, outcomes, consequences*).
- Notice verbs that might signal causes/reasons (e.g., *contribute to, affect, influence, determine, produce, result in*) or effects/results (often these are passive, e.g., *is affected by*).
- Listen for specific phrases that introduce reasons/causes and effects/results.

Giving Causes or Reasons:

The first reason is . . .

This is because . . .

This is due to . . .

This is very important because . . .

Giving Effects or Results:

As a result . . .

Consequently . . .

Another effect is . . .

One consequence is . . .

Therefore, . . .

Understanding Meaning from Context

Speakers may use words that are new to you, or you may not understand exactly what they've said. In these situations, you can guess at the meaning of a particular word or fill in the gaps of what you've understood by using the context or situation itself.

Strategies:

- Don't panic. You don't always understand every word of what a speaker says in your first language either.
- Use context clues to fill in the blanks. What did you understand just before or just after the missing part? What did the speaker probably say?
- Listen for words and phrases that signal a definition or explanation.

Giving Definitions:

. . . which means . . .

What that means is . . .

Or . . .

In other words . . .

Another way to say that is . . .

That is . . .

Recognizing a Speaker's Bias

Speakers often have an opinion about the topic they are discussing. It's important for you to understand if they are objective or subjective about the topic. Being subjective means having a bias or a strong feeling about something. Objective speakers do not express an opinion.

Strategies:

- Notice words like adjectives, adverbs, and modals that the speaker uses (e.g., *ideal, horribly, should, shouldn't*).
- Listen to the speaker's voice. Does he or she sound excited, happy, or bored?
- When presenting another point of view on the topic, is that other point of view given much less time and attention by the speaker?
- Listen for words that signal opinions.

Opinions:

I think . . .

In my opinion . . .

Here's what I believe is happening . . .

Making Inferences

Sometimes a speaker doesn't state information or opinions directly, but instead suggests them indirectly. When you draw a conclusion about something that is not directly stated, you make an inference. For example, if the speaker says he or she grew up in Spain, you might infer that he or she speaks Spanish. When you make inferences, you may be very sure about your conclusions, or you may be less sure. It's important to use information the speaker states directly to support your inferences.

Strategies:

- Note information that provides support for your inference. For example, you might note that the speaker lived in Spain.
- Note information that does not support your inference. For example, the speaker says she was born in Spain (maybe she speaks Spanish) but moved away when she was two (maybe she doesn't speak Spanish). Which evidence is stronger—the evidence for or against your inference?
- If you're less than certain about your inference, use words to soften your language such as modals, adverbs, and quantifiers.

She very probably speaks Spanish, and she may also prefer Spanish food. Many people from Spain are familiar with bull-fighting.

Summarizing or Condensing

When taking notes, you should write down only the most important ideas of the lecture. To take good notes quickly:

- Write down only the key words. You don't need complete sentences.

  ~~In~~ Okinawa, ~~people have~~ very low rates ~~of~~ cancer and heart disease compared to Americans. One ~~of the~~ reasons ~~for this is~~ Ikigai, ~~a Japanese word which translates to~~ "reason for living."

- Use abbreviations (short forms) and symbols when possible.

  info = information   dr = doctor   w/ with   < = less than / fewer than   > = more than
  b/c + because   = / → = leads to causes   1/4 = one-fourth

Recognizing Organization

When you listen to a speaker, you practice the skill of noticing that speaker's organization. As you get in the habit of recognizing the organizational structure, you can use it to structure your notes in a similar way. Review the signal words and phrases from the Improving Your Listening Skills section.

Some basic organizational structures (and where they are often used):

- Narrative (often used in history or literature)
- Process (almost any field, but especially in the sciences)
- Cause and Effect (history, psychology, sociology)
- Classification (any field, including art, music, literature, sciences, history)
- Problem and Solution

Using Graphic Organizers

Graphic organizers can be very useful tools if you want to rewrite your notes. Once you've identified the speaker's organizational structure, you can choose the best graphic organizer to show the ideas. See the Resources section starting on page 214 in this handbook for more information.

Distinguishing between Relevant and Irrelevant Information

Remember that not everything a speaker says is important. A lecturer or presenter will usually signal important information you should take notes on.

> *This is important . . .*
> *The one thing you want to remember . . .*
>
> *Let me say again . . .*
> *Write this down . . .*

Instructors and other lecturers may also signal when to stop taking notes.

> **Signals to Stop Taking Notes:**
> *You don't have to write all this down. . . .*
> *You can find this in your handout. . . .*
>
> *This information is in your book. . . .*
> *This won't be on your test. . . .*

In a similar way, they may let you know when they are going to discuss something off-topic.

> **Understanding Sidetracks:**
> *That reminds me . . .*
> *This is off the subject, but . . .*
> *On a different topic . . .*
>
> *By the way . . .*
> *As an aside . . .*

Recognizing a Return to a Previous Topic

When a speaker makes a sidetrack and talks about something that is not directly related to the main topic, he or she will often signal a return to a previous topic.

> **Returning to a Previous Topic:**
> *So, just to restate . . .*
> *Back to . . .*
> *Getting back to what we were saying . . .*
> *To return to what we were talking about earlier . . .*
> *OK, so to get back on topic . . .*
> *To continue . . .*

Using Notes Effectively

It's important to not only take good notes, but to use them in the most effective or helpful way.

Strategies:

- Go over your notes after class to review and to add information you might have forgotten to write down.
- Compare notes with a classmate or study group to make sure you have all the important information.
- Review your notes before the next class so you will understand and remember the new information better.

Independent Vocabulary Learning Tips

Keep a vocabulary journal

- If a new word is useful, write it in a special notebook. Also write a short definition (in English if possible) and the sentence or situation where you found the word (its context). Write a sentence that uses the word.
- Carry your vocabulary notebook with you at all times. Review the words whenever you have a free minute.
- Choose vocabulary words that will be useful to you. Some words are rarely used.

Experiment with new vocabulary

- Think about new vocabulary in different ways. For example, look at all the words in your vocabulary journal and make a list of only the verbs. Or list the words according to the number of syllables (one-syllable words, two-syllable words, and so on).
- Use new vocabulary to write a poem, a story, or an email message to a friend.
- Use an online dictionary to listen to the pronunciation of new words. If possible, make a list of words that rhyme. Brainstorm words that are related to a single topic and that begin with the same sound (*student, study, school, skills, strategies, studious*).

Use new words as often as possible

- You will not know a new vocabulary word after hearing or reading it once. You need to remember the word several times before it enters your long-term memory.
- The way you use an English word—in which situations and with which other words—might be different from a similar word in your first language. If you use your new vocabulary often, you're more likely to discover the correct way to use it.

Use vocabulary organizers

- Label pictures.

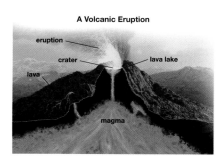

A Volcanic Eruption

- Make word maps.

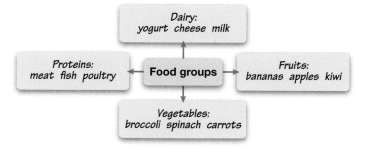

- Make personal flashcards. Write the words you want to learn on one side. Write the definition and/or an example sentence on the other.

Prefixes and Suffixes

Use prefixes and suffixes to guess the meaning of unfamiliar words and to expand your vocabulary. Prefixes usually change the meaning of a word somewhat. Suffixes usually change the part of speech.

Prefix	Meaning	Example
a-	completely	awake
bi-	two	bilingual, bicycle
dis-	not, negation, removal	disappear, disease
pre-	before	preserve, predict
mis-	bad, badly, incorrectly	misunderstand, misjudge
re-	again	research
un-	not, the opposite of	unhappy, unusual

The following are derivational suffixes that change the part of speech of the base word.

Suffix	Meaning	Example
-able	adjective	available
-al	adjective	mental, controversial
-ary	noun	summary
-ent/-ant	adjective	different, significant
-ful	adjective	beautiful, successful
-ed	adjective	endangered, interested
-ical	adjective	logical, psychological
-ize	verb	summarize, memorize
-ment	noun	attachment
-tion	noun	information
-ous	adjective	dangerous

Dictionary Skills

The dictionary listing for a word usually provides the following helpful information:

Synonyms
A synonym is a word that means the same thing (e.g., *significantly—importantly*). Use synonyms to expand your vocabulary.

Word Families
These are the words that have the same stem or base word but have different prefixes or suffixes.

Different Meanings of the Same Word
Many words have several meanings and several parts of speech. The example sentences in a word's dictionary entry can help you figure out which meaning you need.

Collocations
Dictionary entries often provide collocations, or words that are often used with the target word.

Everyday Communication

Summary of Useful Phrases for Everyday Communication

It's important to practice speaking English every day with your teacher, your classmates, and anyone else you can find. This chart lists phrases you can use to perform each communication task—from more formal phrases to less formal.

Getting Clarification
Could you explain what the professor said?
What did the professor mean by that?
Did you catch what the professor said about that?
Did you understand that?
I still don't understand.
Could you explain . . . ?
So what you mean is . . . ?

Agreeing
That's my opinion also.
I think so, too.
I totally agree.
You're right about that.
Right!

Disagreeing
I'm afraid I have to disagree.
I see your point, but . . .
I see what you mean, but . . .
I'm not so sure about that.
I disagree.
No way.

Inviting
Would you like to get a cup of coffee/go have lunch?
Do you have time before your next class?
Are you doing anything now/after class?
What are you doing now?

Showing Surprise
That's unbelievable/incredible.
You're kidding!
Wow!
Really?
Seriously?

Making Suggestions
I recommend/suggest . . .
Why don't I/you/we . . .
Let's . . .

Expressing Thanks and Appreciation
Thank you so much for . . . (e.g., finding it).
Thank you for . . . (e.g., the good advice).
I really appreciate your . . . (e.g., doing that).
I really appreciate your . . . (e.g., help).
Thanks for . . .

Responding to Thanks
You're very welcome.
You're welcome.
No problem.
Any time.

Refusing
Thank you, but (I have other plans/I'm busy tonight/I'd rather not/etc.).
I wish I could, but (I don't have a car/I have a class at that time/etc.).
I'm sorry, I can't.
Maybe some other time.

Voicing a Small Problem
Actually, that's a problem for me because . . .
I hate to say it, but . . .
It's no big deal, but . . .

Congratulating
That sounds great!
Congratulations!
I'm so happy for you.
Well-done!
Good for you!
Way to go!

Expressing Sympathy
Oh, no, I'm sorry to hear that.
That's really too bad.

Asking for Repetition	Making Suggestions
I'm sorry?	*We could . . .*
I didn't catch what you said.	*Why don't you . . .*
What's that?	*I recommend . . .*
I missed that.	*I suggest that you . . .*
	Let's . . .
Staying Neutral	**Asking Sensitive Questions**
Either one is fine with me.	*I hope this isn't too personal, but . . .*
I don't really have a preference.	*Do you mind if I ask . . .*
I can understand both points of view.	*Would you mind telling me . . .*
I think you both make good points.	*Can I ask . . .*
Clarifying	**Interrupting**
What I mean is . . .	*Can/Could/May I stop you for a second?*
Let me explain . . .	*Can/Could/May I interrupt?*
Expressing Understanding	**Giving opinions**
That makes sense.	*I think . . .*
I see your point.	*I feel . . .*
I follow.	*My feeling is . . .*
That's a good point.	*If you ask me . . .*

Doing Group Projects

You will often have to work with a group on activities and projects. It can be helpful to assign group members certain roles. These roles should change every time you do a new activity. Here is a description of some common roles:

Group Leader—Makes sure the assignment is done correctly and all group members participate. Ask questions: *What do you think? Does anyone have another idea?*

Secretary—Takes notes on the group's ideas (including a plan for sharing the work).

Manager—During the planning and practice phases, the manager makes sure the presentation can be given within the time limit. If possible, practice the presentation from beginning to end and time it.

Expert—Understands the topic well; asks and answers audience questions after the presentation. Make a list of possible questions ahead of time to be prepared.

Coach—Reminds group members to perform their assigned roles in the group work.

Note that group members have one of these roles in addition to their contribution to the presentation content and delivery.

Classroom Presentation Skills

Library Research

If you can go to a public library or school library, start there. You don't have to read whole books. Parts of books, magazines, newspapers, and even videos are all possible sources of information. A librarian can help you find both print and online sources of information.

Online Research

The Internet is an easy source of a lot of information, but it has to be looked at carefully. Many Web sites are commercial and may have incomplete, inaccurate, or biased information.

Finding reliable sources

Strategies:

- Your sources of information need to be reliable. Think about the author and the publisher. Ask yourself, "What is their point of view? Can I trust this information?"

- Your sources need to be well respected. For example, an article from a journal of medical news will probably be more respected than an article from a popular magazine.

- Start with Web sites with *.edu* or *.org* endings. Those are usually educational or non-commercial Web sites. Many *.com* Web sites also have good information, for example www.nationalgeographic.com or www.britannica.com.

Finding information that is appropriate for your topic

- Look for up-to-date information, especially in fields that change often such as technology or business. For Internet sources, look for recent updates to the Web sites.

- Most of the time, you'll need to find more than one source of information. Find sources that are long enough to contain some good information, but not so long that you won't have time to read them.

- Think about the source's audience. If it's written for computer programmers, for example, you might not be able to understand it. If it's written for university students who need to buy a new computer, it's more likely to be understandable.

Speaking Clearly and Comprehensibly

It's important that your audience actually understands what you are saying for your presentation to be effective.

Strategies:

- Practice your presentation many times in front of at least one other person and ask him or her for feedback.

- Make sure you know the correct pronunciation of every word—especially the ones you will say more than once. Look them up online or ask your instructor for the correct pronunciation.

- Try to use thought groups. Keep these words together: long subjects, verbs and objects, clauses, prepositional phrases. Remember to pause slightly at all punctuation and between thought groups.

- Speak loudly enough so everyone can hear.

- Stop occasionally to ask your audience if they can hear you and follow what you are saying.

Demonstrating Knowledge of Content

You should know more about your subject than you actually say in your presentation. Your audience may have questions, or you may need to explain something in more detail than you planned. Knowing a lot about your subject will allow you to present well and feel more confident.

Strategies:

- Practice, practice, practice.
- Don't read your notes.
- Say more than is on your visuals.
- Tell your audience what the visuals mean.

Phrases to Talk about Visuals:

This graph/diagram shows/explains . . .
The line/box represents . . .
The main point is that . . .
You can see . . .
From this we can see . . .

Engaging the Audience

Presenting is an important skill. If your audience isn't interested in what you have to say, then your message is lost.

Strategies:

- Introduce yourself.
- Make eye contact. Look around at different people in the audience.
- Use good posture. *Posture* means how you hold your body. When you speak in front of the class, you should stand up straight on both feet. Hold your hands together in front of your waist if you aren't holding notes. This shows that you are confident and well prepared.
- Pause to check understanding. When you present ideas, it's important to find out if your audience understands you. Look at the faces of people in the audience. Do they look confused? Use the expressions from the box below to check understanding.

Phrases to Check for Understanding:

Do you know what I mean?
Is that clear?
Does that make sense?
Do you have any questions?
Do you understand?

Understanding and Using Visuals: Graphic Organizers

T-Chart

Purpose: Compare or contrast two things or list aspects of two things. We often write good things (pros) on one side and bad things or problems (cons) on the other. This can help people make choices.

Advantages of dams	Disadvantages of dams
Provides water for cities	*Might cover historical areas*

Venn Diagram

Purpose: Show differences and similarities between two things, sometimes three. The outer sections show differences.

This information represents information that is true for both earthquakes and volcanoes.

This area represents information that is true for volcanoes.

This area represents information that is true for earthquakes.

Volcanoes — *magma erupts*

occur along the edges of tectonic plates

Earthquakes — *earth shakes*

Grid

Purpose: Organize information about several things. Grids can show information in different groups, different time periods, different processes or different qualities.

Boundary Type	Convergent		Transform
Movement	Plates come together; one plate can move under or over another.	Plates move apart.	
Results		A body of water can form between the two plates.	

Flow Chart

Purpose: Show the stages in a process, or a cause-and-effect chain. Flow charts have many different shapes. Each step or box follows another in a specific time order.

The Memory Process

Sensory Information → Short-Term Memory → Long-Term Memory

Timeline

Purpose: Show the order of events and when they happened in time. Timelines start with the oldest point on the left. Timelines are frequently used to show important events in someone's life or in a larger historical context.

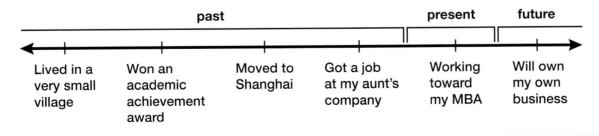

past				present	future
Lived in a very small village	Won an academic achievement award	Moved to Shanghai	Got a job at my aunt's company	Working toward my MBA	Will own my own business

Reading Maps, Graphs, and Diagrams

Maps are used to show geographical information.

The **labels** on a map show important places mentioned in a reading or listening passage.

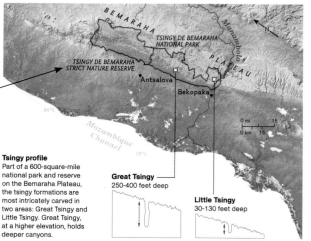

The **key** or **legend** explains specific information about the map. This legend shows the location of Madagascar and the Tsingy de Bemaraha National Park.

Tsingy profile
Part of a 600-square-mile national park and reserve on the Bemaraha Plateau, the tsingy formations are most intricately carved in two areas: Great Tsingy and Little Tsingy. Great Tsingy, at a higher elevation, holds deeper canyons.

Great Tsingy
250-400 feet deep

Little Tsingy
30-130 feet deep

Bar and **line graphs** use axes to show the relationship between two or more things.

Bar graphs compare amounts and numbers.

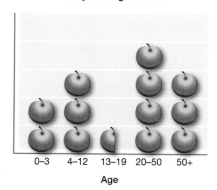

Daily Servings of Fruit

0–3   4–12   13–19   20–50   50+
Age

Line graphs show a change over time.

The **y axis** shows the amount of sugar people eat in pounds.

Sugar Use

Pounds of Sugar

160
140
120
100
80
60
40
20
0

1950 1960 1970 1980 1990 2000
Year

The **x axis** shows the year.

Pie charts show percents of a whole, or something that is made up of several parts.

This section shows that this family spends the most money on meat and fish.

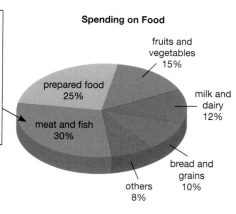

Spending on Food

fruits and vegetables 15%
prepared food 25%
milk and dairy 12%
meat and fish 30%
bread and grains 10%
others 8%

Diagrams are a helpful way to show how a process or system works.

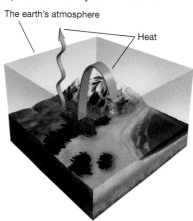

The earth's atmosphere

Heat

Presentation Outline

When you are planning a presentation, you may find it helpful to use an outline. If it is a group presentation, the outline can provide an easy way to divide the content. For example, someone could do the introduction, another student the first main idea in the body, and so on.

1. **Introduction**

   Topic: _____

   Hook/attention getter: _____

   Thesis statement: _____

   _____

2. **Body**

   First step/example/reason: _____

   Supporting details: _____

   _____

   _____

   Second step/example/reason: _____

   Supporting details: _____

   _____

   _____

   Third step/example/reason: _____

   Supporting details: _____

   _____

   _____

3. **Conclusion**

   Major points to summarize: _____

   _____

   Any implications/suggestions/predictions: _____

   _____

   Closing comment/summary: _____

   _____

Research Checklist

☐ Do I have three to five sources for information in general—and especially for information I'm using without a specific citation?

☐ Am I correctly citing information when it comes from just one or two sources?

☐ Have I noted all sources properly, including page numbers?

☐ When I am not citing a source directly, am I using adequate paraphrasing (e.g., a combination of synonyms, different word forms, and/or different grammatical structure)?

☐ Are my sources reliable?

Presentation Checklist

☐ Have I practiced several times?

☐ Did I get feedback from a peer?

☐ Have I timed the presentation?

☐ Do I introduce myself?

☐ Do I maintain eye contact?

☐ Do I explain my visuals?

☐ Do I pause sometimes and check for understanding?

☐ Do I use correct pronunciation?

☐ Am I using appropriate volume so that everyone can hear?

☐ Do I have good posture?

Pair and Group-Work Checklist

☐ Do I make eye contact with others?

☐ Do I pay attention when someone else is talking?

☐ Do I make encouraging sounds or comments?

☐ Do I ask for clarification when I don't understand something?

☐ Do I check for understanding?

☐ Do I clarify what I mean?

☐ Do I express agreement and disagreement politely?

☐ Do I make suggestions when helpful?

☐ Do I participate as much as my classmates?

☐ Do I ask my classmates for their ideas?

Summary of Signal Phrases

Identifying the Topic:
Today, I'm going to talk about . . .
Our topic today is . . .
Let's look at . . .

Introduction (Topic + Organization):
I'll be talking about . . .
My topic is . . .
There are basically two groups . . .
There are three reasons . . .
Several factors contribute to this . . .
There are five steps in this process . . .

Following the Flow of Ideas:
The first/next/final (point) is . . .
Another reason is . . .
However, . . .
As a result, . . .
For example, . . .

Restating/Concluding:
As you can see, . . .
In conclusion, . . .
In summary, . . .
To sum up, . . .

Repetition/Rephrasing:
I'll say this again . . .
So again, let me repeat . . .
What you need to know is . . .
The most important thing to know is . . .
Let me say it in another way . . .

Giving Examples:
The first example is . . .
Let me give you an example . . .
Here's an example of what I mean . . .

Giving Causes or Reasons:
The first reason is . . .
This is due to . . .
This is because . . .

Giving Effects or Results:
As a result . . .
One consequence is . . .
Consequently, . . .
Therefore, . . .
Another effect is . . .

Giving Definitions:
. . . which means . . .
In other words, . . .
What that means is . . .
Another way to say that is . . .
Or . . .
That is . . .

Opinions:
I think . . .
In my opinion, . . .
Here's what I believe is happening . . .
If you ask me . . .
I feel . . .

Signal to Stop Taking Notes:
You don't have to write all this down . . .
This information is in your book . . .
You can find this in your handout . . .
This won't be on your test . . .

Returning to a Previous Topic:
So, just to restate . . .
Back to . . .
Getting back to what we were saying . . .
To return to what we were talking about earlier . . .
OK, so to get back on topic . . .
To continue . . .

Understanding Sidetracks:
That reminds me . . .
By the way . . .
This is off the subject, but . . .
As an aside . . .
On a different topic . . .

Phrases to Check for Understanding:
Do you know what I mean?
Is that clear?
Does that make sense?
Do you have any questions?
Do you understand?

*These words are on the Academic Word List (AWL). The AWL is a list of the 570 highest-frequency academic word families that regularly appear in academic texts. The list was compiled by researcher Averil Coxhead based on her analysis of a 3.5 million word corpus (Coxhead, 2000).

conversations, 19, 20, 26, 30, 36, 40, 48, 90, 159, 177, 179

critical thinking and, 31, 51, 98

descriptions, 153

discussion, 1, 2–3, 5, 7, 12, 13, 16, 17, 20, 21, 22–23, 25, 29, 31, 33, 35, 37, 40, 45, 46, 47, 53, 55, 57, 59, 62–63, 64–65, 65, 68, 69, 73, 74, 75, 76, 78, 79, 82–83, 85, 86, 87, 88, 90, 91, 93, 94, 96, 97, 98, 100, 105, 106, 107, 108, 109, 110, 113, 116, 118, 119, 122–123, 125, 128, 129, 133, 135, 142–143, 145, 148, 149, 150, 151, 152, 153, 155, 159, 161, 162–163, 165, 171, 175, 181, 182–183, 185, 190, 191, 192, 193, 194, 196, 199

explaining, 29, 35, 70, 170

expressing thanks and appreciation, 120

giving advice and suggestions, 39

giving information, 51

interviewing, 10, 139, 195

intonation of finished and unfinished statements and, 106

prior knowledge and, 171

reading aloud, 46, 58, 77

role-playing, 39, 59, 91, 110, 130, 159, 177, 200
    of a meeting, 80

self-reflection and, 11, 31, 98

sentences, 9, 87, 89, 156

taking turns in, 40

talking about assignments, 59

useful phrases for everyday communication and, 210–211

Test-Taking Skills

categorizing, 106, 117

checking off correct answers, 7, 16, 37, 66, 73, 86, 104, 174, 192

circling correct answers, 28, 30, 33, 37, 38, 44, 49, 57, 59, 67, 72, 73, 77, 97, 104, 136, 192

filling in blanks, 15, 16, 17, 25, 27, 35, 95, 115, 125, 128, 138, 145, 152, 165, 173, 195

matching, 4, 12, 13, 14, 24, 26, 32, 34, 37, 44, 46, 52, 54, 64, 72, 84, 113, 114, 115, 118, 135, 144, 155, 164, 172, 179, 184, 194, 198

sentence completion, 5, 7, 9, 13, 15, 18, 33, 45, 49, 50, 53, 55, 65, 74, 77, 79, 85, 88, 104, 109, 113, 119, 135, 137, 148, 155, 158, 174, 175, 189, 196, 198

true/false questions, 33, 47, 53, 64, 86, 93, 112, 117, 133, 153, 157, 169, 172, 193

underlining correct responses, 6, 26, 28, 68, 95, 129, 136, 149, 168

Topics

Ancient Peoples and Places, 141–160

Inside the Brain, 81–100

Culture and Tradition, 41–60

Energy and Our Planet, 21–40

Entrepreneurs and New Businesses, 181–200

Our Active Earth, 121–140

Species Survival, 161–180

Staying Healthy in the Modern World, 1–20

A Thirsty World, 61–80

What We Eat, 101–120

Viewing

charts, 78, 150

checking predictions and, 112

comprehension and, 13, 52–53

critical thinking and, 13, 33, 53, 72, 73, 93, 173, 193

diagrams, 102–103, 132

dictionary use and, 12, 52, 72, 92, 172

discussion after, 113, 153

discussion before, 12

note-taking and, 112

photos, 2–3, 22–23, 41, 61, 62–63, 70, 81, 82–83, 89, 92, 98, 101, 102–103, 122–123, 126, 141, 142–143, 151, 161, 162–163, 181, 182–183

predicting content and, 32, 72, 112, 173

prior knowledge and, 12, 32, 52, 112, 172

self-reflection and, 93, 133, 192

videos, 153, 192

visuals/graphic organizers, 76
    bar graphs, 114
    diagrams, 114
    line graphs, 114
    maps, 25
    pie charts, 22–23, 31
    understanding visuals and, 115

Vocabulary

building vocabulary, 4, 14, 24, 34, 44, 54, 64, 74, 84, 94, 104, 114, 124, 134–135, 144, 154, 164, 174, 184, 194, 208–209
    experimenting with new vocabulary for, 208
    journal for, 208
    organizers for, 208
    prefixes and, 209
    suffixes and, 209
    using new words for, 208

critical thinking and, 35, 44, 125, 135

dictionary use and, 12, 14, 44, 74, 104, 152, 172, 186, 209
    for collocations, 209
    for different meanings of same word, 209
    for synonyms, 209
    for word families, 209

meaning from context and, 4, 14, 24, 34, 44, 54, 64, 74, 84, 94, 114, 124, 134, 144, 154, 164, 174, 178, 184, 194, 204–205

prior knowledge and, 94, 134

self-reflection and, 45, 75, 105, 114, 185

using vocabulary and, 5, 15, 25, 35, 45, 55, 65, 75, 85, 95, 105, 115, 125, 135, 145, 155, 165, 175, 185, 195

Writing

PHOTOS (continued)

86: ISM/PhotoTake, 87: Sportstock/iStockphoto .com, 88: Orange Line Media, 2009/Shutterstock. com, 89: Cornstock/Jupiter Images, 89: VILevi/ Shutterstock.com, 89: Lena S, 2010/Shutterstock .com, 89: Tom Merton/OJO Images/Jupiter Images, 90: Sherwin mcGehee/iStockphoto.com, 91: Scott Quinn Photography/Jupiter Images, 91: Iofoto, 2010/Shutterstock.com, 91: Luminis, 2010/ Shutterstock.com, 91: Jiang Dao Hua, Shutterstock .com, 91: Martina Ebel/iStockphoto.com, 92: Andresr/Shutterstock.com, 92: Mark Herreid/ Shutterstock.com, 92: Trapp/Caro/Alamy, 93: AVAVA/Shutterstock.com, 94: Melissa Farlow/National Geographic Image Collection, 95: Sawayasu Tsuji/iStockphoto.com, 97: Diego Cervo, 2009/Shutterstock.com, 98: Ian Shaw/ Alamy, 99: Derek Latta/iStockphoto.com 99: StockLite, 2010/Shutterstock.com, 99: Niko Guido/iStockphoto.com, 99: Kim Ruoff, 2010/ Shutterstock.com, 99: Robert Kneschke, 2010/ Shutterstock.com, 99: Francisco Romero/ iStockphoto.com, 101: Maria Stenzel/National Geographic Image Collection, 102-103: Thierry Bornier/National Geographic My Shot/National Geographic Image Collection, 103: 2005 Peter Menzel/Hungry Planet: What the World Eats/ www.menzelphoto.com, 103: Peter Menzel/ www.menzelphoto.com, 104: Elena Aliaga, 2008/ Shutterstock.com, 105: Morgan Lane Photography, 2010/Shutterstock.com, 105: Cat London/ iStockphoto.com, 107: Kheng Guan Toh, iStockphoto.com, 107: wish white/iStockphoto.com, 107: WizData, inc./Alamy, 108: PBNJ Productions/ Getty Images, 109: Stocklite/Shutterstock.com, 112: Raul Touzon/National Geographic Image Collection, 112: Kathy Tarantola/Photolibrary, 113: Richard Gunion/iStockphoto.com, 113: JTB Photo/JTB Photo Communications, Inc./Alamy, 116: Image copyright Viktor1 2009/Used under license from Shutterstock.com, 116: Kheng Guan Toh/Shutterstock.com, 116: John Wynn/ Shutterstock.com, 116: kentoh/Shutterstock. com, 116: Oliver Hoffman, 2009/Shutterstock. com, 117: British Retail Photography/Alamy, 121: John Stanmeyer LLC/National Geographic Images, 122-123: Carsten Peter/National Geographic Image Collection, 126: Jacques Descloitres, MODIS Land Rapid Response Team, NASA/GSFC/NASA Images, 127: James P. Blair/ National Geographic Image Collection, 129: Robert Asento/Shutterstock.com, 130: National Geographic Image Collection, 131: Waldermar Lindgren/National Geographic Image Collection, 132: Carsten Peter/National Geographic Image Collection, 132: Carsten Peter/National Geographic

Image Collection, 133: Steve Raymer/National Geographic Image Collection, 133: Carsten Peter/National Geographic Image Collection, 134: John Stanmeyer/National Geographic Image Collection, 135: John Stanmeyer/National Geographic Image Collection, 136: Hans F. Meier/ iStockphoto, 137: James P. Blair/National Geographic Image Collection, 138: Liba Taylor/ PhotoLibrary, 138: Richard Baker/Alamy, 138: Danita Delimont/Alamy, 140: Mike Theiss/ National Geographic Image Collection, 140: Medford Taylor/National Geographic Image Collection, 140: Rowan Bestmann/National Geographic Image Collection, 141: Simon Norfolk/National Geographic Image Collection, 142: rj lerich/Shutterstock.com, 142: Ned M. Seidler/National Geographic Image Collection, 143: Kenneth Garrett/National Geographic Image Collection, 143: alandj/iStockphoto.com, 143: James L. Stanfield/National Geographic Image Collection, 143: James L. Stanfield/National Geographic Image Collection, 144: Dumitrascu, Vlad/National Geographic Image Collection, 144: Kenneth Garrett/National Geographic Image Collection, 144: Kenneth Garrett/National Geographic Image Collection, 145: Kenneth Garrett/National Geographic Image Collection, 145: National Geographic Image Collection, 146: Kenneth Ginn/National Geographic Image Collection, 147: Ralf Broskvar/iStockphoto.com, 148: Jennylynn Fields/National Geographic Image Collection, 148: Richard Nowitz/National Geographic Image Collection, 149: Taylor S. Kennedy/National Geographic Image Collection, 149: Kent Kobersteen/National Geographic Image Collection, 149: Michael S. Yamashita/ National Geographic Image Collection, 151: Ira Block/National Geographic Image Collection, 151: Kenneth Garrett/National Geographic Image Collection, 151: Otis Imboden/National Geographic Image Collection, 152: Tritone Images inc./National Geographic Image Collection, 153: Ralph Lee Hopkins/National Geographic Image Collection, 154: Kenneth Garrett/National Geographic Image Collection, 154: Kenneth Garrett/National Geographic Image Collection, 155: National Geographic Image Collection, 156: National Geographic Image Collection, 157: Hoang Dinh Nam/Staff/ Getty Images, 160: Bob Krist/National Geographic, 161: Dordo Brnobic/National Geographic My Shot/National Geographic Image Collection, 162-163: Frans Lanting/National Geographic Image Collection, 163: Frans Lanting/National Geographic Image Collection, 163: Paul Nicklen/National Geographic Image

Collection, 163: Michael Nichols/National Geographic Image Collection, 166: Lynn Johnson/ National Geographic Image Collection, 167: Lynn Johnson/National Geographic Image Collection, 167: FotoVeto/Shutterstock.com, 169: Michael Zysman/Shutterstock.com, 169: Eric Isselee/ Shutterstock.com, 170: Beverley Vycital/golfadi/ iStockphoto.com, 170: Linda Drake/National Geographic My Shot/National Geographic Image Collection, 170: Thomas Barrat/Shutterstock.com, 171: Oxford, Pete/National Geographic Image Collection, 172: Michael Nichols/National Geographic Image Collection, 172: Michael Nichols/National Geographic Image Collection, 173: Michael Nichols/National Geographic Image Collection, 173: George Steinmetz/National Geographic Image Collection, 174: Frans Lanting/ National Geographic Image Collection, 174: Joel Sartore/National Geographic Image Collection, 175: Joel Sartore/National Geographic Image Collection, 175: Joel Sartore/National Geographic Image Collection, 176: Lajos Repasi/ iStockphoto.com, 178: Tim Laman/National Geographic Image Collection, 178: Tim Laman/ National Geographic Image Collection, 179: Ted Spiegel/National Geographic Image Collection, 180: Maria Stenzel/National Geographic Image Collection, 181: James L. Stanfield/National Geographic Image Collection, 182-183: Sisse Brimberg/National Geographic Image Collection, 182: George Steinmetz/National Geographic Image Collection, 182: Michael Nicholsl/National Geographic Image Collection, 184: Shawn Baldwin/Corbis, 185: Justin Guariglia/National Geographic Image Collection, 185: Susan Seubert/National Geographic Image Collection, 186: Ingram Publishing/Photolibrary, 186: National Geographic Image Collection, 186: Andre Nantel, Shutterstock.com, 186: Orientaly/Shutterstock.com, 187: Sisse Brimberg/National Geographic Image Collection, 187: David McNew/Getty Images News/Getty Images, 187: Luis Marden/National Geographic Image Collection, 187: Mikhail Zahranichny, 2008/ Shutterstock.com, 187: Konstantin Chagin, 2010/ Shutterstock.com, 188: age footstock/SuperStock, 190: Simon Greig/Shutterstock.com, 190: Rich Legg/iStockphoto.com, 190: Deanna Bean/ iStockphoto.com, 190: iofoto/Shutterstock.com, 192: dbtravel/dbimages/Alamy, 192: Bruno Morandi/Encyclopedia/Corbis, 193: Travelshots. com/Alamy, 193: Lisa Limer/The Image Bank/ Getty Images, 194: Emotive Images, 195: Egon Bomsch/imagebroker/Alamy, 196: x99/ZUMA Press/Newscom, 199: Anton Gvozdikov/ Shutterstock.com, 200: KevinDyer/iStockphoto.com

MAP AND ILLUSTRATION

14: NED M. SEIDLER/National Geographic Image Collection; 23: National Geographic Maps; 25: National Geographic Maps; 42-43: National Geographic Maps; 46: National Geographic Maps; 56: National Geographic Maps; 66: Hsien

Min Yang/National Geographic Maps; 70: Roundabout Water Solutions SA, www. playpumps.co.za; 72: National Geographic Maps; 76: Martin Gamache/National Geographic Maps; 122: National Geographic Maps; 122, 132, 208: Bob Kayganich/illustrationonline; 122: National Geographic Maps; 124-125: Christie, Bryan/National Geographic;

132: National Geographic Maps; 142-143: National Geographic Maps; 144: National Geographic Maps; 152: National Geographic Maps; 163: National Geographic Maps; 164: Charles W. Berry/National Geographic Maps; 165: National Geographic Maps; 172: National Geographic Maps; 192: National Geographic Maps